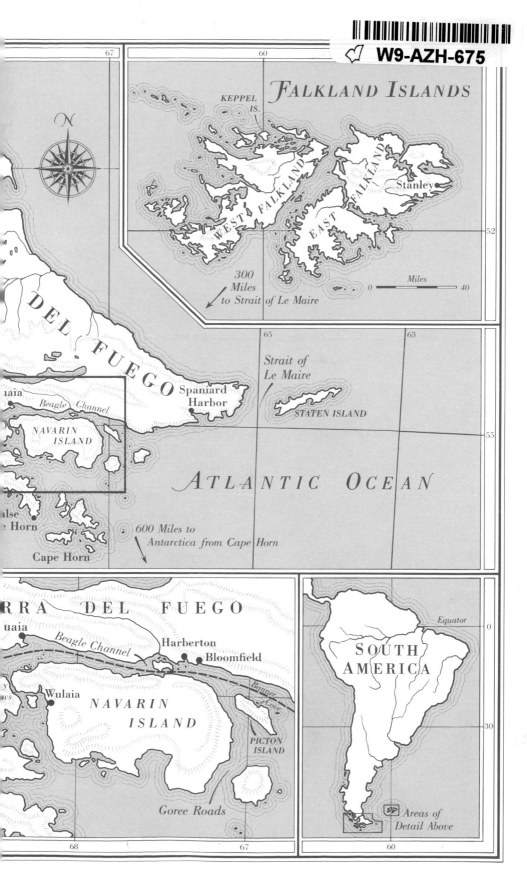

N

FALKLAND ISLANDS

KEPPEL IS.

WEST FALKLAND

EAST FALKLAND

Stanley

52

300 Miles
to Strait of Le Maire

Miles
0   40

DEL FUEGO

Beagle Channel

NAVARIN ISLAND

uaia

Spaniard Harbor

65   63

Strait of Le Maire

STATEN ISLAND

55

ATLANTIC OCEAN

lse
e Horn

Cape Horn

600 Miles to
Antarctica from Cape Horn

67   60

RRA DEL FUEGO

uaia

Beagle Channel

Harberton

Bloomfield

Banner Cove

Wulaia

NAVARIN
ISLAND

PICTON
ISLAND

Goree Roads

SOUTH
AMERICA

Equator   0

30

Areas of
Detail Above

68   67   60

THREE MEN OF THE *BEAGLE*

THREE MEN
OF THE *BEAGLE*

Richard Lee Marks

 Alfred A. Knopf New York 1991

THIS IS A BORZOI BOOK
PUBLISHED BY ALFRED A. KNOPF, INC.

Copyright © 1991 by Richard Lee Marks
Endpaper map copyright © 1991 by Anita Karl and James Kemp
All rights reserved under International and Pan-American
Copyright Conventions. Published in the United States by
Alfred A. Knopf, Inc., New York, and simultaneously in Canada by
Random House of Canada Limited, Toronto. Distributed by
Random House, Inc., New York.

Library of Congress Cataloging-in-Publication Data
Marks, Richard Lee.
Three men of the *Beagle* / by Richard Lee Marks.—1st ed.
p.   cm.
Includes bibliographical references and index.
ISBN 0-394-58818-5
1. Beagle Expedition (1831–1836).   2. Darwin, Charles, 1809–1882.
3. Fitzroy, Robert, 1805–1865.   4. Fuegians.   I. Title.
QH11.M27   1991
508.8—dc20   90-5139
                                                    CIP

Manufactured in the United States of America
First Edition

To my brave son

PAUL

LIST OF ILLUSTRATIONS

The endpaper map, drawn by Anita Karl and James Kemp, is based in part on a map surveyed and charted by Captain Robert FitzRoy, R.N., and the officers of H.M.S. Beagle, *1830–1834. Staten Island was surveyed by Lieutenant E. N. Kendal in 1828.*

The Beagle Channel. Photograph by the author.   1

Yahgan Indians in a "wigwam." Photograph by the French   10
Scientific Expedition to Cape Horn in 1882.
   (Courtesy of the Museo Territorial, Ushuaia, Argentina.)

Yahgan Indians in a canoe. Photograph by the French   11
Scientific Expedition to Cape Horn in 1882.
   (Courtesy of the Museo Territorial, Ushuaia, Argentina.)

Seals on an island in the Beagle Channel. Photograph by   13
the author.

Penguins on an outcropping off Navarin Island. Photograph   17
by the author.

A whale in the Beagle Channel. Photograph by the author.   20

H.M.S. Beagle *in the Strait of Magellan,* by Conrad Martens.   24
   (By permission of the Darwin Museum, Down House, courtesy
   of the Royal College of Surgeons of England.)

Tierra del Fuego from Navarin Island. Photograph by   26
the author.

Robert FitzRoy, by Philip Parker King.   30
   (Courtesy of the Mitchell Library, Sydney, Australia.)

Jemmy Button, York Minster, and Fuegia Basket, by Robert   41
FitzRoy. From *Narrative of the Surveying Voyages of His
Majesty's Ships "Adventure" and "Beagle" between 1826 and
1836.*
    (Courtesy of the New York Public Library.)

Charles Darwin in 1840, by George Richmond.   49
    *(Courtesy of the College of Mount St. Joseph,
    Mount St. Joseph, Ohio.)*

A Heavy Gale Off Cape Horn, by Capt. W. Parker Snow.   58
From *A Two Years' Cruise Off Tierra del Fuego* by
W. Parker Snow.
    (Courtesy of the New York Public Library.)

Jemmy Button in 1834, by Robert FitzRoy. From *Narrative   74
of the Surveying Voyages of His Majesty's Ships "Adventure"
and "Beagle" between 1826 and 1836.*
    (Courtesy of the New York Public Library.)

Spaniard Harbor, by Capt. W. Parker Snow. From *A Two   85
Years' Cruise Off Tierra del Fuego* by W. Parker Snow.
    (Courtesy of the New York Public Library.)

Commander Allen Francis Gardiner.   89
    (Courtesy of the South American Missionary Society.)

A recent view of Spaniard Harbor. Photograph by the staff   106
of Museo el Fin del Mundo.
    (Courtesy of the Museo Territorial, Ushuaia, Argentina.)

Down House. Photograph by the author.   115

Banner Cove on Picton Island, by Capt.   132
W. Parker Snow. From *A Two Years' Cruise Off Tierra del
Fuego* by W. Parker Snow.
    (Courtesy of the New York Public Library.)

Page from Appendix of *Narrative of the Surveying Voyages   137
of His Majesty's Ships "Adventure" and "Beagle" between
1826 and 1836*, by Robert FitzRoy.
    (Courtesy of the New York Public Library.)

A view of the Falkland Islands, by Conrad Martens. 140
From *Narrative of the Surveying Voyages of His Majesty's
Ships "Adventure" and "Beagle" between 1826 and 1836,*
by Robert FitzRoy.
  (Courtesy of the New York Public Library.)

A Cove on the Beagle Channel, by Conrad Martens. From 152
*Narrative of the Surveying Voyages of His Majesty's Ships
"Adventure" and "Beagle" between 1826 and 1836,*
by Robert FitzRoy.
  (Courtesy of the New York Public Library.)

Button Sound, by Capt. W. Parker Snow. From *A Two Years' 159
Cruise Off Tierra del Fuego* by W. Parker Snow.
  (Courtesy of the New York Public Library.)

A Yahgan Indian in his native state in 1882. Photograph by 163
the French Scientific Expedition to Cape Horn.
  (Courtesy of the Museo Territorial, Ushuaia, Argentina.)

Robert FitzRoy as an older man. 187
  (Courtesy of H. E. L. Mellersh and the Misses E. and M. Smyth.)

Cartoon of Charles Darwin from *Hornet.* 205
  (Courtesy of the American Philosophical Society.)

Caricature of Charles Darwin from *Vanity Fair.* 210
  (Courtesy of the American Philosophical Society.)

Cormorants on an island in the Beagle Channel. Photograph 227
by the author.

Charles Darwin in 1881. 235
  *(By permission of the Darwin Museum, Down House, courtesy
  of the Royal College of Surgeons of England.)*

Darwin's study in Down House. Photograph by the author. 240

Emma Darwin. 245
  *(Courtesy of the College of Mount St. Joseph,
  Mount St. Joseph, Ohio.)*

ACKNOWLEDGMENTS

In connection with the research for this book, I would like to thank for their exceptional courtesy and helpfulness: Oscar Pablo Zanola, Director, Museo Territorial, Ushuaia, Argentina, and his staff; Héctor Julio Alvarez, *Capitán de Fragata*, of the Argentine Navy; Paul Nikitovich of Perfiltra, S.A., Buenos Aires; Solene Morris, Curator, The Charles Darwin Museum, Down House, Kent, England; and Gene Kritsky, Professor and Chair of Biology, College of Mount St. Joseph, Mount St. Joseph, Ohio.

I am also indebted to the staffs of the Public Record Office in England, the British Library, and the New York Public Library.

R.L.M.

AUTHOR'S NOTE

This story, to my knowledge, has never before been told as a narrative. It is based scrupulously on historical facts mostly recorded by the participants and is enhanced only by reasonable presumptions to fill out the pictures and by reasoned speculation about the essence of past times. For this enhancement I have relied on my experience with Indians on both American continents (from the Assiniboin of Alberta to the Calchaquí of Tucumán), on the advice of my seafaring brother Bob with whom I have sailed along the American coasts, and on my familiarity with the locales where these happenings took place.

Part One

FROM THE BEGINNING TO THE FALSE ENDING

OVERLEAF: *The Beagle Channel after a storm.*

THE SETTING OF
THE CRIME

I PREFER to get to this place the way I first got there more than forty years ago.

The initial lap was aboard a Norwegian freighter called the *Reinholt* from a dock in the Red Hook section of Brooklyn to Montevideo, Uruguay. The ship carried fewer than twelve passengers, including a Canadian missionary and his family returning from a sabbatical at home to their mission in Jujuy, Argentina; an Argentine doctor who had been studying for a year in the U.S.; and several others. We all watched from the rail while two determined tugs nudged our rusting freighter past the Statue of Liberty and headed us out into the North Atlantic. (The last use of the *Reinholt* was as an expendable supply ship in the Korean War.)

Then we were three weeks at sea without a stop—through a rough blow around Bermuda and eerie calm in the doldrums and reasonably pleasant pushing against the wind-driven waves in the South Atlantic before we reached Montevideo on the northern bank of the wide estuary of the Río de la Plata. (When we were off the hump of Brazil, after a night when all of us except the missionaries had quite a lot of akvavit and beer, the Argentine doctor hysterically begged the captain to put him ashore; the doctor was unbearably homesick and was only diverted from diving overboard when the first mate pointed out to him that the constellations had changed and the Southern Cross was in the sky where previously the Big Dipper had been, proving that we were now in southern latitudes; the mate gently assured the doctor that he would be home sooner if he stayed with the ship and did not swim for shore.)

In those years Uruguay was a lucky and lovely country and we spent a beautiful day there. My young wife and I had a long late lunch in Carasco on a patio under trees filled with cooing doves and afterward, on the streetcar ride back to the harbor, we passed under a banner advertising the convention of the Communist Party of Uruguay, decided to report on it, and promptly got off to join the festivities. The Uruguayan Communists— idealistic kids full of life who unfortunately were destined to disappear—gave my wife a huge corsage of jasmine and we drank white wine with them until the early morning hours. When we returned to the *Reinholt* we found that the whores the sailors had brought aboard had stolen my wife's stockings which she had left in the head to dry.

After crossing the Río de la Plata diagonally upriver to Buenos Aires and spending some time in that shabbily splendid replica of Paris which was exploding with excitement in the heyday of the Peróns, we faced the challenge of getting ourselves about 2,000 miles to the south overland (since the only ship that traveled that route by sea had just burned up).

From the terminus of the Southern Railroad in the great gray Plaza of Depots, still echoing for us with the cheers of a mass meeting we had attended there for Eva Perón, we could take the train only as far as San Vicente, a short distance from the capital. From San Vicente it was a trip of weeks by bus and truck from one dusty town to another, across the fertile pampa which is so flat that it seemed concave and made us feel as if we were standing on our knees, and then across bleak windy Patagonia. (At Comodoro Rivadavia someone put a good-sized fish aboard our bus, stowed it unwrapped on the floorboard beside the driver; then, as we jolted along, the fish slid toward the back of the bus and became wedged beside a crate of live chickens, and the chickens by craning their necks between the slats began to peck at it; then some children took the fish to the back seat of the bus and played a game that involved holding the fish by the tail and whacking one another with it; but finally, when we stopped for the fourth or fifth time at some tiny inland settlement, the driver came for the fish and delivered it to a waiting crowd of half a dozen grinning women who happily carried it off to be the *pièce de résistance* at a local wedding.)

Eventually we reached the town of Río Gallegos in the narrowing southern end of South America. There we had to buy a little Chilean money for the ferry-crossing of the Strait of Magellan and the subsequent bus ride across the Chilean part of Tierra del Fuego, then back into Argentina to bounce across the Argentine part of Tierra del Fuego to Ushuaia, the southernmost town in the world. It had become chilly, and even our resilient young bones and healthy kidneys had reached their limits.

So there we stood facing southward on the shore at Ushuaia, at the very bottom of the habitable earth, with the Americas and the island of Tierra del Fuego behind us, and before us only the narrow Beagle Channel and the few small islands ending with Cape Horn that were like the vertebrae in a tail bone and diminished and sank beneath the polar sea. Beyond those islands, some 600 miles further south, lay only Antarctica buried under mile-deep ice.

I HAVE mapped out this journey from many years ago in discursive detail simply to make the point that, by the time you got to Tierra del Fuego in this way, the sounds of Brooklyn were long gone from your ears, you were able to question your own mindset, and you knew you were far, far from home in a strange land where the strangeness had to be respected. Nowadays, when you can jet from New York to Buenos Aires to Ushuaia with a stopover in Comodoro Rivadavia, all within twenty-four hours (if your connections are excellent), you may still stand there on the shore looking across the gray-green water of the Beagle Channel at Navarin Island—but you may be less respectful of the strangeness and your mind-set may be more intractable, less susceptible to the great questions of human existence.

In this place so far from home there are reminders all around of the beginning of life on earth, even of the emergence of land, particularly of the beginning of human life at its difficult dawning. Great glaciers still cover much of the surface of this southern tip of the Americas. In frigid caves along the coast the remains of once-living things tend to endure because the caves act as refrigerators (as such remains endure in the dryness of the coastal desert of Peru and in Egypt and Palestine) and in the caves of Patagonia have been found the remains of hairy mylodons, long-extinct giant land-sloths that once munched the foliage here. Still stuck between the ribs of the mylodons are arrowheads made by men.

Yet Tierra del Fuego is a place where human life can barely be sustained, so close to the frozen pole. The water in the Beagle Channel during the long dark winter is only two degrees Fahrenheit above freezing. There is precipitation, on the average, three hundred days a year, and it is often icy rain, sleet, snow and hail coming in galvanic storms that blast up continuously from the pole. The seas off Cape Horn, where the Atlantic and the Pacific meet in a ferocious clash, are said to be the most awesome in the world. The waves reach a height that has been calculated at more than 100 feet, mountainous waves which despite their size have a dangerously short pitch between crests. And from the channels between the sinking and fractured land come powerful tiderips that are difficult to see on the surface. All around Tierra del Fuego the bottom of the sea is a graveyard of ships, of sailing ships and of steamers, too.

On the polar side of these ultimate rocks human life cannot endure; it would be blasted and beaten to death by the storms. But here along the Beagle Channel, on the first sheltered channel north of the South Pole, human life did endure, does endure.

And it was here—in what has aptly been called the "uttermost part of the earth" — a horrific crime was committed, a crime that, because its elements are primeval, does not suggest the conflict of good and evil but instead may reveal in depth, if you choose so to view it, the nature of the human soul.

THE PEOPLE OF
YAHGASHAGA

O NCE a boy stood over there, on Navarin Island, on the shingle beach — and he was of the poorest, most primitive people on earth.

Totally naked, he stood and stared in rapt curiosity, goggle-eyed and agape. The slanting rain swept in by the Antarctic wind did not chill him or affect in the least his almost catatonic concentration. With his splayed prehensile toes he clung to the rounded stones of the beach and by so clinging, it seemed, kept his amazement from lifting him up and letting him be carried off by the wind.

(From the rounded stones on these shingle beaches of Patagonia and Tierra del Fuego, Charles Darwin, the most acute observer in the nineteenth century, deduced that, in some past time, the ocean floor had been thrust up, as evidenced by the calciferous strata of marine shells and fish bones which could be seen high on the cliffs; all this land then had been covered by glaciers, some of which remained, and, as the glaciers had slowly melted — as they would in a climate even a few degrees above freezing — the stones had been worked smooth by the continuous runoff. From these same stones, however, Robert FitzRoy, also a most astute and eminently respectable observer, commander of the *Beagle* and one of the finest sailing captains of his time, co-founder of modern meteorology and a driven man devoted and dedicated to science, concluded that stones thus rounded were clear evidence of The Flood.)

In equatorial Africa there are extremely primitive tribes whose way of living is almost as simple as it can be and still enable the people to endure. Many of these African tribesmen are Pygmies (with males up to only fifty-nine inches in height) or pygmoids (with males slightly taller). The people inhabit the forests of central Africa and live around the Kalahari Desert. These primitive people vary slightly, in aspects other than height, from the accepted norm for *Homo sapiens*. The Bushmen of the Kalahari Desert, for example, have a few extra vertebrae that protrude and form a small but observable tail at the base of the spine; the females have vaginal flaps like dewlaps that hang between their legs; and both males and females develop on their buttocks large hard humps of fat that sustain them through periods of famine and drought.

In the Philippines there are also very primitive people, jungle tribes that exist on worms, fungus, almost anything barely edible they can find. Their weapons and tools are rudimentary. They plant nothing. They simply wander, hunt a little and gather what they can.

In the desert regions of Australia, too, the aborigines endure in an extremely arid environment, hoarding water, tracking lizards for food.

But in the jungles and deserts of Africa, in the Philippine jungle, in the outback of Australia and in similar regions, the weather is warm. The climate is mild. And the poorness, the basic primitiveness of a people depends in large part upon the relationship between the people and their environment.

In Africa, in the Philippines and in and around Australia the challenge of the environment is not so formidable as to threaten the existence of human life. (In the northern lands around the Arctic Circle where the challenge of climate is extreme, the Eskimos with their fur clothes, igloos, kayaks and hunting instruments have a culture which places them far above the most primitive people on earth.)

This boy on the beach of Navarin Island in the lee of Cape Horn was naked, as were all his people, and there were thousands of them spread along the Beagle Channel. In spite of the weather with its cold and rain and snow, it had never occurred to these people to make clothes for themselves. The most they ever did to protect their bodies against the weather was to put an otter skin over their shoulders, and this only a few of them did casually and rarely. Obviously here were people on the very edge of survival.

The racial strain of these people was American Indian, and in the late nineteenth century an Englishman with a hobby of linguistics conferred upon the boy's tribe the name "Yahgan," which was an Anglicized version of a place-name in the tribal language, Yahgashaga, for that part of the channel the English called the Murray Narrows. These Indians really had no name for themselves. They were pygmoid people; the boy on the beach at fourteen or fifteen years old had just about reached his full height of five feet two inches and seemed smaller because it was the habit of these people to walk in a semi-crouch, a kind of cringe. The boy had a mass of black hair which was matted and snarled, a low forehead and a broad flat face with a dark complexion that was naturally reddish, though both the darkness and the color of his face were heightened by white stripes made from riverbank clay and by stripes of red and black organic dye made from the sludge of microscopic organisms that accumulated in the creeks (not unlike the mash of shellfish which gave the ancient Phoenicians Tyrian purple). In the structure of the boy's body there were no unusual physical characteristics.

The Yahgans did not live in caves nor did they build huts or houses; they had "wigwams" but that word is misused to describe their shelters. They would find some fallen wood, a few boughs to pull together to serve as a support, and would pile tall grass and reeds against the sticks to make a kind of windbreak. The Yahgans knew how to weave reeds to make baskets, but it never occurred to them to make thatch.

The Yahgans slept on the ground, sometimes in the shelter of their wigwams but often simply huddled together on the grass or

Family of Yahgan Indians in a "wigwam" and in a canoe.
The Yahgans depended on fire for their survival, but
the "wigwam" had neither chimney nor smoke hole, and
in the canoe the wood-coals were carried on a bed of sand

mud of the bank or on the stony beaches—naked, exposed to the
weather, warmed only by each other.

They knew how to make boats from the bark of trees, crude
heavy leaky canoes in which they would venture into the channel,
never out to sea. The Yahgan women were the boat-handlers. The
women would sit in the middle of the boats and row with improvised paddles and they were responsible for tying the boats to
the kelp in the algae-clogged inlets. The women were the only
ones who could swim effectively for any distance and in the
nearly freezing water they would swim out to collect the boats

and turf in the center of the leaky boat. These photographs, on emulsified glass plates, were taken by the French Scientific Expedition to Cape Horn in 1882–83. The Yahgans then were still living in their native state.

for fishing and later, after tying up, would swim back to shore. The men rode in the prow of the boats. In the stern huddled the children and dogs.

The Yahgan men used a crude harpoon as their hunting weapon for spearing big fish; it was merely a long stick with a sharp piece of bone bound to one end. They were just beginning to experiment with bows and arrows for shooting birds, in imitation of the Fuegians very similar to them who inhabited the western end of the Beagle Channel; and the Yahgans had simple slings and snares for catching sea-birds. For fighting among themselves the Yahgans used clubs. For both hunting and fighting, though, their favorite weapons were those that came easiest to hand—the stones of the beach, the size of oranges, heavy and hand-filling. The Yahgans could throw these stones with great force and accuracy.

Mostly the Yahgans ate the stuff that clung to the rocks along the channel or that they could dig from the mud, chiefly mussels. In addition, while the men tried to spear large fish, the women caught small fish on hookless lines made of their own plaited hair (when a small fish would sink its sharp teeth into the bit of bait, the fisherwoman would pull up the fish and catch it in hand, bite out its belly and lay the fish near the fire in the center of the boat). Occasionally the men were able to spear or brain with a stone a dozing seal or an otter. The Yahgan dogs would chase the seals and otters when the sea-mammals were ashore and the untrained dogs would compete with the humans for the meat. Regularly the Yahgans searched for the eggs of birds and turtles. Sometimes a dead sea elephant or small whale would wash ashore and then the Yahgans would gorge on blubber. During the short summers the people stuffed themselves on wild berries. Almost certainly, though rarely, they would eat a human corpse. They put to death their old and infirm by smothering and strangulation.

The Yahgans lived in small inbred family groups that had little cohesion and no social structure. Each group numbered from a few up to twenty or thirty, and each group would move every few days. Thus the Yahgans were nomadic but purposeless in their movement. They did not follow herds like hunting people or pursue good grazing like shepherds. Whenever a spot became filthy from mussel shells and themselves (which took only a few days), they would move but never far. The little groups were in a nervous, restless, irritable, kinetic state, restricted as they were by the oceans and the forests to a fixed geographical area where their population seemed to remain stable.

The tribe had no organization. Language and physical characteristics and social familiarity bound them together, but there

Seals on an island in the Beagle Channel. The Yahgans would utilize every bit of a seal: They would eat even the hide if they were hungry enough in the winter, or they would cut the hide into strips and tie the strips together to make a rope by which a man could be lowered from a cliff to look for birds' eggs in the nests on the ledges.

was no acknowledged leader. The little groups squabbled continuously, individual with individual, and often fought, one group against another, yet there was never any extension of a group's hegemony. It has been said that excess production is a prerequisite for civilization (there must be a little surplus food to support a chief, a priest, an artist, even an artisan). The Yahgans had no chiefs, no priests, no medicine men, no one to paint on the walls of a cave.

The Yahgans did have a distinct language of their own, a

language with a huge number of words estimated at over thirty thousand, with all kinds of variations to describe the weather, the water, the birds, the fish—and the danger.

Terror was a constant in their lives. They lived in fear of the awful storms and of the tribes of bigger men who came from the woods to the north and preyed on them. A tribe called the Ona often fell upon the Yahgans (the Ona wore fur clothes and had better weapons). Perhaps the Yahgans never built better houses or settled more permanently because at any moment and frequently they could be sent fleeing and screaming.

Like the algae, the kelp and the mussels, the Yahgans clung to the rocks of this uttermost channel in their effort to survive.

WHAT occupied the minds of these people who, despite the inclemency of their weather, had made for themselves neither clothing nor adequate shelter?

The culture of the Yahgan Indians was so simple that it antedated the cultures that we conceive for the noble and ignoble savage. We usually think of savagery as a condition preceding the advent of civilization—civilization commencing with the development of agriculture and the building of cities and the tempering of human behavior. The examples of savagery with which we are familiar generally involve people who have invented gods to inspirit the terrifying forces of nature and who have devised magic to propitiate the gods. But the Yahgans predated magic, and the notion of a god had never entered their minds. The Yahgans feared the storms because the storms battered them and so limited their movement that each winter they nearly starved. The Yahgans were afraid of the woods because that was where the Ona were. But the Yahgans never imagined unperceived realities.

The Yahgans did not have words in their language for God or a god, nor words to describe divine concepts. Even the Englishman with the hobby of linguistics who had been raised with Yahgans and who with Victorian assurance spent most of his life in an effort to convert them to Christianity eventually had to give up because the Yahgan language with all its words was inadequate to convey his meaning.

The Yahgans had no oral history. They had no myths. They told no stories. They had no music or poetry. They had no rituals of any sort, no ceremonies, not even for eating, and none for mating.

What the Yahgans did have was—fire.

Flints were common all along the rocky shore and in a cove at the western edge of Yahgan territory there is a deposit of iron pyrite which is better than flint for striking sparks. The worn trail to this deposit as well as the depth of the dung and the size of the mess of mussel shells is evidence of long usage by the Yahgans. For tinder to light their fires the Yahgans used the fluff from puffball weeds.

The Yahgans would keep their fires going endlessly and would carry the fire with them when they moved. They even made little beds of sand and wet turf in the middle of their canoes and on these beds took live wood-coals with them when they went out onto the water. If a fire went out ashore, the women would borrow a glowing coal from the nearest fire to get a flame going again. And the greatest assertion of the Yahgans—their sign of warning, of greeting or farewell—was made by piling onto the fires heaps of greenery to send skyward great towers of smoke.

This was the way naked human beings could stay alive in Tierra del Fuego—by huddling close to a fire and never venturing far from it. They would always keep water boiling in a seal's skull with foodstuff in the stew. Over the flame they warmed and lightly roasted seal meat, fish and blubber.

FOR many centuries these canoe Indians of Tierra del Fuego had been having periodic contacts, though at very long intervals, with civilized men and with the accoutrements of civilization.

In the second century A.D. Egyptian navigators, sailing eastward and exploring the Indian Ocean and the Pacific, sighted

Tierra del Fuego, and their discovery was recorded on a map drawn by a Greek-Egyptian astronomer and geographer called Ptolemy, like the Greek-Egyptian kings who preceded him. This geographer who worked in Alexandria believed that the world was round, though he believed the globe of the earth was the fixed center of the universe, and he could roughly calculate longitude and latitude and thus was able to place the island of Tierra del Fuego and the strait to the north of it without knowing anything of the huge continents that lay further north. I suppose it is chauvinism which inclines us to presume that the Americas were discovered by Europeans voyaging westward across the Atlantic, the Vikings and then Columbus, but the Map of Ptolemaeus is evidence that the Egyptians found at least the southern tip of South America many centuries before the Vikings discovered Greenland. There is, however, no evidence that the Egyptians landed in Tierra del Fuego or that there was any invigorating cross-fertilization with the Fuegians.

(Acknowledgment of the existence of Tierra del Fuego, following the Egyptian discovery and mapping, has an interesting history. In the year 833, Al-Hwarizmi of Baghdad drew a map which in all likelihood was derived from the old Map of Ptolomaeus and his map showed the island of Tierra del Fuego and the western opening of a strait to the north of the island as the only fixtures in an otherwise unknown vastness. In 833 Europe was in the depth of its long intellectual sleep, but the maps of Al-Hwarizmi and Ptolemy endured probably in the library at Alexandria and were discovered by Europeans during the Renaissance; indeed, it was the Greek knowledge from the library at Alexandria, knowledge which had been lost during the Middle Ages, that in large part inspired the Renaissance. Then in 1428 an Italian mapmaker working from one of the two maps made another that showed Tierra del Fuego, and in 1487 a mapmaker named Ericus Martellus Germanus made yet another map showing Tierra del Fuego. And in 1514 two Portuguese ships sailed from the Atlantic into the strait and back out of it without

*Magellan penguins, with a few king penguins, on an outcropping
off Navarin Island in the Beagle Channel. The Yahgans
occasionally ate penguins.*

realizing that here was a through passage that connected the
oceans. So when Magellan went in search of Tierra del Fuego and
the interocean sea-passage to the north of it, he was not without
clues that led him to his find.)

After Magellan in 1520 knowingly sailed through the strait
later named after him, he was followed by other Portuguese and
by Spanish and English and Dutch. It was the Dutch who braved
the open-sea route around the cape and named the cape for the
town they came from in Holland, Hoorn. The Dutch place-name,
Hoorn, translated easily into the similar English word Horn, all
of which made some sense because the cape does look a little
like a horn and perhaps so did the original site of the town in Hol-

land. But the Spanish agreeably called the cape Hornos, which in Spanish means "ovens," and this makes no sense at all and pays no homage whatever to the birthplace of the brave Dutch captains.

After whaling became lucrative in the late eighteenth century, American ships from the ports of New England en route to the whale-rich waters off Chile would take the route through the Strait of Magellan to avoid the terrible seas off Cape Horn.

This sea-traffic past Tierra del Fuego was infrequent but unceasing. And many of the ships did not make it. They were smashed on the rocks and the pieces washed ashore. Sailors were shipwrecked and met awful fates at the hands of the Indians. Armed sailors occasionally ventured ashore and clashed with the Indians. All of this, however, stimulated nothing in the Yahgans.

In spite of their contacts with civilization (there had been about eighty expeditions over three centuries) the Yahgans remained as they were: human beings just hanging on, unable to do more than just hang on.

ONE might reasonably ask: Where did the Yahgan Indians come from and why were they there, at the bottom of the world?

The answer generally offered and accepted is that tens of thousands of years ago a land bridge existed where the Bering Strait is now, linking Siberia and Alaska. Either the land was then higher or the level of the water lower, and Asian people simply walked across to the unpeopled Americas. These people of Asian stock spread southward and eastward, propagating, and went through the narrow neck of Panama (which may have been wider then and less difficult to traverse) and the people spread across South America and eventually reached Tierra del Fuego.

But does this make sense? There are many mysteries aroused by this explanation. We are asked to believe, for example, that the land bridge linking Siberia and Alaska submerged and the Americas were isolated for a period long enough for the people in the

Americas to become a distinctive race. We must believe this because, despite variations, the American Indian is a race similar to perhaps but certainly different from the Asian.

Yet there is evidence of ebb and flow in the peopling of the Americas. When the Arabs invaded Europe, when the tribes from northern Europe invaded the British Isles, the immigration came in waves. But it is hard to account for waves of people coming to the Americas from Asia when Asia had to have been cut off from America for a period long enough for the American stock to achieve its uniqueness.

The greatest American Indian civilizations were built over millennia, with rises and falls, periods of enlightenment and dark ages, in the high valley of Mexico, in the scrub-jungles of the Yucatán, Guatemala and Honduras, and in the high valley of Cuzco in Peru. But there is no path of development leading from the Bering Strait to these sites in the middle of the American hemisphere. Instead, in Casa Grande in Arizona were found a rubber ball and a ball-court, clearly items which traveled north-ward to Arizona from Mexico. Yet the llama, one of the most useful native animals in the Americas, never found its way north from Peru, and the guanaco, which is the root-stock of the llama, is found all the way down to Tierra del Fuego.

So there isn't any pattern of evidence to support the theory of a dispersion of people crossing from Siberia.

There are so many mysteries.

Why did *eohippus*, the little horse of the Argentine pampa, become extinct in the midst of one of the greatest grasslands in the world? Why, in spite of many areas where the environment was ideal for horses, were the Americas horseless?

Why twenty-five million years earlier did the dinosaurs, then the most successful animals on earth, all die out within a rela-tively short period of time?

We simply don't know.

But of the Americas we probably can presume, in spite of the lack of a developmental trail, that Asian people—prior to the

A whale traveling comfortably through the Beagle Channel after bucking the ocean's waves. The canoe Indians could not kill or capture a whale, but when a dead whale washed ashore or a whale beached itself and died, the Yahgans would feast on the blubber.

evolvement of the existing races of today—once crossed the land bridge from Siberia to Alaska and filtered all the way down to Tierra del Fuego, slipping along the coasts and following the mountain ranges to bypass the deserts. It is reasonable to presume that human beings at the hunting and gathering stage would move southward from Alaska toward warmer weather, richer vegetation and better hunting.

But why keep going after the temperate zone of the southern

hemisphere had been reached? Why keep going into ever-colder and bleaker surroundings until, from Tierra del Fuego, there was no place further to go? (Antarctica is unpopulated and uninhabitable.)

Population pressure could not have forced the people onward because the Americas were never more than sparsely settled. There were very few human beings spread over the two fertile continents. So what drove people southward until they were literally clinging to land's end?

One is tempted to think of people coming to the Americas from the east like the Egyptians (Thor Heyerdahl's theory in reverse) or even inhabiting the continental plates eons earlier when South America and Africa, which fit together like pieces of a jigsaw puzzle, were joined. If the latter were the case, a kind of human life like so many other forms of life would be native to the Americas.

Of these unfathomable speculations, though, the one most defensible, it seems to me, is that there was a dynamic drive in the human beings who were peopling the Americas—and I suggest that it was an irrational, compulsive, nomadic, periodic urge. In New Mexico, for example, the Zuni claim to be the original inhabitants of their region. It is part of the Zuni cosmology that where they live is the center of things. Yet within tribal memory they have moved a number of times. They moved when some inspired member of their medicine clan would announce, after perhaps a half-century or more during which the tribe had done nothing but chant memorized prayers, that the center of things was not where they were but somewhere else not far away. And the tribe packed up, sledged off and reestablished itself in a new place. Among the Indians on the *altiplano* of Bolivia and Peru one hears similar recollections of spasmodic tribal movements wholly unsupported by logic.

That's how I think the Americas were peopled—by random movement of one group and another and another, by spasms of the primitive mind. This was the dynamic of their nomadism. It was not at all a steady or planned movement but a series of irrational twitches that revealed an underlying restlessness which might lie dormant for a very long time but then would assert itself for no comprehensible reason at a moment no one could have foretold.

In this way the Yahgans ended up in Tierra del Fuego. And the naked Yahgan boy stood on the stony beach. He was at a stage of human development before people had begun to dream.

And what stupefied him, amazed him, baffled and dazzled him was thus not a figment of his own making, neither vision nor nightmare, but a real thing—a thing out there in the bay, a marvelous thing, not a seal, not a fish, not a whale, but bigger, with huge bladders like lungs, strung with cords that were like the intestines of seals, with round shining eyes on its sides, and with men like lice running all over it.

Reality was the cause of his astonishment—for he was looking at the *Beagle*, a ship considered modern by the standards of the early nineteenth century, built by people on another side of the earth who had millennia of reasoning behind them, people for whom agriculture and the development of cities had led to scientific progress and industrialization, people who long ago had begun to wear clothes and build houses and long ago had begun to dream and then had begun to think and for whom the intertwining of faith and reason had led to explosive human progress.

If the Yahgan boy had not so tightly held with his toes to the stones of the beach, he might have been blown off the beach not by the Antarctic wind but by the force of modern humanity.

The boy's people were behaving naturally; they were wildly excited and were out in their bark-boats, circling the strange thing, trying to pick whatever they could from it, screeching taunts at it; they were beside themselves with curiosity. The Beagle carried six cannons, and the British sailors were armed with muskets and pistols and several times had fired their pistols into the air to dissuade the Yahgans from coming too close. But the Yahgans had had so little contact with people armed with modern weapons that they did not comprehend the potency of the cannons, and the explosions of the pistols amused them. The Yahgans almost always seemed good-natured in the hunt; hunting lifted them from their torpor; they were grinning, mocking, spears at the ready, stones in hand.

But the naked boy was dumbstruck.

NOBLESSE OBLIGE

ENTER NOW Robert FitzRoy, commander of the *Beagle*, not only wearing clothes but clothes that conveyed a meaning, the items of uniform of the Royal Navy, which entitled him to give orders. He was at twenty-four years of age one of England's most competent sailing captains. His ship which lay in the bay off Tierra del Fuego was, as a result of its design, so susceptible to capsizing that the sailors of the Royal Navy called this class of ships "coffins." But not with Robert FitzRoy in command. FitzRoy in the *Beagle* had doubled Cape Horn, he had fought off the worst of the storms; he had sailed around the Cape of Good Hope and across most of the seas of the world; and the men who served under him now all acknowledged that their lives were dependent upon him.

In this year of 1830 Captain FitzRoy was on the cutting edge of modern science and his cabin was filled with the latest gadgets, called barometers. One of the secrets of his success was that from the barometers he could tell when a storm was imminent and consequently was never caught by surprise. Then his orders were rapid and sure—and his mainsails were furled, his ship headed into the wind, when the hurricane's fury which would have capsized an unprepared ship fell upon it.

FitzRoy was an English aristocrat, descendant of a bastard of Charles II, the rakehell king; he was an exemplary representative of the energized elite that had established England's dominance and had now maintained it for two hundred fifty years. FitzRoy

A drawing from Down House, Charles Darwin's home, entitled
H.M.S. Beagle in the Strait of Magellan. *This drawing may be*
mistitled. The little boat seems to be a Yahgan canoe (which
would only be in the Beagle Channel) and the landscape looks
like that to the west of Ushuaia.

was of medium height, wiry and strong, and he had aquiline, fine
features and an oversensitive, though tautly controlled face. He
had begun his training for command at sea when he was twelve.
He had been sent to the Royal Naval College at Portsmouth
where he had received the finest available education in mathe-
matics, geometry, mechanics, French and fencing; he had been
first in his class. Since he was fourteen, he had been tested and
toughened at sea. He thought and talked quickly, sometimes
brilliantly, and never questioned his right to command. He was a
noble Englishman inspired and propelled by his own vitality.

And on that day when the *Beagle* was lying off Tierra del

Fuego, he was fit to be tied because the Indians had stolen one of his two whaleboats.

He needed his whaleboats to establish the points of reference for mapping, which was the *Beagle*'s assignment. As an act of noblesse oblige appropriate for the world's reigning naval power, the British navy for the benefit of civilized mankind was engaged in mapping all the hitherto-uncharted and most difficult coasts of the world. But mapping from an unwieldy square-rigged sailing ship was an arduous and frustrating job. Even when the weather allowed the main ship to remain at anchor, smaller boats, usually with sailors pulling hard on the oars, had to establish the points for triangulation. The preceding commander of the *Beagle,* a career officer named Pringle Stokes whom FitzRoy had recently replaced, had been so undermined by his problems, had become so unbearably annoyed—by the desolation of the land, by the unceasing rain and sleet, by the roughness of the sea, and by the larceny of the Indians—that he had broken down, had become emotionally erratic, veering from fear of mutiny to hyper-eagerness for his next assignment to mute depression, and he had committed suicide, mortally wounding himself in the head with a pistol.

Of course the Fuegians had stolen FitzRoy's whaleboat—if "stolen" is the right word. The Fuegians were trying to pinch everything they could; the Indians were enchanted by all the things they saw, and they especially loved the whaleboat which was like a pup of the big ship. After a few English sailors had beached the whaleboat and gone to poke around inland, the Indians in their bark-boats promptly had towed it away.

At first blush the rare meetings of Europeans and Fuegian Indians had a similarity which was engaging: The first response on both sides would be a childlike hilarity. The Indians would seem to beg for and would try to pilfer all the bright belongings of the Europeans. For the Indians this promised to be the easiest method of acquisition. The Europeans for their part would show off for the Indians, would sing, dance to a hornpipe and indulge

A view of Tierra del Fuego from Navarin Island.

in hijinks as if for children. And the Indians would mimic the Europeans; the Indians were good at it (mimicry was an important means of communication for them). The meetings were swathed in good humor, as if the Indians had come upon a washed-up dead whale and a gorging was at hand.

At first blush. In the aftermath, however, there was intimidation on both sides.

It has always seemed to me that with primitive people the moment of first meeting is usually not dangerous. People accustomed to a very simple life are so surprised by anything they have not imagined or expected that they are initially immobilized. And often they are pleased by a little variation in their routine. It is after they have had time to think up some scheme unfettered by civilized restraint that the element of danger intrudes. Thus the trick to achieve safe passage, in an encounter with primitive people, is to move on quickly before they have time to conspire.

When the Indians would come upon shipwrecked, often injured sailors or a small band of sailors detached from their ship, then the Indians could contemplate the men who were at their mercy—and the inventions of the Indians were not kindly. Shipwrecked sailors had almost always been killed and sometimes eaten. (Christian missionaries to the Fuegians have been eager to deny that cannibalism ever existed and to blame the evidence on the Fuegian dogs or foxes, but the Fuegian Indians whom FitzRoy encountered, when they were denied whatever they wanted and were angry, mimed precisely how they would eat the sailors if they could.) At the least, shipwrecked sailors were stripped by the Indians and left to die of exposure and starvation.

Europeans, on the other hand, when in lands that were strange to them, were primed to cope with the unexpected and, if they didn't have plans in mind at the outset, they made plans quickly and acted upon them.

FitzRoy and his crew were at the point when the first stage of surprise and hilarity was merging into the second stage of quarreling, which was the Yahgans' habitual condition when they were by themselves. In the western part of the Beagle Channel, where the Indians were bolder and more sullen, Europeans and Fuegian Indians were having frequent conflicts.

In a fury over the theft of his whaleboat FitzRoy in the remaining whaleboat with a squad of armed sailors set off to get his boat back. And he found pieces of the missing whaleboat in almost every canoe and wigwam he came upon—the lead line in one canoe, the broken mast in an abandoned wigwam, canvas from the whaleboat in another canoe. With each finding he would try to lay hands on the nearest Indians to force them to tell him where those with the stolen whaleboat had gone. Nearly as fast as he grabbed these Indians, however, they escaped, mothers even abandoning their children.

(The Fuegians seemed not fully to comprehend the usefulness of tools in production or seriously to value trade goods. Unlike the Patagonian Indians, the Fuegians did not ask for knives and axes. The Yahgans begged for everything and anything. FitzRoy thought the Fuegians stole his whaleboat because it would be better for fishing, seal-hunting and transport between the islands than the leaky canoes they had, but the Fuegians were never seen using any of the many whaleboats, longboats and dinghies they stole. When the Fuegians were given or stole bright-colored cloth or canvas, they would snatch the goods from one another with wild hilarity, fighting among themselves over the pieces, ripping them into progressively smaller pieces, and running off with the little pieces until only shreds were left and these were lost. To the Yahgans the English boats were no more than prizes in a game, even though the Yahgans were extremely possessive of the bark-boats they built for themselves for their own use. Each family was fiercely defensive of its own canoe.)

FitzRoy determined to take hostages to be held against the return of his whaleboat. So he led a party ashore and surreptitiously encircled some Fuegian wigwams where he knew he would find at least pieces of equipment from the whaleboat. Then a dog barked and the Indians fled screaming as they would from the Ona. The whaleboat had been stolen from the Beagle's master, Mr. Murray, and it was Murray with two sailors who chased after and discovered three Fuegians hiding in the lee of a huge boulder over which a waterfall was cascading into the channel. The Indians had with them bits of canvas from the whaleboat. But these three Indians let loose a volley of stones that battered the Englishmen and smashed the eye of one of the sailors named Elsmore whom the Indians attacked and tried to drown. In the melee Murray shot one of the Indians, who flung two more stones and dropped dead.

Though it was a male Indian whom Murray shot, the Englishmen were surprised to realize that they had been fighting two men and a woman. The Fuegian women were quite as strong fighters as the men; they were stout and heavy in the arms; and FitzRoy himself, after wrestling to tie one's hands at the back, was astounded when his coxswain pointed out to him that he had been wrestling a woman.

FitzRoy returned to the *Beagle* with two hostages—western Fuegians, apparently healthy men in their twenties—and in addition he kept one of the children who had been abandoned, a girl about nine.

Venturing out in the remaining whaleboat again, FitzRoy had his sailors raise oars when another of the Indian canoes came near him.

In this canoe was the boy who had been staring from the beach; he had come out onto the water to be closer, to see better.

With a gesture FitzRoy ordered the Indian boy into the whaleboat—and the boy willingly came aboard, leaving two older men in the canoe.

When a sailor in the whaleboat observed that the older Indians would think the boy was being stolen, FitzRoy, still fuming, tore a large mother-of-pearl button from his coat and flipped it into the Fuegian bark-boat as payment.

Which is why the Englishmen took to calling the boy Jemmy Button.

T O T H E Yahgan boy this was all amazing. These white men were not the forest Ona. They were not horrible wild men from the north. These creatures were like dragonflies come to play.

And this fabulous thing on the water—he had to climb a kind of tree to board it and then he could stand on it as firmly as he could stand on land.

He was pleased, delighted, enchanted by all that was happening to him.

On the deck of the *Beagle* were the three Fuegians from the

*Robert FitzRoy, as drawn by Capt. Philip Parker
King during the first voyage of the* Beagle.

western islands, two grown men and a girl. The western
Fuegians, the men, both sneered at him. The Indians who inhabited the shore of the Beagle Channel at its western end were
distinct from the Indians on and around Navarin Island. The
language of the westerners, although understandable to the boy,
was a little different from his own. Yet the beginnings of trade
existed between these two tribes, neither of which had any
organization. Sometimes chips of iron pyrite from the deposit
that lay between them would be exchanged, and sometimes
mates were taken, eastern women by western men and western

women by the easterners. The western Fuegians were called Alacaluf; the eastern Fuegians were Yahgan.

These sneering western men called the boy *iapoo,* which meant "otter"—fit to be hunted.

The little girl, who FitzRoy thought was Alacaluf, was actually Yahgan from a western island where the Alacaluf and Yahgans mixed, but she spoke the Alacaluf dialect.

Captain FitzRoy, polite even in his anger, ordered that food be given to the Indians.

The four Fuegian Indians were absolutely dumbfounded when these elaborately adorned white men—all of whom weirdly had thick hair all over their faces—brought them fish and mussels, more thoroughly cooked than the Fuegians were used to but definitely food, and also salt pork which they had never seen or tasted before, on smooth white disks. With their fingers the Indians gingerly picked at the fish and mussels and tried the salt pork, while they squatted on the deck, munching.

At the rail FitzRoy waited for other Indians to come and negotiate for the return of the four he held.

He waited in vain.

After an hour Indians in bark-boats did again approach the *Beagle,* circling round it, but the Indians only stared without apparent feeling at the four on the deck of the ship and proceeded to beg, half-threateningly, for presents.

The family ties of these Fuegian Indians in their incestuous groupings were too slight, the expected independence of offspring came too early, the loss of family members was too common, for the separation of the four FitzRoy had taken as hostages to cause any commotion. The Indians simply didn't understand the significance of four of their kind being aboard this strange thing. And they would not be distracted from their begging and probing.

Finally FitzRoy left the rail and, with his crew on guard, went into his cabin and closed the door.

Then, with aristocratic finesse, with the aplomb that came naturally to him, FitzRoy transformed his frame of mind.

If he were to take these four aborigines back to England, they could be taught some English, they could be taught how to plant and how to build, and they could be instilled with the basic tenets of Christianity. Then, if he were to bring them back here again, they could pass on their knowledge to those of their kind.

Shipwrecked sailors might then be better treated. Ships passing through the straits north of the cape might be assisted rather than hindered. Eventually farms might be started here and ships could be provisioned for their long trip across either ocean.

In his cabin FitzRoy calmed himself and felt better. He had not acted out of frustration and anger. He had acted upon a noble impulse which was expected of him and which he expected of himself.

So he called for Mr. Murray and explained his plan in detail, practicing his rationalization verbally before writing it down in the ship's log. The *Beagle* was executing its mapping mission in tandem with a larger sailing ship, the *Adventure,* which was operating on the Pacific side of lower South America. In command of the *Adventure* was FitzRoy's superior officer, Captain Philip Parker King, who would eventually review FitzRoy's log.

Once his entry was completed, FitzRoy went back on deck and gave orders for his ship's departure.

VARIOUS GROUNDS FOR INDICTMENT

OBVIOUSLY various criminal acts had already been committed and many seeds of crime had been sown, but these were all of a commonplace sort and were not remarkable.

Primitive Indians who did not at all understand crime were stealing in a most natural, predictable way.

When pursued, as the Indians expected to be, they fought back ferociously—and the English sailor, Elsmore, had been blinded in one eye.

Mr. Murray, ship's master of the *Beagle,* had killed the Indian who had blinded Elsmore.

And Commander Robert FitzRoy, nephew of the Duke of Grafton, either (1) had kidnapped four Fuegian Indians or (2) had undertaken to transport the four Fuegians to England to educate them for their own betterment so that, when he returned them to their own land, they could pass on their enlightenment to their own kind for the convenience of his own kind.

FitzRoy did unquestionably try to explain to the four Indians on board his ship that after a while—perhaps within a couple of years—he would bring them back and they would bring with them iron tools and clothes and useful knowledge and knowledge of God.

It is equally unquestionable that the four astounded Fuegian Indians whom FitzRoy harangued on the deck of the *Beagle* did not understand him.

But there was, as yet, no consciousness of crime.

Nor was there a consciousness of crime in the events that ensued. In fact, on the contrary, there was a patent though unexpressed assertion of virtue in a sequence of events which nevertheless may be regarded as germinal to the ultimate crime. And these events attracted, from time to time, the attention of the Fleet Street press and the press of the world with tabloid intensity because this beguiling sequence clearly had a classical narrative pattern—a distinct beginning, a middle, and a false ending that achieved an emotional effect.

When the *Beagle* hoisted anchor and set sail from Tierra del Fuego, the four Fuegian Indians aboard understood that they were being taken out to sea—and that meant death. As the *Beagle* picked up the ground swells of the open ocean, the Indians were terrified. Where they had been—clinging for dear life to the coast of their channel—they had at least drawn a sense of security from the rocks. They knew what storms were and they knew they needed something to hold on to when it stormed, but there was nothing to hold on to in the open sea. So they vomited from fear as well as from seasickness as the *Beagle* with its lungs fully expanded made its way northward.

With glazed eyes the four Fuegians looked out at Montevideo when the *Beagle* anchored in the harbor there. What they saw—a town built by Europeans—was completely beyond them and outside their interest. The crew had given them a few clothes for the sake of decency and the Indians compliantly wore them.

The English sailors had named the four Indians:

The stolid surly man, estimated to be about twenty-six years old, was called York Minster because the sailors had named a rock near where he had been captured after the glowering English church of that name.

The younger man, around twenty, was called Boat Memory because he somehow could not seem to remember where the stolen English whaleboat had been taken, even though Mr. Murray's empty beer bottles had been found in his canoe.

The girl, about nine, was called Fuegia Basket because a few of the sailors from whom the whaleboat had been stolen had made their way back to the *Beagle* afloat in a canvas-lined framework of twigs and vines that looked like a big basket.

Jemmy Button was named for the price FitzRoy had paid for him.

York Minster's real name, phonetically transcribed by FitzRoy, was *ĕl'lĕpăru;* Fuegia Basket's name was *yŏk'cŭshlu;* Jemmy's name was *o'rŭndĕl'lĭcŏ.* FitzRoy did not transcribe Boat Memory's name.

While the *Beagle* was in harbor at Montevideo, the Fuegians were vaccinated against smallpox. This was done in a sensible and usually effective way. The doctors would draw some of the pus from the sore of someone who had smallpox, and a bit of this pus on a needle, when scratched on the skin enough to draw blood, served for the vaccination. (Benjamin Franklin—who, like FitzRoy and Darwin, was a champion of science in his time— although he understood the purpose of vaccination, failed to have his four-year-old son vaccinated, and the boy consequently died during an outbreak of the disease.) FitzRoy oversaw the vaccination of the Fuegians. It was as fierce a battle as when poor Elsmore was blinded, but vaccinated the Fuegians were. The Fuegians, for their part, seemed to fear that they had become burdensome to this strange white tribe and were being put to death, as the Fuegians put to death their own old and infirm when they became burdensome.

Nothing the Fuegians had seen yet, however, compared to the crossing of the Atlantic. Their seasickness and terror went on for weeks. The crewmen of the *Beagle* could not tell if the Fuegians were awake or asleep as the Indians squatted in their misery on the deck of the ship.

The eyes of the Fuegians were nearly closed when the *Beagle* entered the harbor at Falmouth. But then they saw something that amazed them, popped open their eyes, and brought them goggling to the rail.

A steamship was passing through the water near them.

FitzRoy was amused by their wonder at this fantastic thing, which was more fantastic than the boat they were on. The boat they were on had lungs like a whale or a seal or a corpse, but this other boat sending up a tower of smoke—was the smoke a signal of warning or greeting or farewell? Or a sign of sickness or anger? Or was the boat on fire?

The Indians were baffled. But reality, FitzRoy noticed, was what intrigued them, reality that they tried to fit into the realm of their comprehension.

And it was the shock of the sight of the steamship that brought the Fuegians back to life when the *Beagle*, along with the *Adventure*, arrived in England.

THE COST OF
NOBLESSE OBLIGE

W HILE at sea, FitzRoy had written an elegant letter
to Captain King which he knew King would forward to the
Admiralty. In his letter FitzRoy felt obliged to announce that he
assumed personal responsibility for the four Fuegians he had of
his own volition taken aboard and he would at his own expense
provide for their maintenance and comfort in England and for
their eventual return to their own country (presumably on the
next voyage of the *Beagle* to complete its mapping assignment).
With Victorian gentilesse, FitzRoy pointed out for the attention
of the Lords of the Admiralty that by educating and equipping
these natives prior to their return to their own country great
benefits to modern commerce might accrue.

While the *Beagle* and the *Adventure* were being decommis-
sioned in Falmouth, Captain King wrote a covering letter in
which he highly praised FitzRoy (describing one instance in
particular when FitzRoy on an exploring expedition away from
the safely anchored *Beagle* had spent thirty-one days in foul
weather in an open boat) and King sent both letters on to the
Admiralty.

The Lords of the Admiralty in turn agreed not to interfere
with Commander FitzRoy's plan—but allotted not a penny to
further it.

The Lords of the Admiralty, with some reason, might have
interfered because Boat Memory was taken into the naval hospi-
tal at Plymouth and died there of smallpox.

That FitzRoy was left financially responsible for the Indians
came as no surprise to his crew. Sailors of the Royal Navy in the
early nineteenth century were a cynical lot; in many ways they
were abused and sometimes sailors were still shanghaied into
service (although not into service on the *Beagle*); flogging was

still the usual form of punishment; and the last thing the sailors expected was generosity from high command. That FitzRoy, whom they knew to be an aristocrat and a martinet, was entrapped by his own generous gesture, his crew regarded as ironic. Yet the English sailors had become fond of the Fuegian Indians, and perhaps the sailors appreciated the benefit to themselves and to all seamen that FitzRoy's plan for the Indians might achieve. So the crewmen, at least several of them, volunteered their own time in the efforts FitzRoy now had to make in the Fuegians' behalf.

Immediately, the Fuegians had to be taken off the *Beagle* and FitzRoy paid for their installation in a boardinghouse in the port town. FitzRoy's coxswain, James Bennett, who made the arrangements, thought it fitting to rent two rooms, one for the men and one for the girl, but the Indians objected to being separated. So all three were installed in one room. The Indians did not take readily to sitting on chairs; they preferred to squat. And beds above the floor disturbed them, although they had become used to the hammocks at sea.

Whenever the Indians were in the midst of a town, they simply withdrew, their eyes glazing, their faces becoming slack and expressionless. All that was around them then seemed of no interest because there was too much for them to absorb and they appeared to lose their alertness.

A few of the sailors of the *Beagle*, carousing in the town, gave out that the Fuegians were fierce cannibals, the worst they had ever seen, liable to break loose at any moment, and the first news sheets appeared describing the fearsome savages. Soon FitzRoy had to move the remaining three Indians to a farmhouse outside the town.

Though the sailors of the *Beagle* caroused, there is no evidence that FitzRoy did so, even though he had been away at sea for years. After this first voyage of the *Beagle* under his command, he was twenty-five years old. And upon his return he probably went to call on his sister or other members of his family. After the second voyage of the *Beagle* when Charles Darwin went along—

a voyage of nearly five years' duration—FitzRoy on the day following his return took tea in Falmouth at the home of a Quaker scientist who had invented a dipping-needle deflector for use in barometric readings; the Quaker had a comely daughter, so FitzRoy, having come for tea, stayed until after eleven. But in fact, FitzRoy did not marry until several months after the second voyage. And Darwin, returning from the second voyage to a cousin who had been chosen for him and who had been waiting for him, took three years to get around to marrying her. In his notes Darwin made it clear that it took him that long to talk himself into marrying, although he enthusiastically announced the conclusion he had reached and congratulated himself for having reached it.

These men of scientific genius—FitzRoy and Darwin— seemed to be so intensely concentrated upon the world as it is, upon the quintessential reality of the world which they tried to see with greater accuracy than had ever been achieved before, that they tended to regard sex as a distraction from that concen- tration. For many men of artistic genius who try in one form of art or another to capture the world that is in their minds, sexuality of whatever bent is the source spring of their inspiration. But for these men of scientific genius—these intense realists—sexuality was unworthy as a preoccupation and definitely was not the driving force essential to their originality, so absorbed were they in perceiving deducible facts. For FitzRoy and Darwin the immi- nent onset of Victorianism also may have encouraged their sexual restraint.

The Fuegian Indians FitzRoy brought back, on the other hand, were behaving with utter naturalness. In spite of their terror at sea and their seasickness, they had all fattened up on a steady diet which they did not have to collect or catch. Jemmy Button—like most boys, wanting to be liked by the men around him—was the good-natured favorite of the crew. And York Minster was jealous of Fuegia Basket. He combatively kept the sailors, innocent and not so innocent, away from her (and thus provided basis for the reports of a few of the sailors to the press). There were no marriage formalities among the Fuegians, no ceremonies of any sort, no dowry or bridal purchase, no troth. York threateningly kept all other men away—while he waited for Fuegia's breasts to swell and for her to begin to menstruate.

FitzRoy approached the Church Missionary Society for help in the religious and practical education of the Fuegians, and the Church Missionary Society promptly turned him down. Their attention at that time was directed toward those parts of the East where the British Empire was embellishing its establishment and toward the British holdings in Africa; these were the places— with names like Mandalay and Zululand—that had romantic appeal and attracted funding.

FitzRoy persisted, however, and eventually the Church Missionary Society referred him to the National Society for Providing the Education of the Poor in the Principles of the Established Church. This was an odd connection and it set in motion an odd pecking order, which nonetheless worked. The clergyman who was the secretary of the National Society, Reverend Joseph Wigram, was the son of the squire of Walthamstow House, Sir Robert Wigram. Walthamstow was a pleasant residential suburb of northeast London. Reverend Wigram, a young man who with many of his sisters and brothers still lived in the parental home, talked to his father who in turn talked to the Rector of Walthamstow whose name was William Wilson, and the rector talked to the schoolmaster who ran the local "infant school" for the benefit of the neighborhood poor—a school for children not yet of boarding age who came from worthy but needy families. The schoolmaster's name is unrecorded in history but he was the one on whom was bestowed the obligation and opportunity of accepting into his home and family the three well-publicized savages from the other end of the earth, for the purpose of having these Fuegian Indians attend his school.

When plans for the transfer of the Indians were worked out, Murray and Bennett from the *Beagle* took York Minster, Jemmy Button and Fuegia Basket by coach from Plymouth directly to Piccadilly where FitzRoy met them at the coach depot.

Piccadilly in 1830 was, as it is now, a central hub of London life, a riot of activity, the bustling hive where people who held an empire were collecting and exchanging goods from all over the world.

The Fuegian Indians withdrew into themselves as soon as they left the quiet of the farm outside Plymouth.

Then what attracted their attention on the ride in the coach to Piccadilly was the periodic changing of the horses. This intrigued them. Horses, which were strange to them, were not wholly unlike the guanacos that inhabit the forests of Tierra del Fuego and Navarin Island, and these horses that obediently pulled the coach were changed when they became tired. To the Indians this was most interesting.

And FitzRoy, when he accompanied them in the coach to which they were transferred for the ride from Piccadilly to Walthamstow, sensed the interest of the Indians in this puzzling reality, likened their interest to many reactions of his own, and empathized with them.

In Walthamstow the three Fuegians were installed in the schoolmaster's small house where they remained for ten months. FitzRoy paid a modest amount for their keep and set the pattern for their education. Sensibly FitzRoy ordered that they should be instructed in English, in Christianity, in the use of tools, and in the basics of farming and husbandry. This education was given them by the unnamed schoolmaster in his school where the three dark-skinned Fuegian Indians—one full-grown and sullen man, one nearly full-grown boy, and a fat girl rapidly approaching womanhood—sat each day in their newly bought English clothes among the pale and staring small children of the English poor in their patches.

At this time the Industrial Revolution was in full swing in England; the country was thriving and paying scant attention to the social effects of the shift from agriculture to manufacture and trade; schools of this sort for the poor were tokens of a social conscience that was much discussed and very little regarded.

Fuegia Basket, in an English dress.

Jemmy Button, in his English clothes, as sketched by FitzRoy.

York Minster, while in England.

Nevertheless, the education of these Fuegian Indians as prescribed by FitzRoy progressed.

Fuegia was the quickest at learning English. She even learned a little French.

Jemmy was the most eager to please, and he excelled in manners. He loved to shine his shoes (Murray and Bennett had taught him how) and took great care of his clothes. He obviously liked the English crewmen and had endeared himself to the farmwife in whose home he had been kept; he had brought her bouquets of wildflowers.

York, who was never pleasant, was like a captured warrior biding his time. But even he showed interest in the tools and in construction. With reading, he had no patience.

All three Indians perked up as the months passed; they withdrew less or were withdrawn for shorter periods and less frequently. They became more generally interested in the details of their surroundings.

Occasionally the squire dropped by. The secretary and the rector—both young clerics—visited the school regularly and oversaw the Fuegians' education, giving emphasis to their religious instruction, although this had to be carried on by verbal repetition and rote.

And FitzRoy came often. He was excited because already he could see that these Indians would serve as interpreters. He could see the link being forged between the darkness they had been born to and the brightness of civilization.

FitzRoy would come in a coach and take the Fuegians to visit his sister Fanny. The Indians liked that; they liked his sister whom they called "Cappen sisser." She was brimming with energy and vitality like her brother but was less formal, and she would romp with them, inviting the laughter and play which was the first and most pleasant stage between people on radically different levels of human development. Obviously the Indians liked to get away from the dreariness of English clerics and the English poor.

Church notices and newspaper reports about the Fuegians

continued to appear and the public responded with enthusiasm and generosity. Many people came to the infant school just to see these Indians and brought the kind of presents the English would give one another—gloves, cravats, scarves, purses, stockings, hats, wicker baskets filled with knickknacks. Formerly the Indians would have torn these things into pieces, each taken a piece and eventually thrown it all away. But now they looked at each thing, turned it over and over, and tried to understand its purpose.

REX ET REGINA

ENTER NOW the King of England.

Finally the King heard about the Fuegians. Consequently in the summer of 1831 FitzRoy received a magnificently engraved summons to a royal audience for himself and his Indian wards.

So the Fuegians were most carefully dressed in their finest English clothes. There is no word for "king" in the Fuegian language, or even a close equivalent, so the Indians could not have really comprehended what was happening except that they were about to go on an outing of some importance. Jemmy applied several coats of polish to his best boots and he carefully selected from the pile of gifts the Indians had been given a pair of yellow chamois gloves that fit him tightly and well. The schoolmaster's wife helped dress Fuegia in a new dress and bonnet. York was dressed like an English cleric.

It was one of the crewmen from the *Beagle* who remarked that the Fuegians stood upright now; they no longer half-crouched as they had in Tierra del Fuego.

In the finest coach FitzRoy could hire, with every bit of brass gleaming and the varnish reflecting the dim summer sun (the Fuegian Indians thought the English climate was very nice), FitzRoy and his wards went to St. James's Palace, down edged paths paved with stones, pulled by sleek animals bigger than guanacos, into ever-wider paths, then passing through a wall of stiff straight black sticks, part of which was opened for them by gorgeously adorned men (some of whom held odd harpoons but not in a threatening way), to stop before an enormous building and to climb down and walk through rooms with decorated roofs, with walls and floors that were decorated, too, all fantastically ornate (to Indians who had never made or seen even a totem), with detail that strained their eyes (and the Fuegian Indians had exceptionally good eyesight), past other gorgeously adorned men in huge room after room, up a ridged hill to the upstairs audience chamber where waited King William IV and Queen Adelaide.

William IV had been King of England for only a year. He was the last of England's profligate kings, but he was sixty-five years old and was resigned to slowing down. His father, King George III, who lost the American colonies, had been a stubborn, hard-working, strait-laced incompetent whose ineffectual diligence, combined with a hereditary blood condition, had brought about four episodes of violent insanity which had periodically incapacitated him during his reign. The sons of George III perversely had opted for the dissolute life.

William's brother George IV, who had preceded William on the throne (George IV is the one who imported all the finery of the East for his *folie* at Brighton), used to leave boxes of official papers unopened for weeks on end, state papers that required his signature. William, especially since it seemed unlikely he would ever succeed to the throne, was a drunkard from the time he was a boy and cohabited with a succession of mistresses, giving his children by them the name of FitzClarence since he was the Duke of Clarence prior to becoming king. Having fallen impossibly behind in his obligations to moneylenders by the time he was about forty-five, he determined to make a good match for himself financially, but heiress after heiress rejected him until finally, when he was fifty-three, he had been accepted as husband for the daughter of a German duchess.

It is entirely likely that the King was well soused when he received FitzRoy and the Fuegians. FitzRoy's name must have amused William because it marked this rigid young sea-captain as some king's bastard descendant, like so many of William's own. The King, who when he was a young man had been to sea "long enough to hate it," took pains to discuss with FitzRoy the importance of surveying strange coasts and the problems of life at sea.

FitzRoy, although he was by nature a most perceptive observer, was excusably overwhelmed.

Queen Adelaide with her German accent was totally unintelligible to the Indians, but she laughed and made a big fuss and she was vivacious, like the Captain's sister, so they liked her.

The Fuegians showed off some of the English they had been taught (six months before, they would have withdrawn and not uttered a word). Fuegia was the most voluble; Jemmy was the proudest.

Delighted, the Queen went to her personal chambers and brought back a fine silk bonnet. She removed the simpler and smaller bonnet Fuegia was wearing and put onto Fuegia's head the Queen's own hat. Not knowing what else to give her, the Queen took a ring from her finger and gave it to Fuegia and also gave her an embroidered purse.

The King was enormously amused. In the spirit of the party, he filled Fuegia's purse with coins and proclaimed that this was money with which Fuegia could buy her trousseau.

The Indians never understood the significance of money. The notion of a trousseau, of course, was completely beyond them. But this audience with the King and Queen was undoubtedly the high point of the Fuegians' time in England.

THE FURTHER COST OF
NOBLESSE OBLIGE

F ITZ ROY was bedeviled by the cost of keeping the
Fuegians in England with no help or interest from the Admiralty
and, after Boat Memory's death, he feared for the Indians' health.
So he inquired of the Admiralty when he might expect the *Beagle*
to be sent back to Tierra del Fuego, assuming that he would be in
charge since Captain King was retiring.

To his surprise and disappointment FitzRoy learned that the
attitude at the Admiralty had changed and now there was no plan
to send the *Beagle* on another voyage.

FitzRoy was a man who accepted disappointment stoically, yet
each disappointment left its scar upon him.

He complained to some of his relatives in high places; it was a
reaction of pride because he and his relatives were better born
than many of the Lords of the Admiralty. But he proceeded with
other arrangements to accomplish his aim.

He unquestionably felt obligated by his promise to return the
Indians to their homeland and he was resolved to do so sooner
rather than later. So he petitioned for a year's leave of absence
from the Royal Navy during which at his own expense he would
take the Indians back to Tierra del Fuego.

Never inclined to interfere with his plans, and ignoring his
plea for financial support, the Lords of the Admiralty granted his
petition.

Then FitzRoy promptly went down to the London docks and
found a merchant vessel which was scheduled to leave for Valparaiso, Chile; the vessel was owned by a London trader named
John Mawman. For one thousand pounds sterling payable in
advance, John Mawman undertook to have FitzRoy, two aides
(probably Murray and Bennett) and the three Fuegian Indians
transported to Tierra del Fuego where at two places of FitzRoy's

choosing (at the eastern end of the Beagle Channel for Jemmy, at the western end for York and Fuegia) the Indians would be left ashore and FitzRoy and his aides taken back aboard and carried on to Valparaiso. FitzRoy promised there would be no unnecessary delay in landing the Fuegians. Mawman was to pay for the food and drink of FitzRoy and his party en route, but FitzRoy was to pay for the provisions, equipment and whatever else the Indians would take ashore with them, as well as for whatever incidental port charges and pilotage there might be.

A contract was signed by Mawman and FitzRoy. And at FitzRoy's order Bennett went out and bought a herd of goats for the Indians to take with them to Tierra del Fuego.

Then, unexpectedly, the Admiralty, possibly influenced by one of FitzRoy's relatives, changed its collective mind. The *Beagle*— without the *Adventure*—was ordered to return to Tierra del Fuego to continue with the mapping. FitzRoy, promoted from the official rank of commander to captain, was to be in charge, his year's leave of absence rescinded. This, of course, suited FitzRoy; this had been his expectation all along. And he was pleased by his promotion.

But Mawman would not revoke the contract that had been signed, and FitzRoy lost most of the thousand pounds he had paid.

The goats, likewise, had to be sold at a loss.

Nonetheless, FitzRoy's spirit rose as he engrossed himself in preparing the *Beagle* for another voyage. This time he was neither replacing a previous officer (and the replacing of a suicide had had its eerie aspect) nor under the command of a superior.

FitzRoy foresaw and had no doubt that the future of the Royal Navy—and, hence, the future of England—was tied to the advancement of science. So he proceeded carefully to buy and to install aboard the *Beagle* twenty-two chronometers with which he would confirm the longitudinal measurements of the earth.

And he had another noble idea. He would take with him this time a scientist—a naturalist who could investigate and attest to the strangeness of the lands they were about to explore.

THE requirements for this position of naturalist may seem odd to us now but were completely reasonable in FitzRoy's eyes. Whoever was chosen to be the naturalist to go on a voyage of more than two years would work for nothing, for no remuneration whatsoever. There was an opportunity here to be of service, which FitzRoy and the Royal Navy regarded as more than sufficient.

That the voyage would certainly be dangerous was regarded by FitzRoy and the Admiralty simply as an added incentive. It was expected of those who sought to be England's heroes that they would court danger.

And the naturalist, whoever was selected, would, of course, be expected to pay his own expenses, even his own mess bill aboard ship, and to equip himself, to buy the paraphernalia he required, to support himself when ashore.

It is a measure of the strength of England at its peak that there were many applicants.

THE VITAL ASSOCIATIONS

CHARLES DARWIN had a hard time making it. Darwin was not an aristocrat. On his father's side he was the son and grandson of practicing physicians, and his mother was a Wedgwood. In the Midlands the Wedgwood potteries were pouring out vases, dishes, cups and saucers that were being sold all over England and the Continent. Darwin's forebears were all brainy men. His grandfather, Erasmus Darwin, had written books on natural philosophy, and his other grandfather, Josiah Wedgwood, founder of the potteries and a stalwart of the Industrial Revolution, had introduced modern kiln techniques and introduced as well the use of classical Greek motifs to adorn the

*Pencil-portrait of Charles Darwin as a young man in 1840,
by George Richmond.*

crockery. All of these Darwin forebears, however, and especially Darwin's father, were believers in profit, at the least in ample recompense, and not in noblesse oblige.

Besides, Charles had failed to pursue his study of medicine at Edinburgh University, which had disappointed his father, and he had been sent to Cambridge to become a clergyman. But he had not responded to his religious studies either, and his career at Cambridge had been mediocre; he had ended up tenth on the list of those who had not sought honors.

Charles was a pleasant, unassuming young man, a good rider, a good shot, high-colored, with a bland disposition, excellent digestion and dependably regular bowel habits. And he had an extraordinarily equable temperament.

He was not by nature a spendthrift and his father had always given him an adequate allowance; there was more than ample money all about him; and economic ambition seems never to have occurred to him, even though England as a nation was in a frenzy of money-making (as exemplified by the Wedgwoods) and was driving to assert its power in the world (as exemplified by dedicated naval officers like FitzRoy).

Unaffected by economic pressure, uninspired by patriotism, uninterested in the ailments of the body or the soul, and most importantly not egocentric, Darwin was ideally suited *to see clearly*. And this is what, even as an undergraduate, he had done. At Cambridge he had fallen in with the professors who specialized in the natural sciences, in observing the realities of the earth. These professors liked him, though he was not an ambitious student; they liked his easy manners, his utter lack of affectation, and his most remarkable quality: the fact that he was not absorbed with himself.

Darwin at twenty-two—with no other call upon his time and with a seeming infinitude of time at his disposal—was the perfect fertile soil in which to plant a great idea.

FitzRoy's solicitation for someone to be the naturalist on the *Beagle* had been passed by the Royal Navy to Cambridge University, the more scientific of the two great English universities, and eventually the Cambridge professors recommended Darwin.

Darwin had no actual experience as a naturalist. All that could be said in his favor was that, when a student, he had shown interest in the natural sciences.

Darwin had to overcome his father's disapproval of the project—Dr. Darwin regarded it as lunatic—and his father's general disapprobation of Charles's impracticality and aimlessness. Charles's uncle, the second Josiah Wedgwood, helped bring round his father. Uncle Jos's opinion carried considerable weight because he was so rich, yet he was an easygoing man and was responsive to his nephew's enthusiasm. Moreover, Uncle Jos had a plain, even-tempered daughter only a little older than Charles and he foresaw the possibility of a match between his nephew and his daughter. A stint as a naturalist would provide Charles as a potential husband with some needed solidity.

Finally Darwin had to meet with FitzRoy's approval in order to win out over the other applicants. But FitzRoy and Darwin hit it off from the start. They were both wellborn young Englishmen in their prime—Darwin at twenty-two, FitzRoy at twenty-six—and they shared a greatness of vision; they wanted to analyze and explain the course of life on earth. That Darwin had once shown an interest in becoming a clergyman brought him favor in FitzRoy's eyes, not because FitzRoy liked clergymen (he didn't), but because FitzRoy in accepting and championing the various elements of his life—England, the Navy—was inclined to accept the literal word of the Bible. And it was the resolve of both FitzRoy and Darwin, both of them instinctive and compulsive scientists, to use the irrefutable logic of science to prove the Biblical account of creation.

This was their joint undertaking.

A FURTHER addition to the *Beagle*'s sailing list was suggested by the Rector of Walthamstow. He thought that a couple of young clerics, good at catechism, ought to accompany the three Indians who were to be returned to Tierra del Fuego, the clerics to remain there to establish a mission for continued teaching and preaching among the Indians. So certain was the rector of the acceptance of his suggestion that he had already organized a subscription for funds to support the missionary effort.

For this missionary effort, however, there was not a rush of applicants. With some difficulty one applicant was finally found, a young and eager catechist named Richard Matthews.

I T I S doubtful that Jemmy, York and Fuegia quite realized what was going on. They had been away from Tierra del Fuego for nearly two years. After they had been taken aboard the *Beagle*, most of a year had passed while the ship worked its way northward, mapping the lower east coast of South America, with prolonged stops for refitting in Montevideo and Río; then there had been the crossing of the Atlantic and the time spent in England. What the Fuegians did now realize, of course, was that another important excursion was in the offing, and they liked excursions. But, considering how they had suffered from seasickness and fear during their first crossing of the Atlantic, it is not likely to have occurred to them that another such crossing would willingly be planned.

Responding to the celebratory atmosphere, though, Jemmy shined and reshined all his boots and shoes. And Fuegia reexamined all her dresses.

Then Murray and Bennett showed up, and the Walthamstow schoolmaster and his wife pitched in, and all the presents that had been given to the Fuegians were packed into trunks or crated and prepared for shipment.

Reports had appeared in the press that the *Beagle* would soon be sailing to take the Indians back to their homeland, and a great volume of new presents arrived, presents absurdly unsuited for an expedition to Tierra del Fuego—tea sets, wineglasses, lace cloths, table linen, chamber pots, many small items of furniture—presents that English people thought would decorate the Indians' houses, except that there were no houses in Tierra del Fuego, no huts, not even cozy caves. (It unduly strained the imagination of English people of the nineteenth century to envision the life of these Indians at the bottom of the human ladder, at the bottom of the earth, as it strains our imagination today.) Yet none of these presents could be refused because the gifts were given in pure generosity, openhandedly, by the kindhearted English public whose sentiments had been whipped up by the exuberant English press.

Eventually all the crates, trunks and boxes—along with Jemmy, York, Fuegia, Murray, Bennett, and the bewildered cleric, Richard Matthews—were carted to a London dockside and were loaded aboard the London-to-Plymouth steamship.

The Indians hadn't seen the steamship since their arrival in England when, belching smoke, it had passed by the *Beagle* in the harbor. Now they were able to study this weird thing in some detail.

As in their canoes, the fire obviously was taken onto the water. But what for? Perhaps to send a signal; this is what a tower of smoke meant to the Indians; or perhaps for some other purpose. York and Jemmy peered at the glimpses of flame to be seen near the boiler; but why let the blaze flare up? Even Fuegia came and stared with them. They could not figure out the purpose of the fierce fire in the belly of this boat with so much smoke rising above them.

A year before when they had seen the steamship, they had not controlled their amazement or analyzed their wonder. But now, acclimated as they were, civilized as they were, they were puzzled and pleased by their reacquaintance with the steamship. And they thoroughly enjoyed their first (and only) steamship ride when they and their associates with their mountain of baggage were transported from London through the Strait of Dover to Plymouth where the refitted *Beagle* was docked.

The Indians were happy to see FitzRoy, and with him was a new young man of an even lighter color. The full crew was there, bustling about, because into this square-rigged sailing ship less than one hundred feet in length, with a beam of twenty-five feet, had to be packed seventy-four people with adequate provisions to last for eight to ten months, although the *Beagle* would restock en route; all the ship's equipment (including spare sails, six cannons with cannonballs, and a forge with iron ingots and coal); the expedition's scientific equipment; four whaleboats, a yawl and several dinghies on deck; plus the mountain of presents the Fuegians brought with them.

In all the hubbub, at Walthamstow, in London and Plymouth, it is reasonably certain that no one ever asked Jemmy, York and Fuegia if they wanted to be taken back to Tierra del Fuego.

This seemed an unnecessary question.

Captain FitzRoy's firm resolve, ever since he had picked up the Indians, was to take them to England for education and training and then to return them to their home. Besides, it would have been premature to discuss resettlement in Tierra del Fuego with these three Indians, two of whom were still young enough to be thought of as children.

The return of the Indians to their own country had been FitzRoy's primary motivation in pleading with the Admiralty for a second voyage. Once the second voyage was agreed upon, however, an elaborate assignment for the *Beagle* had been worked out. This assignment now became the focus of FitzRoy's attention; and, according to the Admiralty's plan for the second voyage, another year would pass—a third year away from home for the Fuegians—before the *Beagle* would again reach the southernmost tip of South America. The *Beagle* was to visit several islands in the Atlantic, then go to Brazil and survey the coast north and south from Rio, then proceed with the mapping of the Patagonian coast, confirming all previous measurements and filling in missing details, before reaching Tierra del Fuego.

So, from the Indians' point of view, all that was happening now was a continuation of this strange nomadic trek, this seaborne odyssey, among people who were so incredibly kind, people who fed them and gave them so many things and who required hardly anything from them. Even the little the Indians were asked to do, like learn English, seemed a game. By nature the Fuegians were nomads with only the slightest link to their homeland, to their families, to their tribes—they were rootless like tumbleweeds blowing about in a world far kinder than the world they had known.

The three Fuegian Indians seemed contented, unalarmed and unquestioning when the great lungs of the *Beagle's* sails filled once again and the ship headed southward from England, then turned west to the open sea.

RETURN TO THE
SETTING OF THE CRIME

A NOTHER year of voyaging passed for the Indians. FitzRoy was absorbed with his surveying and mapping; he kept his crew constantly busy. Little attention was paid to the Fuegians. Only Matthews bothered them occasionally, insisting that they recite the incomprehensible catechism, and they tried to oblige him.

The *Beagle* reached Brazil at Bahia. FitzRoy took measurements to the north and south, then moved the base further south to Rio. But when FitzRoy decided that the measurements he had taken at Bahia were incomplete, he returned in the *Beagle* to Bahia, and for nearly two months the Fuegians were left ashore in Rio, lodged in the home of yet another kindly Englishman.

From Rio the *Beagle* worked its way down to Montevideo and stayed there for some time, while FitzRoy updated the old Spanish charts for the Río de la Plata.

Then the *Beagle* continued southward off the coast of Patagonia, far out to sea because only one sizable river vents into the Atlantic along this desolate coast; there are few adequate bays for harbors; and FitzRoy, perhaps in belated eagerness finally to take his Indians home, intentionally bypassed the Strait of Magellan.

WHEN you approach Tierra del Fuego by sea from the east sailing toward the projecting hook of the island at its southeast corner, even in midsummer (December) as it was when the *Beagle* approached, the usual weather is dismal—the Atlantic blue-gray and covered with a skein of gray foam, strongly surging with oceanic ground swells that oddly have a short, rapid, dangerous chop, the surface of the water roiled by the wind or dappled by rain, and from the fog the ragged silhouette of the land emerging and developing its patina of massed Antarctic beech trees that in the cold and wet never shed their foliage but are always gray-brown, and the rocky, snowy remains of the peaks scarcely visible in the gray sky.

South America, when approached by sea, can be austere and proud, as when you come to the palisade coast of Peru at Mollendo and beyond the blazing strip of coastal desert you can see the looming massive ranges, row upon row of peaks, snow-crowned, rising to a dazzling white skyline etched against a brilliant, clear, infinite blue.

Not so in Tierra del Fuego. There everything to be seen is generally gray, and depression is the prevailing mood—the mood of profound melancholy that drove FitzRoy's predecessor to suicide. The cracked, faltering peaks of these islands at the tapered bottom of South America are not proud; they are like broken old teeth, soon to disappear.

Tierra del Fuego is an apt setting for a crime of ponderable proportion.

SURELY, while the *Beagle* plowed through the sea and the outline of Tierra del Fuego became bigger and clearer and the smell of the land was pungent in the wet, chilly air, Jemmy, York and

Fuegia came to realize fully what was happening: They were being brought back to their home.

In response to teasing and goading by the sailors, Jemmy and York had taken to bragging about their land and their people. But the first contact was traumatic.

After the *Beagle* anchored in a small bay, FitzRoy led ashore a substantial party, including Jemmy, York and Darwin—and on the beach they encountered the eastern Ona, huge Indians of the forest who had no canoes and never went onto the water and who sometimes hunted the little canoe-people. To York and Jemmy the sight of these eastern Ona brought a wave of sickening, primal fear.

With the Englishmen present, a kind of standoff took place. The Ona were puzzled to find canoe Indians with the English; they were especially puzzled because these two canoe Indians were wearing English clothes. The eastern Ona—who averaged about six feet in height—were dressed in fur capes, fur hats and foot-coverings, and they carried bows and arrows that they were able to use expertly. In the forest the Ona built substantial wigwams and they were proficient guanaco-hunters. They also were more responsive to their contacts with civilization than were the smaller Fuegians to the west. When the Ona asked the English for knives and hatchets, they used the Spanish word *cuchillo*. The Ona were painted, wild, raucous and intimidating.

The English reacted as they usually did and played with the Ona, in the pleasantness of first contact. FitzRoy, seeing that these were not the Indians he was seeking, cut short the encounter.

The reactions of FitzRoy and Darwin were interesting opposites: Darwin, who was not sentimental, was shocked by the Ona; he was shocked to see the extent of difference that existed between savage men and civilized men living contemporaneously. FitzRoy, on the other hand, thought well of the Ona and regretted he could not stay to help them. He felt that these Ona confirmed his notion of the universality of being human and

*A Heavy Gale Off Cape Horn, by Capt. W. Parker Snow, who
doubled and redoubled the cape many times. Snow reported that,
when a storm was blowing up from Antarctica, the sea undulated
with crests that were one-quarter mile apart, "like rolling Alps,"
and a sailing ship was becalmed in the troughs only to be blown
nearly to pieces when caught by the shrieking wind on the crests.
These waters south of Cape Horn, where the Pacific and Atlantic
clash, are acknowledged to be the most dangerous in the world.*

encouraged his hope that his effort with Jemmy, York and Fuegia
would prove constructive.

FitzRoy then decided to take the *Beagle* round Cape Horn as
the shortest route to the western end of the Beagle Channel.
(The South American mainland ends at the Strait of Magellan,
which runs to the north of the large, roughly triangular island of
Tierra del Fuego; the Beagle Channel runs to the south of Tierra
del Fuego; and there are many small islands, including Navarin
and ending with Cape Horn, south of the Beagle Channel and in
a fragmentation to the west.) This being summer, FitzRoy hoped

for at least bearable weather. The western islands were York's and Fuegia's country, and FitzRoy made it clear to them that this is where they would be taken. Then FitzRoy planned to go through the Beagle Channel with the current from west to east to reach Jemmy Button's country at the eastern end of the Channel.

Luck was not with him.

For more than a month FitzRoy kept the *Beagle* at sea trying to round the Cape. He fought off the worst storm he had ever been through. He was forced to seek shelter in inadequate little nooks like False Cape Horn. While at sea fighting the storm to make headway, the *Beagle* was washed over by a huge wave that nearly sank her. Darwin, who was prone to seasickness anyway, expected to die. But FitzRoy remained firm in his resolve—until finally York with a kind of elementary sensibleness came to him and, through gestures and broken English, conveyed that he and Fuegia preferred to be landed in Jemmy's country, so it wasn't necessary to round Cape Horn.

FitzRoy accommodated York, turned the ship about and sailed to the eastern end of the Beagle Channel.

Then out came the Yahgans, Jemmy's tribe, in their bark-canoes—yelling, naked, painted, with their mops of tangled hair, beside themselves with excitement, other Yahgans running about on shore in their cringing half-crouch. When the sailors left the *Beagle* in their whaleboats, they had to fend off the beseeching, intimidating Indians. And when the English went ashore, they were mobbed by the threatening Yahgans who came pouring at them from all directions—screaming, howling, bleeding from the nose in their frenzy, grabbing, stealing, tearing. Neither a warning shot from a pistol nor the waving of a cutlass affected the Yahgans. The English could not find a defensible place in which to establish themselves. And towers of smoke rose from Yahgan fires, summoning more Yahgans, signaling that something rare and strange had been come upon. Maybe a dead whale had been found and a feasting was at hand. There was only one signal: the smoke.

The Englishmen and Jemmy, York and Fuegia retreated, with

difficulty, to the *Beagle*. Near tears, Jemmy tried to explain that these were his people but not his family.

So FitzRoy hoisted anchor and moved on, dropped anchor in another cove, and again a multitude of crazed Yahgans came across the water, surrounded the ship, pursued the whaleboats to shore and nearly overwhelmed the landing party.

When Jemmy's mother appeared, she looked at Jemmy for no more than a few seconds, then went to tie up her canoe so that she could join in the fierce begging and stealing and the ripping to shreds of the red cloth the English sailors handed over to the Indians.

When Jemmy's oldest brother came forward, Jemmy and his brother said very little to each other, and what Jemmy said in his embarrassment was mostly in English with the common jargon of sailors' Spanish thrown in (*"No sabe?"*).

To Darwin the two Yahgan brothers looked like strange horses meeting in a field—though one was naked, painted, unkempt and unwashed, and the other was clean, with his hair cut and combed, and was dressed in English clothes.

But there wasn't a range of expression in the Yahgan language to bridge all that had passed; the Yahgan language was simply inadequate to bridge the difference which now existed between these brothers; nor was there between the brothers a strong sense of kinship. Also, Jemmy regarded the English language as his key to civilization; English was the main subject he had been taught in the last three years; and he was ashamed of the Yahgan language and was reluctant to speak it before his English friends.

This was a fair stretch of coast where FitzRoy had chosen to land. It had an accessible beach and behind the beach one of the rare strips of flat grassy ground where a crop could be raised. The English had no name for the place but Jemmy called it Wulaia, the *-aia* ending in Yahgan indicating a bay. This was not where FitzRoy had picked up Jemmy; that was further south in water the English called Ponsonby Sound. But this bay on Navarin Island south of the Murray Narrows was declared by FitzRoy under pressure to be suitable for a settlement.

So, with the *Beagle* at some distance offshore safely anchored and guarded, the English land party went at it—unloading from the *Beagle* all the goods which were considered to belong to Jemmy, York and Fuegia. While the sailors worked, marines guarded the yawl and the beached whaleboats, and boundary ditches were dug to mark off the area FitzRoy had selected.

With dispatch the sailors built three well-thatched huts, then spaded the earth behind the huts and planted two gardens. They brought planks from the ship and in the huts built lofts where some supplies were stored and they buried in the earth floor of the huts the supplies they wanted to protect from fire.

The work went quickly because there were twenty hours of daylight. And during the daylight and the few hours of dimness and darkness the sailors and marines from the *Beagle* tried to keep the Yahgans away.

But the Yahgans would not be kept away. There were thirty Englishmen and over three hundred Yahgans. The Indians never ceased to wheedle and steal and scream in their hoarse voices. Their language sounded to the Englishmen like a cacophony of guttural grunts and noises that the English could not utter. When a marine pushed off an old Yahgan man, the Yahgan spat in his face and in pantomime killed and ate the marine.

FitzRoy, in spite of the uproar, attended to his wards. And Jemmy, York and Fuegia were not terrified. They were ashamed of their own people. But the outcry and tumult were not strange to them. Jemmy, York and Fuegia were not disturbed, as were the English, by the lack of decorum and the absence of order, or by the seeming craziness of the Yahgan behavior.

AFTER five days and four short guarded nights, the English finished the camp for the three returned Fuegians and their tutor, Richard Matthews. Everybody was jumpy. The fervor of the Yahgans had passed through several stages. There had been almost no initial playfulness. When the Yahgans had descended upon the English, the Yahgans had in their hands and in their slings large round beach-stones and they had been diverted only by the gifts the sailors had proffered. Yet the frenzy of the Yahgans had, from time to time, flagged, and then they had passively watched from behind the boundary ditches.

At dawn on the fifth morning almost all the Yahgans were gone, and later only the Yahgan men—and more Yahgan men than the English had seen before—returned. The atmosphere was tense.

But the final step of FitzRoy's original plan had now been reached, and FitzRoy could not resist taking it.

FitzRoy asked York, Jemmy and Fuegia if they were afraid to stay. They said no. York said no because he was not afraid; he was eager to be free again. To him his experience with civilization had been captivity. Fuegia, who had come into womanhood, was utterly compliant to York's wishes. And Jemmy still tended to be defensive of his own people. He was sickened by the behavior of the Yahgans but he was not afraid of them, and that was FitzRoy's question which Jemmy understood. Also, Jemmy adored FitzRoy, knew what FitzRoy expected of him, and did not want to disappoint the captain.

Then FitzRoy asked Matthews if he would stay. Matthews had not impressed the men of the *Beagle,* though it is fair to say that to impress men with the energy and intellect of FitzRoy and Darwin was a formidable challenge. Matthews had done very little during his year aboard ship except to catechize the Indians. Apparently Matthews was a young Englishman of ordinary strength of spirit who did not question the worth and efficacy of the religious questions and answers he had learned by rote and taught by rote. True to his obligation, Matthews told FitzRoy he would stay.

Still, FitzRoy was uncertain. He put all his crewmen and Darwin back into the boats and they rowed out of sight, spent the night on another beach, and returned again in the morning.

Nothing much had happened during the night. Matthews repeated to FitzRoy that he was prepared to go on with the Lord's work which had been entrusted to him. York, Fuegia and Jemmy were unchanged.

So FitzRoy sent most of his men in the yawl and a whaleboat back to the *Beagle,* and with a dozen men including Darwin in two whaleboats FitzRoy departed and went westward against the current on an exploring trip along the Beagle Channel.

AFTER nine days FitzRoy and the exploring party returned— to find Matthews hysterical.

Once the boats from the *Beagle* were out of sight—and the departure was confirmed by Yahgans on the headlands who had watched them go—the Yahgans had invaded the camp, paying no attention to the boundary ditches or to Matthews' authority. They had stolen from him, threatened him with clubs and stones; they had kept him from sleeping by screaming into his ears and poking him all through the night. They had bent back his head until his neck was strained. They had pantomimed pulling all the hair from his beard and head and chest and groin and then killing and eating him, as if hair-pulling were their preparation of a human body, like the scaling and cleaning of a fish prior to a meal. In his year aboard the *Beagle* Matthews had learned nothing of the language of the Fuegian Indians, so he could neither under-stand the Yahgans nor speak to them. That the Yahgans hadn't killed him was apparently because their frenzy had abated temporarily (frenzy is exhausting and the Yahgans tired) and the Yahgans who kept arriving were more interested in the ever-smaller pieces of English goods than they were in him. But Matthews had no doubt that, if he stayed, he would be killed.

So FitzRoy without hesitation took him back for return to the *Beagle.* Matthews' assignment to preach among the Indians had not been FitzRoy's idea, nor had Matthews been his choice, and the failure of Matthews' mission did not affect FitzRoy's hope for the success of his original plan.

Unlike the catechist, York, Fuegia and Jemmy were not upset. They still had much of the goods that had been left with them; the huts were still standing. FitzRoy examined the gardens which had been trampled by the Yahgans and found that the planted seeds might still produce.

Jemmy said that his mother and his brothers had done much of the stealing, perhaps thinking that the goods were Jemmy's and they were welcome to whatever they could take. His mother and brothers had bragged to other Yahgans and had brought in many new family groups. Jemmy knew how the English condemned stealing and he, too, deplored it and complained about the behavior of his own relatives. Yet the truth seemed to be that, to Jemmy, York and Fuegia, this sharing of everything—even the repeated tearing and sharing until only bits were left—was not unreasonable. They did not regard the mountain of useless presents the English public had given them as their own property, nor did they place much value upon it. There was actually very little that the Yahgans regarded as personal property—a boat if one had built it, a few weapons if one had made them, maybe a hastily thrown-together wigwam.

York clearly conveyed, for himself and Fuegia, that he did not feel threatened and that they were content to remain.

Jemmy found it hard to hide his feelings. To Darwin it was clear that Jemmy wanted to rejoin them. But FitzRoy's question to Jemmy was the same: Was Jemmy afraid to stay?

And Jemmy's response was the same: He was not afraid. The wildness of his own people that so bothered the English did not bother him in the same way. And Jemmy knew that FitzRoy wanted him to stay. He knew that was what all his English friends expected of him.

So he stayed. Thus FitzRoy's original plan was put to the test.

Perhaps it can be said that at this point—when Jemmy Button, after three years of being embraced by civilization and warmed by the kindliness of the English, was left to fend for himself among his own uncivilized people—the basis for a crime was established, the foundation for crime was laid, in the bestowal and withdrawal of a dream.

Their work done, the Englishmen departed and did not return for more than a year.

THE TEST OF TIME

E VER DILIGENT, FitzRoy spent the next year in astonishingly hard work, carrying out the assignment that had been given him by the Admiralty, of completing the survey and perfecting the mapping of lower South America as well as confirming the longitudinal measurements of the world.

Initially, after leaving Jemmy and the others on Navarin Island off the Beagle Channel south of Tierra del Fuego, FitzRoy sailed to the Falkland Islands (the Admiralty had ordered him to check out the Falklands while he was at it). In the Falklands he encountered a veteran sea-captain of the South Atlantic named Low whose sealing schooner had nearly been wrecked in the storm the *Beagle* had endured off Cape Horn.

FitzRoy needed the schooner. He needed another base ship from which he could send small boats to establish the points for the angles on which he based his mapping. Captain King, FitzRoy's superior officer in command of the *Adventure* on the previous voyage, had faced the same problem, even though King had both the *Adventure* and the *Beagle* at his disposal; and King, when he wanted to purchase an auxiliary schooner, had sent off a letter to the Admiralty (by way of a merchantman from the port of Valparaiso) and had waited six months for his answer before making the purchase. FitzRoy, free from the control of a superior on the second voyage, had already hired two tiny sailboats and, with his usual aristocratic high-handedness and ultra-politeness, had sent off a letter to the Admiralty from Montevideo to the effect that, although he was certain that his need for these boats would be recognized and he would be reimbursed for their expense, if the Admiralty thought otherwise he was willing and able to pay for them because admittedly he had proceeded with the hiring on his own initiative. He had not yet received an answer from the Admiralty when he bought the schooner in the Falklands for 1,300 pounds sterling plus another 400 pounds for canvas and tackle (which he scavenged from two other ships that had been wrecked in the storm).

FitzRoy renamed the schooner the *Adventure* and with astute seamanship prepared her to sail alongside the *Beagle* en route around the world. At the outset this involved sending the newly christened *Adventure* from the Falklands to the Río de la Plata, where a fresh sheath of copper could be put on the hull of the *Adventure* below the waterline. (The coppered bottom would not attract barnacles, and a sailing ship with such a bottom was able to sail much faster; this was a secret of the Royal Navy's success for many years.) After completing his measurements in the Falklands, FitzRoy was to follow in the *Beagle*.

The difficulties with which these men contended cannot be overestimated and, in fact, can hardly be comprehended. The Falkland Islands lie 300 miles east of the Strait of Magellan. Montevideo is 1,000 miles to the north. And this is not a part of the world where sailing is easy. The seas are almost always high. A square-rigged ship is very hard to maneuver and cannot sail close to the wind. And in the Falklands it has been measured that, on the average, there are winds of gale force on one out of every five days.

FitzRoy demanded of his officers and men nearly as much as he required of himself. One of the little sailboats he had hired had a cabin only 30 inches high, and FitzRoy kept a crew on that sailboat, surveying the coast of Patagonia, for months without return to the *Beagle*. Again and again, FitzRoy led exploring parties in open whaleboats on expeditions that kept them from the mother ship for more than a month.

So across 1,000 miles of open ocean between the Falklands and Maldonado (a little harbor in the estuary of the Río de la Plata near Montevideo) went the *Adventure* and then the *Beagle* to rendezvous with the two tiny sailboats that had also been at sea during the storm that nearly sank the *Beagle* and nearly wrecked the *Adventure*.

It has been said of the Spanish *conquistadores* who subjugated

Mexico and Peru that they were ironmen, and to anyone who has spent much time in Mexico and in the Andes this is undoubtedly true: Those men in their armor, many of them middle-aged and one in advanced age, went up and down the massive mountains and forced multitudes of Indians of complex civilizations to yield to them.

But these English sailors of the Royal Navy, led by inspired aristocrats, assisted by scholarly plutocrats, were remarkable for their caliber, too. They operated in peacetime; they were the generation after Nelson; they fulfilled a mission of noblesse oblige, furthering civilization's comprehension of the physical world—and they did what they did without the lure of gold or the lust of conquest.

During their stay in the Falklands, the work load for the men of the *Beagle* was extremely heavy. FitzRoy had to spend many days and nights in his cabin, which he shared with Darwin, compiling and assembling all the mapping computations he had accumulated and keeping up to date his log and journal. FitzRoy had to see to it that each day, when the weather permitted, boats under commanders he had accurately instructed went out to gather more surveying details. At all times FitzRoy had to make sure that the *Beagle* and its boats were well maintained and in good repair. He had negotiated the purchase of the schooner and the equipment for it. In his cabin he was crowded in with the twenty-two chronometers and the barometers and many of the specimens that Darwin kept collecting. Darwin would go ashore almost every day regardless of weather to gather flora and fauna which he would sort out and dry on the scrubbed deck (to the disgust of the officer on watch) and then would come below to bottle and crate his catch and to work on his own diary and journal.

In addition, FitzRoy had to attend to the problem of government on the Falkland Islands.

There *was* no effective government on the Falkland Islands. For two hundred fifty years France, Spain and England had alternated in asserting sovereignty over these islands, complete with the raising of national flags and the occasional placing of plaques, only to come, each empire in its turn and repeatedly, to the realization that these miserable, windswept, rainswept islands were next to worthless, used only as a refuge by seal-hunters.

By 1820 Spain had lost its grip on South America but the nations of South America had not yet formed. In 1828 the "United Provinces of the Río de la Plata" based in Buenos Aires had sent a governor for the Falklands and with him a small troop of soldiers who built a fort and some gauchos to corral the cattle that had become feral and ran wild on the islands. The Argentine governor imprisoned a few American sealers for seal-hunting without a license, so an American warship, the *Lexington,* had sailed in and blasted the little fort to pieces. The American captain, Silas Duncan, had proclaimed that the Falklands had no government, and the Americans had sailed away.

Then a British warship had visited the islands. The British disapproved of Captain Duncan's assertion; the British regarded the Falklands as British territory (and somewhere on a rock there was a lead plaque to prove it). The British also refused to recognize Argentine control. The governor from Buenos Aires had gone home but the British found in residence a British citizen who was the governor's business partner, a gnarled old sailor named Brisbane. So the British, dismissing both the American contention and the Argentine claim, reasserted their sovereignty and left Brisbane in place as Britain's representative. The British forced the remaining Argentine soldiers to go back to Buenos Aires. Then the British sailed away.

A short while after the departure of the British warship, the *Beagle* on its mapping assignment anchored in Berkeley Sound.

FitzRoy took a liking to Brisbane, who had been shipwrecked several times. And FitzRoy, to whom authority came naturally, tried to help in the establishment of order and the fostering of productivity.

The Argentine gauchos, left stranded after the British had

forced out the troop of Argentine soldiers, were about to embark for the mainland themselves. FitzRoy, however, liked the gauchos and felt that their departure would weaken the Falklands, so he harangued the gauchos and induced them to stay— to bolster the population and to continue in their roundup of the wild cattle.

Darwin liked the gauchos even more than FitzRoy did. With two gauchos (and six horses) in bad weather Darwin made a trip of several days around East Falkland Island. Darwin was used to living outdoors and his prowess as a rider was noticed by the gauchos, who have their own distinctive riding style, sitting high over a horse like Arabs astride camels, and they accepted and respected him.

The gauchos killed and ate the wild cattle for sustenance on the trip. They introduced Darwin to *asado con cuero*, beef with the hide still on (which is delicious, slow-cooked over a fire, and the hide, hardening into leather, acts as a bowl to catch the juice from the meat, and the meat softens in the natural gravy; in the countryside of Greece, lamb cooked on a spit the way in Homer's time "hundred-beast sacrifices" were prepared has the same kind of intense flavor).

Argentine gauchos are among the cruelest handlers of animals (I once saw a gaucho nearly cut a dog in half with a whip-stroke). When an old bull got in the gauchos' way and seemed stubborn about moving on, the gauchos emasculated him.

IT IS amazing, in the circumstances under which FitzRoy and Darwin lived aboard the *Beagle*, that they got along as well as they did. They were living in terribly close quarters. Both were men of genius or formidable intelligence; both were fantastically energetic and dedicated, each to his own calling. They had to eat in the little cabin in which they worked and slept and washed and defecated. They both kept accumulating more and more papers and paraphernalia. With increasing frequency FitzRoy had fits of temper that offended Darwin and adulterated the pure admiration, almost adulation of FitzRoy with which Darwin had begun the voyage. It was remarked by many on board including FitzRoy that Darwin always seemed to keep his good humor. But FitzRoy was the one solely responsible for the whole venture while Darwin was free to quit at any port. FitzRoy, like most disciplinarians, was relentless with himself and was firm and often irascible with his officers and men. But under the burden of that work load, confined as they were, through all the dangers and difficulties, the voyage of the *Beagle* went on for nearly five years.

Obviously, FitzRoy and Darwin liked each other very much. While the *Adventure* was being recoppered and later while they were proceeding with the mapping of the Patagonian coast, FitzRoy and Darwin would often go out by themselves to pursue their speculations. Of all the young Englishmen on that voyage, theirs were the minds that met.

Sometimes they would sit in a dinghy in calm water at the mouth of a river, patiently sounding the bottom — and pondering how this river had been created or affected by The Flood.

Another time, assisted by some crewmen, FitzRoy and Darwin hauled a whaleboat up a river for sixteen days by pulling it from the shore like Volga boatmen because the current downriver was too strong for them to make headway on the water — and they wondered about the origin of the mountains and the land. On that hauling trek, Darwin, who with his hunting background was the best shot in the company, kept guard on the flank and brought down the game they needed. FitzRoy took his turn in the traces.

They had fun, these two brilliant young Englishmen, straining as they were with their bodies, their brains and their beliefs.

In their twenties, at peak strength physically and intellectually, FitzRoy and Darwin were not yet fixed in their points of view: They were squinting, peering, trying to fathom the most profound mysteries.

Once, in a discussion aboard ship when other officers were present, an argument was peremptorily terminated by a quotation from the Bible as an authoritative closing of the subject—and it was Darwin, the prospective clergyman, who quoted the Bible.

On another occasion, when FitzRoy and Darwin were crossing a dry riverbed of rounded stones, one of them, taking up a stone and turning it in his hand, said, "This could never have been effected by a forty days flood." The doubter was FitzRoy.

As they veered with their thoughts, though, Darwin tended more and more toward skepticism, even toward an assertion of disbelief in the literal word of the Bible, while FitzRoy, overcoming his occasional spasms of doubt, tended in the end to stand by his loyalties—to England, to the Navy, to the accepted Word of God.

But from all our knowledge of human history, from the whole known span of it, do we know of many young men who equal these two, working as they were, thinking as they were, bending all the strength of their minds and spirits over the grandest questions they could conceive, and sticking at it for years on end, in spite of the perils, without assurance of reward and without economic incentive?

Can we think of the like of FitzRoy and Darwin afloat in their boat off the coast of Patagonia, sounding for Truth?

THE SEARCH FOR JEMMY

I T W A S summertime again when the *Beagle* reached the Strait of Magellan. FitzRoy had sent the *Adventure* from the Río de la Plata to the Falklands to finish up the work there. In the *Beagle* FitzRoy went through the Strait of Magellan as far as Port Famine, about a hundred miles, to redraw the old Spanish maps. Then he brought the *Beagle* back to the Atlantic and, in the mild weather which he hoped would hold, went southward around the hook of Tierra del Fuego in search of Jemmy Button.

THIS time FitzRoy did not anchor the *Beagle* in Goree
Roads and proceed from there in the whaleboats; he brought the
Beagle into and through the Beagle Channel. From the deck of
the ship with the gun ports open, the Yahgan-filled canoes which
promptly came out to meet them did not seem so menacing.

FitzRoy anchored the *Beagle* off the shingle beach behind
which the three huts could be seen. Then with Darwin and an
armed party he went ashore.

The place was deserted, the huts ransacked and empty, the
roofs fallen in. FitzRoy poked about in the gardens that had been
planted. He pulled up a few potatoes and turnips that were big
enough to eat, and he and Darwin took them back to the *Beagle*
and had them for supper.

The Yahgans were in awe of the big ship or had not yet adjusted
to it, so the men of the *Beagle* spent a fairly quiet night aboard. It
seemed too quiet to FitzRoy and Darwin as they wondered what
had happened to Jemmy, to York and Fuegia.

In the morning FitzRoy raised anchor and with a light breeze
moved the *Beagle* slowly past the islands in Ponsonby Sound
where there were a few Yahgan canoes on the water and the
Indians were fishing.

What first startled the men aboard the *Beagle* was that the
Yahgans in these canoes called out to them not in their guttural,
unintelligible language of coughs punctuated by shrieks but with
a modulated English "halloo." And several of the Indians, with
gestures to come closer, said clearly, "Over here!"

While the *Beagle* was again dropping anchor, FitzRoy, Darwin
and the others saw a canoe being paddled rapidly from the shore
and in the prow with his back toward them was a Yahgan who was
dipping his hands into the water and washing the paint from his
face. When the Yahgan turned, they recognized Jemmy Button.

The ladder was lowered and Jemmy came aboard. He was
naked, emaciated, starved. He no longer stood upright, and the

cringing Yahgan half-crouch conveyed his defensiveness, his frailty and vulnerability.

Jemmy's frame was so thin that his penis and scrotum appeared to be swollen as a sign of sickness. He was half-blind, his eyes bleary and rheum-filled from the smoke of the perpetual fires. His hair was long, dirty and tangled, his greasy skin gritty from the earth.

But it was Jemmy—and he was so pleased to see FitzRoy again. And Murray. And Bennett. And Darwin. All his old friends.

Jemmy's grin of welcome was unchanged.

FitzRoy hurried Jemmy below, put him into some britches, and had food served.

The Englishmen were shocked.

Jemmy was not. Although he had been ashamed to show them his painted face, he quickly overcame his shyness at the table, spread his napkin and meticulously took up his knife and fork. And his English, which he said he was teaching to the other Yahgans, easily came back to him.

What he told them then was vivid.

After the *Beagle*'s departure, while pilfering of the stores by the Yahgans continued, York Minster had built for himself a large bark-boat. York had asked Jemmy and Jemmy's mother to come with him and Fuegia to their homeland in the west, and Jemmy and his mother had put all their belongings into York's boat. After they had paddled away from the settlement for a day and had gone to sleep ashore for the night, York and Fuegia had risen during the night and had pushed off in their boat with all the goods, leaving Jemmy and his mother to find their way back as best they could to the ransacked settlement. Nothing had remained for Jemmy from the mountain of gifts the English had deposited.

Still, Jemmy smiled and to himself repeated the names of his friends. FitzRoy (Cappen). Murray. Bennett. Bynoe, the surgeon. Darwin. Not Matthews, the catechist, who was still aboard but whom FitzRoy had not invited to his cabin.

*Jemmy, in his reversion to his native state,
as FitzRoy sketched him in 1834.*

Jemmy had not settled again in one of the huts, he said, because nothing of value remained, yet the huts kept attracting other curious Indians of a bad sort. Besides, he couldn't keep warm in the large high-roofed huts. So he had moved to this small island which did not attract others and had built for himself the usual wigwam, just a windbreak of rushes around a fire.

Jemmy couldn't eat much of the food. He ate a little of each dish but soon stopped and said he had "too much." Starved men are usually incapable of eating amply.

In spite of Darwin's politeness and his bourgeois decency, this pitiful Indian seemed to him an example simply of mistaken transplanting: Wild things were best left in their native habitat; when they were transplanted, damage was done to them, often irreparably, and they died.

FitzRoy, on the other hand, behind his mask of aristocratic rigidity, was overcome by his own affection for Jemmy and by his sense of responsibility for what had happened.

FitzRoy asked Jemmy if he would like to return with them to England (FitzRoy did not say but he meant that Jemmy would be his lifelong guest).

Jemmy looked about at his English friends and he took a minute to think it over. Then he shook his head, not impulsively but conclusively, only lightly moving his head from side to side.

No more cross ocean, he said.

Have plenty to eat here, good people here, he said.

Am not cold, he assured them.

With his reluctance ever to say anything he knew would displease the English, Jemmy did not say to them that he could not bear to go into the light and to be brought back to the darkness again.

When they heard loud crying outside the ship, they all went on deck, and the men of the *Beagle* could see another cause for Jemmy to remain here. In a bark-boat alongside the *Beagle* was a little naked Yahgan girl, and she was crying loudly and gesturing for Jemmy to rejoin her.

Darwin thought: Here in his native habitat Jemmy was taking root.

Grinning, nodding his thanks, Jemmy went down the ladder to the girl, promising FitzRoy (Cappen) that he would return in the morning.

That night, in their cabin on the well-guarded *Beagle*, Darwin worked on his specimens, preserving some in jars, boxing others, annotating everything.

FitzRoy was in one of his moody silences. After sitting for a while, he went out on deck and he saw Matthews standing at the port rail. So he turned to starboard and went aft.

As a naval officer, FitzRoy had been trained in strategy. Now he fully recognized that York had his scheme in mind ever since York had come to FitzRoy to make clear that he and Fuegia preferred to be put ashore in Jemmy's country. Had York and

Fuegia been landed first, they would have been given their fair share of the presents as determined by FitzRoy. But if York and Fuegia were landed with Jemmy in Jemmy's country, York knew he would be able to steal the bulk of the goods and escape (free again) to the west. Mercilessly FitzRoy rebuked himself for his own failure to see through York's scheme.

And FitzRoy grieved for Jemmy.

IN THE morning shortly after dawn the Yahgan canoes came out from shore and Jemmy climbed on deck again, wearing the britches FitzRoy had given him.

This time Jemmy brought presents—an otter skin for Murray, another otter skin for Bennett, a spearhead and two arrows he had made for Cappen.

Once again FitzRoy asked Jemmy if he would like to come with them to England. FitzRoy was careful now not to ask if Jemmy was afraid to stay here. He asked clearly if Jemmy would come back with them.

But already there was loud crying from Jemmy's girl in their canoe alongside (she refused to come aboard). And Jemmy again shook his head.

So FitzRoy, heartily assisted by the others, heaped Jemmy with presents, sensible presents from the ship's stores, tools and food, more than Jemmy could carry so he had to make many trips down the ladder to his canoe and back.

While Jemmy was carrying away the last few loads, the sailors hoisted the anchor and the *Beagle* began to drift in the water.

Then Jemmy's girl became wild in her pleading and Jemmy hurried, bade the Englishmen a quick good-bye, and left the *Beagle* for the last time.

FitzRoy with crackling orders sent his men into the rigging to set sail.

As the *Beagle* moved through the channel, the men aboard all watched the great tower of black smoke that Jemmy was sending up by throwing fresh leaves onto his fire, in token of farewell.

ILL WINDS

FITZROY then took the *Beagle* back to the Falklands to rendezvous with the *Adventure,* also to reconfirm finally all the measurements of the islands. As a perfectionist, FitzRoy was continually reconfirming his mapping and remapping of this part of the world.

In the Falklands both FitzRoy and Darwin found horror that redounded upon themselves.

Going ashore, after the *Beagle* was anchored, FitzRoy and Darwin came upon the bare feet of Brisbane protruding from the soggy earth. The old Englishman, Britain's resident representative, survivor of shipwrecks, had been murdered by the gauchos.

FitzRoy had the whole body exhumed. The gauchos had dragged Brisbane with a lasso round his neck from the back of a galloping horse, probably from several horses; it had been a better game than the *bolas.* The vertebrae of Brisbane's neck and upper spine were displaced and shattered. The gauchos had buried him in a shallow grave; dogs or foxes had found the body and fed on it.

A shore party from the *Beagle* reburied the body at a proper depth, in a flag-draped coffin.

It was a sickening experience—the discovery of the old man's body, with the comprehension of what had happened, and the reinterment of the corpse. At sea since he was fourteen, FitzRoy, while in command, had had men washed overboard and lost, but he had never caused the death of a man—and he had urged the gauchos to stay.

After the emotionally rending experience of seeing Jemmy again and of leaving him, FitzRoy was affected noticeably by tragic turns that he might otherwise have shrugged off, that he could have been expected to accept simply as twists of fate. But these occurrences now stayed with him, weighed heavily upon him and depressed him.

At long last he received a reply from the Admiralty regarding his hiring of the two tiny sailboats: His proposal was rejected; he had not been authorized to hire any additional vessels; having done so on his own initiative, and having said that he was willing and able to pay for the sailboats himself, it was expected by the Lords of the Admiralty that he would do so. And this judgment was rendered after the Royal Hydrographer had appended to FitzRoy's petition a note to the effect that the *Beagle* was the only surveying ship in the Royal Navy that did not have assigned to it auxiliary vessels.

So FitzRoy from his private funds paid for the sailboats a total of 1,680 pounds sterling when, prior to leaving Patagonia, he returned the sailboats to the Englishman in Bahía Blanca from whom he had rented them.

FitzRoy had been waiting for this reply from the Admiralty, assuming approval, before writing for permission to purchase the *Adventure.* Now that loss as well had to be coped with.

Nevertheless, FitzRoy took the *Adventure* with him on the last voyage of the *Beagle* down the coast of Patagonia, through the Strait of Magellan and into the Pacific.

FitzRoy felt he could not dispense with the *Adventure* because the coast of Chile at the tapered bottom of South America is extremely fragmented; it was part of FitzRoy's assignment to survey this coast; and he could not do the work he felt necessary with only one base ship. Thus FitzRoy took his assignment more seriously than did the frugal Admiralty. Furthermore, the *Adventure,* which he had so carefully refitted, was vital to his plans for the remainder of the voyage, on a route that was to traverse the Pacific to New Zealand, to visit Australia, to explore the islands of the Indian Ocean, to round the Cape of Good Hope, to visit the islands of the South Atlantic, to call at Brazil again, then to proceed homeward across the Atlantic. This was an incredible voyage for a ship like the *Beagle* to undertake alone; for safety's sake, ships sailed in tandem or in squadrons on long voyages so there would always be a ship to come to the aid or rescue of another. But where victories were sought at any cost in wartime, economies were the trophies sought by the Admiralty in peace-time. Only reluctantly had the *Beagle* been sent out at all.

For four months the *Beagle* and the *Adventure* proceeded northward along the Chilean coast, trying to map the countless islands, and going finally into harbor at Valparaiso.

Darwin, delighted to be ashore again, went off by himself on one of his expeditions, affording FitzRoy more room on board. But FitzRoy said he needed still more room where he could spread his charts and papers and compile the results of these years of surveying. So FitzRoy left the ship and rented quarters for himself in the town.

FitzRoy said he had to get away from the annoyances on board—calls by officers from other ships, courtesy calls from the local people, the details of shipboard life. FitzRoy always seemed to attract or to have connections to the aristocrats in the port towns; perhaps his manner identified or ingratiated him; but now he found the gestures of courtesy required of him to be an insufferable strain.

Yet separation from the ship did not suit FitzRoy. He could not sleep ashore. His appetite failed him and he lost weight to such an extent that Bynoe cautioned him and told him he was suffer-ing from overwork and exhaustion. FitzRoy said he had to com-pile all these records, even though the sedentary life ashore sapped his strength and he was less able to do the work.

FitzRoy's manner had always been self-disciplined and sure. Now he was so irritable as to be unstable.

He decided he had to sell the *Adventure*. He may have heard from his solicitors in London who honored his drafts that they would have to borrow on his landholdings since he had used up his cashable assets. Or he may simply have forced himself to the realization that this was his predicament. In any case, he did sell the *Adventure* at a loss because, as he said, he was too dispirited and distracted for a prolonged negotiation which might have brought him the profit he deserved for having considerably improved the ship. He sold the schooner at a loss of 300 pounds from the purchase price, plus a loss of 400 pounds he had paid for canvas and tackle, plus the cost of coppering the bottom, plus the cost of the crew he had hired (Wickham, his own senior lieutenant, had been in command of the *Adventure*).

That was it, a dead loss forced upon him by the Admiralty, and with it went his dream of being able to complete his voyage around the world with the efficiency and thoroughness he expected of himself.

Not only did the Admiralty not care about his dream, but the Admiralty had been affected by a political change which Darwin fully recognized and FitzRoy chose to ignore. In England the Whigs had come into power (Darwin's people were Whigs) and Tories were out of favor (FitzRoy's people, of course, were Tories). An ambitious young Tory like FitzRoy, though supposedly apolitical as a Navy officer, was now regarded as a threat.

Ashore, alone, FitzRoy worried about money. He worried that without the *Adventure* he could not set an example for Navy surveyors of the future to follow. He worried that he would not be able to fulfill the role he knew he was capable of playing—for England, for the Navy, for maritime science in the service of mankind.

He tried to turn from his thoughts—about Jemmy, about Brisbane, about his mistakes. If he were to return to Tierra del Fuego (as his crew and Darwin feared he might), he could see Jemmy again—if Jemmy were still alive.

FitzRoy worried about his own sanity.

His uncle, Lord Castlereagh, had committed suicide when FitzRoy was seventeen years old and already a midshipman at sea. There had been a great scandal and FitzRoy had heard all the variations of the gossip. When FitzRoy was a child, Castlereagh (his mother's brother) had been an austere, imposing presence of great handsomeness and regal grandeur. His manner was "frosty" even to his fellow-members of Parliament. Castlereagh had fought Napoleon, had directed English policy through critical post-Napoleonic years, had been England's dominant minister—until, when he was in his early fifties, he had been entrapped.

While walking from the House of Parliament to his home on St. James's Square, he had been approached on the street by a whore. The whores knew who he was; he had patronized them before; and he had gone with this whore to a nearby flat. (Castlereagh had a childless marriage to a wellborn lady who had been a beauty and was known to be high-strung and demanding.) When the whore's accomplices broke into the flat, the whore with Castlereagh, having taken off a skirt and shift, was seen to be a naked boy.

The accomplices had blackmailed Castlereagh—and he had paid, again and again. But oddly Castlereagh, although famous for his icy reserve, and despite the fact that he was paying to keep the matter from becoming public, told all his close friends about it; he told the Duke of Wellington (who, like Castlereagh, was one of the English lords of Ireland), Sir Walter Scott, even King George IV, all of whom advised him not to pay another penny and to place himself under medical care because he was distraught.

Castlereagh's garrulousness about his entrapment caused some of his friends to recall that, when he had been a young officer, he had once seen a ghost. Then, too, he had talked volubly about his experience, insisting that he had seen a true ghost and had not had a nightmare—and the ghost he had seen had been, in Castlereagh's words, "a radiant boy" who, having originated as a tiny figure in a fire and having grown larger as he came closer, was naked and had a slashed, repellent face.

Castlereagh became paranoid in the belief that his friends suspected him of homosexuality, an unspeakable crime throughout the nineteenth century. And he feared that he would be openly accused by those who had entrapped him. Eventually, at the age of fifty-three, he killed himself by cutting his own throat.

FitzRoy had been deeply impressed by the loss of his most famous close relative under these circumstances.

There are times in life when a man has to bear too much.

FitzRoy declared himself ill, classified himself as invalided, and resigned his captaincy of the *Beagle,* naming Wickham to command.

But FitzRoy was not yet thirty, and those around him would not stand for his withdrawal. Wickham, disregarding his promotion, went to FitzRoy's house ashore and argued with him. What was to be accomplished by resigning? FitzRoy's career would be over; his file would be closed in the Admiralty; who would notice? Bynoe joined in the argument. This depression was nothing but exhaustion from overwork. Murray, Bennett, the whole crew demanded that FitzRoy take back his resignation (which had not yet been forwarded to the Admiralty) and lead them the rest of the way around the world and home. In triumph. Triumph over problems which they at least realized were monumental.

The strength of FitzRoy's youth reasserted itself. He returned to the ship and resumed command. His black thoughts—about Jemmy, about the rest—receded.

Darwin came back from his Andean expedition sick with the fever that was to recur through the rest of his life.

Though the *Beagle* was ready to sail and Valparaiso was a port from which Darwin, once recovered, could easily have arranged transport for himself to England, FitzRoy would not go on without Darwin and waited until the strength of Darwin's youth prevailed.

Then the *Beagle* sailed on.

Without the *Adventure* FitzRoy was unable to survey the coast of Peru as he had intended, but his assignment, his commandment from the Admiralty, was to survey as much of the western coast as he had time for. Originally this was expected to be a voyage of two years or a little more, and already, as a result of FitzRoy's perfectionism, over three and a half years had passed.

So FitzRoy, with the wholehearted support of everyone with him on the *Beagle*, finally turned the ship toward the Galapagos Islands, and their westward crossing of the Pacific began.

ON AND ON, the *Beagle* sailed, to round the world—captained by a stalwart young champion of orthodoxy who strove to the very limits of his endurance, and bearing a mild-mannered, dispassionate young observer for whom the world seemed on display and in whose clear mind was irresistibly forming an overview of life no one had ever had before.

BANNER HEADLINES

IN OCTOBER 1835 the *Beagle* returned to home port in England, completing a voyage of nearly five years, and in the ensuing months and years many men of the *Beagle,* not only Darwin and FitzRoy, polished and published their diaries and journals. The files of the Admiralty filled with reports, charts, compilations.

So it was only gradually, as the substance of these reports sank in, that the Fleet Street press and the press of Europe became aware of the poignant ending to the story of Jemmy Button.

Then the press responded enthusiastically.

The press had an investment in this story. While Jemmy, York and Fuegia had been in England, the press had written feature stories, background stories, daily reports, about how savage these Fuegians were, then of how kindly they were treated, of how they responded to the education which was given them, both practical and spiritual. There could be no doubt of how grateful these poor savages were.

And now, based on the new revelations (because nothing was reported about the Fuegians while the *Beagle* was away from England), the overwhelming sentiment was that it was a crime, what had been done to Jemmy Button—how he had been taken from the gloom of his dripping native beech woods, from the darkness of his savagery, and had been fed, clothed, civilized, Christianized, brought fully into the light and presented to the King and Queen, only to be transported back to the darkness, abandoned and left there.

This was the story, and it was such a delicious story, the most unusual crime story to come along in a great while. The press of Europe took it up and echoed the sentiment of Fleet Street. Although the story placed ultimate blame on the agents and agencies of civilization for hurling Jemmy back to savagery, still the story reflected so well on the desirability of the civilized world; it reflected so well on English great-heartedness, even on the motives (undeniably constructive, unselfish and noble) of those who had befriended Jemmy and had helped him. The aim in trying to replant him in his homeland for the benefit of shipwrecked sailors and the world's commerce and for the eventual good of his own people was undeniably worthwhile. So the awful crime done Jemmy could be blamed only on impersonal Fate.

For the Fleet Street press, Jemmy's story ideally conformed to the classical pattern of a news story—with a distinct beginning, a middle, and an end. The beginning was dramatic (in the primitive barbarity of Tierra del Fuego); the middle was glorious (with Jemmy's elevation in England and his audience with the King and Queen); and the ending was sure to swell the throats of all civilized readers (with Jemmy thrust back into darkness, the overambitious plan confounded, and Jemmy politely but firmly declining another invitation to return to the light).

There was only one trouble: This was a false ending.

Because Jemmy's story did not end in this way. It ended, to the extent that it ended, in a completely different way that did not attract the attention of the Fleet Street press and the press of Europe. As a story that went against the grain of popular sentiment, it was of little journalistic interest.

Part Two

THE TRUE MIDDLE

OVERLEAF: Spaniard Harbor, *by Capt. W. Parker Snow.*

THE CATALYST

M ORE THAN twenty years passed after FitzRoy and Darwin left Jemmy Button in Tierra del Fuego, and no one from the civilized world saw Jemmy or thought to look for him. To look for him would have been like looking for a particular squirrel in a forest filled with squirrels; the Fuegian Indians were all homeless nomads and could hardly be distinguished, one from another. If FitzRoy or Darwin or Bennett or Bynoe thought about Jemmy, they surely presumed he was dead. Undoubtedly the average life span of a Fuegian Indian was short. The awful weather, the dangers of fishing and hunting, the incidence of illness, the incessant fighting among the clans and tribes, all made logical the assumption that Jemmy would be dead.

After a little more than twenty years had passed, however, a search for Jemmy was precipitated by the death of an Englishman named Allen Francis Gardiner.

Gardiner's life actually parallels FitzRoy's, though the passion that drove Gardiner was quite different from any of FitzRoy's drives. Where FitzRoy and Darwin were men of science trying to reconcile fact and faith, Gardiner was inspired by a faith which flashed so brilliantly in his mind that it blinded him to the restraints of common caution.

Eleven years older than FitzRoy, Gardiner when a boy was trained for command at sea; he eventually had a career in the Royal Navy and became a captain. Also, like FitzRoy, Gardiner while he was in the Navy immersed himself in the Bible—as he worked, as those young sailing captains worked, with Herculean effort to meet all the challenges and to discharge all the responsibilities that were heaped upon them.

It was on March 5, 1834, that FitzRoy and Darwin last saw Jemmy in Tierra del Fuego.

And, by coincidence, it was in 1834 that Allen Gardiner, while at home port in England, when he was forty, resigned from the Navy to respond to his calling, which was like a church bell tolling inside his head—his calling to be a missionary, to bring the Word of God to those who had never heard it, and to be a missionary in the hardest way, to seek out and convert those at the very bottom of the human ladder, those for whom the darkness was most abject.

Although Gardiner and FitzRoy did not know each other, they shared a profound belief: Both Gardiner and FitzRoy believed without question or qualification in the humanness of each of the most abject people on earth and in the inestimable value of each human soul.

Gardiner was fit for the challenge he chose for himself, toughened by his years at sea, used to command, used to applying himself with all his might, and now propelled by his eagerness to obey—not the commands of the Navy—but the commandments of God. His wife had just died, leaving him with three young children, but her death seems not to have restrained him but rather to have freed him to throw himself headlong into his new endeavor.

From the very beginning of his career as a missionary (a career distinguished not by his success but by his fantastic energy and bravery and the intensity of his dedication) Gardiner worked in the most difficult and dangerous places where human beings moved like shades in infernal darkness.

The Church Missionary Society sent him first to Africa—to Zululand, which was at that time recognized by all nations, even by England, as an independent state ruled by a barbarian king, the successor to the great Zulu king Chaka.

Capt. Allen Francis Gardiner.

Landing at Grahamstown on the southeast coast of Africa, Gardiner hired wagons, drivers and an interpreter, loaded the wagons with trade goods to be used as presents, and set off for the Zulu capital in the interior. When his way was blocked by a flooded river, he abandoned the wagons and forded the river with the unharnessed horses, one of which drowned. Another horse died in quicksand. Gardiner was collapsing from exhaustion when he reached a white settlement but after two days he was off again in a borrowed wagon, only to abandon the wagon at another flooded river, to proceed with a single horse and his interpreter astride the horse with him.

This was the way Gardiner always went ahead, recklessly, fearlessly, with the goal so clear in his mind that nothing could deter or distract him.

When he was finally brought before the Zulu king, the king was disgusted because Gardiner had no presents, no homage to offer. What Gardiner had to offer and what he tried to offer was the Word of God. But he encountered, as did many missionaries, a technical difficulty. There were not adequate words in the Zulu language to comprehend his message. A vast gap separated Europeans from the Zulus, a gap in all forms of cultural development and in practical implementation (guns, plows, horses). Hopefully the Word of God would be like a rope that could be thrown across this chasm, to bridge the gap and to save those in darkness on the other side. But saving by this act of grace required language; language was the rope of communication; and the two languages, English and Zulu, could not reach each other.

The Zulu king wanted Gardiner to teach his people musketry. The king knew what guns could do.

Gardiner refused.

So the Zulu king had Gardiner taken to the small white settlement on the coast in Zululand where a few traders lived in temporary shacks at the sufferance of the king. There Gardiner built a mission on a hill and began to preach to the local blacks and to the few whites, coming down considerably harder on the whites, who were a rough-and-ready frontier lot.

Before long, Gardiner came to the conclusion that Zululand—both the black and the white of it—could be made receptive to the Word of God only if England would annex it (a conclusion that came easily to an Englishman of Gardiner's time).

So he set out to see the British governor of the Cape Colony, received a negative response from him, caught a ship for England, and advocated annexation before a Select Committee of the House of Commons in London. Since annexation cost money, his suggestion was firmly rejected, but Gardiner was officially appointed a justice of the peace with authority over the resident British citizens in Zululand.

While in England, Gardiner found a second wife, who with the three children of his first marriage returned with him to Africa, one of the children dying en route.

Then, as justice of the peace with authority under English law and as spokesman for the white traders to the Zulu king, Gardiner was in a situation not unlike Brisbane's in the Falkland Islands: He had responsibilities with no power whatsoever to impose his will.

The British and Boers and Zulus and other blacks of many tribes were all fiercely fighting each other now.

And after four years all of Allen Gardiner's strenuous striving for African betterment—his heroic attempt to bridge the chasm with the Word of God—was coming to nothing, as the bloodletting went on uncontrollably and was to continue for many years and may be considered to be continuing into the present.

Gardiner avoided Brisbane's fate by packing up his family and boarding a schooner bound for England, just before a Zulu *impi* devastated the whole coast.

UNDAUNTED, Gardiner next tried New Guinea, but the headhunters there resisted even the initiation of a missionary effort.

So he turned to South America, although his support from the Church Missionary Society in London became less than enthusiastic, the Church Missionary Society preferring Africa and the East.

In South America, Gardiner first tried to work among the Araucanian Indians of Chile.

The Araucana are absolutely the toughest Indians in South America. They were not subjugated until 1882. The Incas did not subjugate them. The Spanish ironmen could not subjugate them. After Chile won its independence from Spain, the Chileans could not subjugate them for more than half a century. When Gardiner came to them, the Araucana were fiercely independent. Furthermore, the Araucana, for South American Indians, were fairly advanced culturally, though their modes in religion and in warfare were fanatically their own.

FitzRoy, while working from the *Beagle* mapping the Chilean coast, had encountered the Araucana—and he had liked them.

The Araucana liked Gardiner. They recognized his strength of character and his courage. Faced with the gap of language, however, they could not understand what he wanted to say.

AFTER the Araucana in Chile, Gardiner tried the Chaco.

The Chaco is that hideous region shared by Bolivia and Paraguay where, if it weren't mostly swamp and soft-earthed jungle, the blood would lie in puddles on the ground. The Chaco is a low plain only 450 feet above sea level in the middle of the South American continent. In much of it the average rainfall is 54 inches per year. Two rivers meander through it but flow so sluggishly that almost any rain brings a flood. The Chaco had never been substantially settled. All efforts at colonization had failed. The only stable population was comprised of a few pitifully poor Indian tribes that wandered about the area of approximately 300,000 square miles.

Over this piece of nearly worthless land and on it, Bolivia and Paraguay fought a war that substantially reduced their population of young men.

Bolivia is a weird country, set mostly among the loftiest peaks of the Andes. I have always thought that the strain of the altitude is what makes the history of Bolivia so bloody. And Paraguay is a tough, cattle-raising country comparable to the western U.S. in the mid-nineteenth century. Bolivia and Paraguay are the two landlocked countries of South America, so they are the least susceptible to the moderating, civilizing effects of commerce, and each country has a furious intensity.

Gardiner, when he was in the Chaco, could seldom find the

people he wanted to convert. As soon as he located some Indians, they would drift away from him over the vast lowland plain.

GARDINER spent a few years in each of these efforts, each of which he tried mightily to advance—in Zululand, in Papua, in Chile, in the Chaco. His ardor never flagged. Each time he would fight furiously and race up to the edge of the cliff to throw across toward the side in darkness the rope that was the Word of God— only to find and to have to realize that the rope fell short or was blown by the wind.

Understandably he thought eventually of cooler outlands, of Patagonia and Tierra del Fuego.

Well, the Church Missionary Society in London had also heard of Tierra del Fuego—from FitzRoy, from Matthews—and was definitely uninterested.

Gardiner and another missionary, a man of merely normal dedication named Hunt who was caught up by Gardiner's fervor, went to Port Famine on the continental side of the Strait of Magellan and tried to establish a mission there. At which point the Church Missionary Society in London cut off funding.

Then back Gardiner went to England. He failed to arouse any enthusiasm in the council of the Church Missionary Society. He failed in his appeal for funds with the Foreign Mission of the Church of Scotland. He crossed the English Channel and the Continent to Prussian Poland and appealed to the Moravian Church which also turned him down.

So he returned to England and formed a new society: the Patagonian Mission. Since few people in England knew precisely where Patagonia was, it was Gardiner's intention from the outset that his new society should embrace both Patagonia and Tierra del Fuego.

For Secretary of the Patagonian Mission—to be the administrator of the Mission while Gardiner returned to spearhead the Mission's activity in South America—Gardiner found an obscure and hitherto-modest middle-class man, lower middle-class by FitzRoy's or even Darwin's standards, a man who had been a schoolteacher in Bristol and was now pastor of the tiny town of Lenton in Nottinghamshire. Were it not for extraordinary subsequent events, this man's name probably would never have been recorded. But, in fact, the man Gardiner chose to be administrator of his shoestring mission was the Reverend George Pakenham Despard.

GARDINER was eager to be off again and to concentrate now on Tierra del Fuego. He felt that his previous missionary efforts, all of them, had been tainted by the corruption that already afflicted the native peoples and by the competition he had sensed from rival religious groups. In the Chaco and in Patagonia he knew he had been viewed as an unwelcome competitor by the Spanish Catholic Church, which had not matched him in vitality but which had been an established presence he had to contend with.

It was Gardiner's dream, his particular dream, to bring the Word of God to people who had heard nothing, nothing at all, people who lived in the silence of limbo—and the Fuegian Indians, he felt, in this sense were the ideal potential converts for his cause.

While Despard was padding about England appealing for donations, Gardiner, who could not bear to remain inactive, impatiently booked passage for himself and four of his supporters on a coal ship bound for Lima through the Strait of Magellan. The captain of the vessel agreed to put Gardiner and his party ashore on Staten Island, which lies to the east of Tierra del Fuego. Gardiner and his party brought with them a whaleboat, a dinghy, tents and tools, and enough staple food to last for six months.

It was Gardiner's intention to break into Tierra del Fuego the hard way, which was always the way he chose for himself, by establishing a simple base camp where he and his followers would endure by virtue of their valor and determination.

When the coal ship (a sailing schooner) stopped en route at Montevideo, Gardiner added to the equipage of his party a small herd of goats.

But when the coal ship reached Staten Island there was such a gale blowing that it was impossible to land. Staten Island is fully exposed to the Antarctic blasts that come up from the southwest. Also, around Staten Island are the clashing tides—conflicting, powerfully flowing, even racing sheets of water on and beneath the surface—where the westerly flow from the Beagle Channel pours into the Atlantic. So the buffeted schooner was forced to make its way through the Strait of Le Maire between Staten Island and the hook of Tierra del Fuego and to seek refuge among the islands at the eastern end of the Beagle Channel.

Picton is the first small island encountered and, while the ship with difficulty was holding anchor in Banner Cove on Picton, Gardiner and his party lowered their whaleboat and began to ferry their supplies to shore.

Fighting the storm, Gardiner and his men tried to put up their tents on the beach but the wind ripped the tents from the stakes. They had brought with them from the ship their first load of crated food and, with no place else to put it, they stowed the food in a convenient cave.

The next morning with the rain still falling heavily they ferried another load to shore only to find that the food they had stored the previous day had already been stolen—even though in the noise of the gale and in the rain they had neither heard nor seen any Fuegians.

After three days of trying to set up their base on shore, with the storm still raging, Gardiner had to give up. Much of the food supply had been stolen, the tents ripped to shreds.

So Gardiner and his men were taken back aboard the coal ship, which then went with the wind north to the Strait of Magellan and westward through the sheltered passage to the Pacific.

Gardiner did, however, successfully land and leave ashore on Picton Island the goats he had brought. These goats did not prosper as well as the sheep that were brought later. But the goats endured.

When the coal ship reached Lima, Gardiner hastened to arrange passage for himself and his party back to England.

BY THIS TIME—late in 1848, nearly fifteen years after Jemmy Button had last been seen by an Englishman—the Reverend Despard had collected a little more money for the Patagonian Mission.

Gardiner was more excited than ever. The prospect of finally being able to preach to untainted, untouched souls exhilarated him. This was the service he had been seeking to render through all his striving missionary years—to find those human souls who knew only absolute darkness and to bring to them the enlightenment of God.

On the long voyage back to England Gardiner could hardly bear the enforced inactivity. Yet it was during this time that he conceived a sounder plan, a plan more to be expected from someone who had once been a reliable naval officer.

Gardiner's newly conceived plan was to obtain an adequate ship—either to buy one or to have one built—that he could anchor off one of the Fuegian islands and that he could use as a base for a land station that at first would be only temporary. If circumstances ashore did not prove propitious, he could easily withdraw and move the ship to another spot until a satisfactory station on land was established.

The best kind of ship, Gardiner decided, would be a brigantine, a two-masted schooner with the foremast square-rigged and the mainsail fore-and-aft rigged with square upper sails, so the ship could be trimmed in many ways to cope with the eccentric bursts of wind that sluiced through the fractured and fragmented peaks of the Fuegian islands.

Also, in accord with his new plan, Gardiner wanted facilities in the Falkland Islands, 300 miles from Tierra del Fuego, for the education and training of a few Fuegians at a time whom he would bring over. Gardiner now realized and emphasized the importance of being able to speak and understand the Indian languages so that the rope of the Word of God could be both thrown and caught.

In England Despard had assembled an impressive board for the Patagonian Mission, and these people were deeply affected by Gardiner's passion. At their meetings Gardiner's impatience boiled over. He seemed inspired—and the board members neither could nor wanted to impede him. Gardiner uplifted those around him.

But there was not money enough for a brigantine. There was a new product on the market, though, a small, decked sailing cruiser with one of the first iron hulls, twenty-six feet long with a beam of eight and one-half feet; each cruiser carried its own dinghy. Gardiner had experienced the difficulties of trying to steer a wooden whaleboat past outcropping rocks and over underwater shale to land on the shingle beaches of the Fuegian islands. A wooden hull could be stove in or rubbed ragged against the stone. But an iron hull, though it might dent, would not be pierced or ground away.

The former naval captain was won over to the new product. And the Patagonian Mission, on its severely limited budget, was able to purchase not one but two of the iron-hulled cruisers, which were small enough to be mounted as deck cargo on an ocean-going schooner.

For his second thrust at Tierra del Fuego Gardiner enlisted and took with him a surgeon named Richard Williams who had formerly been skeptical toward religion (he had once called Christianity "absurd"). But four years earlier Williams had had a religious experience when, very ill, he had prayed and recovered, and now he was intensely devout. Gardiner also took along a catechist named John Maidmant to work with the Indians (Maidmant was recommended by the Y.M.C.A.); a carpenter named Joseph Erwin who had been on the previous voyage; and three strong fishermen from Cornwall named Badcock, Pearce and Bryant, all deeply religious men who were stirred by Gardiner.

The trip from England to Tierra del Fuego—crossing the Atlantic diagonally from east to west, from far in the northern hemisphere to the southernmost tip of land in the south—took three months.

It was on December 5, 1850—a suitable time in the southern hemisphere at the beginning of summer—that the schooner bearing Gardiner, his six followers and their equipment reached Tierra del Fuego.

The weather was overcast but it was not raining. Without any trouble the iron-hulled sailing cruisers were lowered into the water off Picton Island (there is a sheltering island that almost landlocks the cove) and the supplies of the missionaries were offloaded into the cruisers.

Gardiner was beside himself with excitement. The brand-new cruisers delighted him. He had planned for this expedition so carefully; everything was labeled and well packed. They had casks of preserved beef and pork, sacks of wheat, oats and rice, tins of biscuits, cheeses, lard, molasses.

Even contingency plans—in the event of unforeseen problems—had been made. Each month a ship from the Falklands came to Tierra del Fuego where trees were cut for timber (the Falklands being nearly treeless) and a letter had been sent to the Falklands (to one of FitzRoy's former lieutenants, Sulivan, who during a brief retirement from the Navy was trying his hand there at sheep-farming) asking that this timber ship should keep an eye out for the missionary camp and should carry emergency supplies. When the schooner bringing the missionaries from England had stopped en route at Montevideo, Gardiner and Dr. Williams had called on a trader, Samuel Lafone, whose ships serviced many of the southern settlements, and Lafone had agreed to have his ships watch for the camp. Thus Gardiner and his party were doubly assured of potential relief, should such relief be necessary.

When the schooner departed and headed for the Strait of

Magellan, Gardiner and his men were exuberant and sang hymns in the pristine solitude of Picton Island.

The weather remained bearable as they set up their tents. In an obscure corner of the beach they buried several casks for safekeeping.

In going over their supplies, however, they discovered that one item was missing: They either had forgotten to unload or had mislaid their reserve ammunition. For their rifles and pistols they had only a few shots. They had expected to be able to use their guns to procure fresh meat—guanaco and fowl. Now they would have to rely on fishing.

Although they never doubted their ability to convey to the Indians the gentleness of their intentions, they had also relied ultimately on their guns if in initial meetings the Indians could not understand them and their situation became perilous.

Suddenly the Yahgans came at them. Gardiner and his party had not noticed the smoke of the signal-fires on the neighboring islands or, if they did notice, had considered the fires neighborly. Now across to Picton came the bark-canoes with the Yahgans screaming, begging, threatening with their spears and stones, gleeful as they always were in the hunt.

Gardiner, Williams and the others attempted to greet the Yahgans as the Indians thronged ashore, to treat with the Fuegians, offering presents, but the Indians, snatching the trade goods from the missionaries' hands, clambered over the heaped crates.

This was the first time Gardiner had actually seen the Yahgans. The Patagonian Indians Gardiner had met in Port Famine had been quite different; along the Strait of Magellan settlements of Europeans or South Americans of European descent had existed for many years and the Patagonian Indians had been affected by this long and stable contact. But these Yahgans were truly the untouched limbo-dwellers Gardiner had always dreamed of saving.

When Gardiner fired into the air in an attempt to regain control, the Yahgans laughed, delighted, and went on prying, stealing. More and more of them kept coming. Towers of smoke were all about.

Gardiner and his followers did not want to dispute with the Yahgans. They wanted to introduce the Yahgans to the grace of their goodness. But the Yahgans would not let them.

Gardiner had to push the Indians away as he tried vainly by gesture to communicate with them. He had to fight his way from tent to tent, trying to protect the piled-up supplies. Dr. Williams and the catechist, Maidmant, were ineffectual but the carpenter and the three Cornish fishermen stoutly defended the camp.

All the Englishmen were shocked by the Yahgans. The missionaries were not taken by surprise; in their minds they had prepared themselves for this meeting—yet the nakedness of these people, their wildness, tossing about their mops of matted hair, the awful smell of the Yahgans, the physical strength of them (both women and men) with no gentleness to be seen in their painted faces, unsettled the Englishmen. In the frenzied atmosphere the composure of the missionaries broke down.

Gardiner called to his men to break camp and reload their supplies. And they did, although some of the tents were ripped to pieces in tugs-of-war with the Indians; some of their goods were scattered and lost.

When most of the equipment had been reloaded, the Englishmen pushed off in their boats, fighting to keep away the Yahgans who tried to climb aboard.

These iron-hulled cruisers—actually tubby sailboats—proved to be very poorly chosen for the task at hand. The Yahgans had bark-canoes over twenty feet long, so the size of these two English sailboats did not impress them. When FitzRoy and his men in whaleboats had encountered the Yahgans, they had nearly been overrun, but when they returned in the *Beagle* and remained aboard ship, the size of the *Beagle* had sufficiently impressed the Indians to keep them in check. That the hulls of Gardiner's sailboats were made of iron meant nothing to the Yahgans. Furthermore, these iron-hulled sailboats, although equipped with oars, could hardly be moved by rowing.

So when Gardiner and his party sought safety in their boats, each boat heavily loaded with supplies and carrying a dinghy on davits, they could push off with their oars but, once the boats were in water more than five or six feet deep, the boats just floated there.

Screaming, the Yahgan men whirled their slings over their heads and brandished their spears, while the women ran about the beach collecting fist-sized stones. The Yahgans, seeing Gardiner and his men floundering with the oars, piled into their own boats—leaky and heavy but familiar and usable, with fire glowing in each boat—and they came after the fleeing Englishmen.

Not until the Englishmen raised their sails and caught the wind were they able to outdistance and evade the Yahgans.

But what sense was there in fleeing from the people they had come to save? This was the dilemma of the savers.

A game of chase ensued—a cruel game that went on for months.

The fixed points of the chase can be identified from the faded, salt-saturated pages of diaries that Gardiner and the doctor kept, making short notes when they could.

From Picton the missionaries went northwestward through the Beagle Channel about fifteen miles to Bloomfield (now Cambaceres), a known cove on the Fuegian side where they landed and rested for the night.

But they were constantly watched by Yahgans who lived along these shores, many of whom, alerted by the signal-fires, were preparing to go to Picton. In the morning Gardiner and his party saw Indians assembling on the heights around them and bark-canoes gathering in the channel.

So Gardiner and his men had to set sail again—with the Yahgans paddling after them.

Again and again the Englishmen tried to hide in small inlets, but each time the Indians would find them.

It was safest for the missionaries to stay on the water where, as long as there was wind, they could use their sails to escape.

Then one night there was too much wind and a gale came up.

Near the eastern end of the Beagle Channel the ground swells of the ocean can be felt. In the calmer water within the channel the Yahgans in their canoes circled and waited. For two days Gardiner and his men had to trim and tack while they rode out the storm, and both dinghies were torn from their davits by the ocean waves and lost. The waves swamped the iron boats and soaked the supplies.

After the storm had abated, the missionaries sought sanctuary in Spaniard Harbor (which is now called Bahía Aguirre). This is a shallow bay on the southern shore of Tierra del Fuego just under the hook of the island, and the Yahgans were afraid to venture so far in their bark-canoes. There are no islands to the south of Spaniard Harbor; it is east of the Beagle Channel and is open to the surging Atlantic. Also, the eastern Ona inhabited the forest to the north and, though the Ona seldom came to the shore, the proximity of the tall, fur-clad Indians was enough to keep away the Yahgans. The land around Spaniard Harbor consequently was uninhabited, which made it appealing to the missionaries.

What Gardiner and his followers did not know about Spaniard Harbor is that under the water of the bay is a continental cliff where the water-depth drops from 100 meters to 4,000 meters. When a storm blows up from the pole, the massive movement of the ocean strikes this underwater cliff and huge waves form that spill over the land in a churning froth. (The Argentine Navy recently lost a ship during a storm at Spaniard Harbor.)

Gardiner and his men tried to settle in. They anchored one of their boats, the *Speedwell,* in a river that flowed into the bay, and their other boat, the *Pioneer,* was anchored just off the beach near a cave.

While the missionaries were storing supplies in the cave, another storm came up, and on the crest of a mountainous wave the *Pioneer* was lifted and smashed against the rocky shore. The cave was flooded. Most of the supplies of the missionary party were ruined or gone. The men retrieved some of the floating casks and crates from the ebbing salt water.

In between storms, while several in the party were developing symptoms of scurvy, Gardiner in the *Speedwell*, keeping careful watch for the Yahgans, returned to Picton Island to retrieve the buried casks and leave messages for the rescue ships. Picton was the place where they expected him to be.

Gardiner painted messages on three boulders around Banner Cove on Picton. He wrote on one of the rocks:

DIG BELOW

GO TO SPANIARD HARBOR

MARCH

1851

In a bottle that he buried in the sand he left a letter addressed to the sailors from whichever ship should come to relieve him, either one of the vessels sent by Lafone in Montevideo or else the timber ship from the Falklands: "Hasten! Haste! We have already been two months in Spaniard Harbor, finding the natives hostile here. We have sickness on board, our supplies are nearly out, and if not soon relieved, we shall be starved."

Actually there were two alternatives available to Gardiner, other than staying at Spaniard Harbor, and they must have occurred to him.

He knew about Jemmy Button from all the reports that had appeared following the second voyage of the *Beagle*. He knew roughly where Jemmy had been left seventeen years before, on an island further to the west along the Beagle Channel. If Gardiner were to continue through the channel, he might if the wind were with him be able to sail past the troublesome Yahgans and, if Jemmy were still alive, be able to locate him. In all probability Jemmy would be attracted to a missionary party. And Jemmy, if FitzRoy's hopes for him were in any way realized, might be able to diminish or control the combativeness of his people. If an atmosphere of reason could be established with presents given and favors returned, then a true missionary effort might be advanced.

Or else Gardiner, who was surely a competent navigator, could put to sea and make for the Falklands. The wind would blow him in that direction.

But Gardiner and his men did not seem to want to extricate themselves through their own ingenuity. They wanted to submit themselves to the will of God, so certain were they that God would intervene and save them. They wanted to show the purity of their faith by their reliance upon divine intervention because such intervention could surely be interpreted as a sign in favor of their mission. In their notes they gave God a choice either to rescue them or to welcome them into Heaven.

So Gardiner returned to Spaniard Harbor, and he and his men tried to endure there. But winter weather—the unrelenting weather of Tierra del Fuego—gave them no respite. During a cold spell, so much ice formed on their fishing nets that they couldn't haul them in. Then a tidal surge tore up the ice-laden nets and ruined them.

Gardiner and his six followers had to eat seaweed, fungus, dead sea-birds that were washed ashore, shellfish.

The flesh of penguins and cormorants had such a fishy taste the Englishmen were nauseated, but they found that if they buried the sea-birds in sand for two weeks, the flesh was less repellent.

When they could no longer swallow mussels, they made a mussel broth to sustain them. They made a broth from seeds they had brought to plant.

They trapped and ate the mice that came into the cave.

Once they saw a guanaco on a distant hill but were too weak to pursue it.

One night they trapped a fox that prowled around the cave, and they ate the fox, a piece at a time, for many days.

As the seven of them starved—acclaiming what they regarded as their testing while they waited with calm assurance for their rescue—they became ecstatic, buoyed by their belief. They identified with God as he weighed various fates for them, each of the fates desirable, and were patient as God took his time in deciding which fate to allot them. Their faith in divine goodness not only never wavered but filled their minds like a flush of polar light.

Gardiner and the catechist, Maidmant, lived in the *Speedwell.*

The doctor, the carpenter and the three Cornishmen lived in the cave, which was about a mile away, and in the wrecked *Pioneer* that lay near the cave on the beach.

But all of them went back and forth between the boats and the cave as long as they could.

The first to die was the Cornishman named Badcock. He died on June 28, 1851, and they buried him on the bank of the river that flowed into the bay.

Then Erwin, the carpenter, died on August 23, and Bryant, another of the Cornishmen, on August 26. These were the men who were physically strongest but they had been strained by their exertions. The catechist, Maidmant, buried them in the same grave.

With only four of the group still alive, Gardiner and Maidmant were living in the *Pioneer,* Williams and Pearce in the *Speedwell.* All were extremely weak.

Maidmant fashioned a crutch for Gardiner to use in an attempt to walk to the *Speedwell* to see after the doctor and Pearce. But Gardiner could not go that far and, hobbling back, found that Maidmant had wandered away.

Pearce and the doctor were already dead. Gardiner was so weak he could not crawl into the beached boat. Maidmant lay dead in the cave.

Gardiner died on the stones of the beach next to the *Pioneer.*

Gardiner's final notation, once more proclaiming his happiness and affirming his faith in God, was written in the wavery hand of a starving man and was dated September 5, 1851.

O N October 21 an American ship, the *John E. Davidson,* under the command of its owner, Captain William H. Smyley, came into Spaniard Harbor while a storm was beginning to blow. Smyley,

The shallow bay of Spaniard Harbor, as shown in a recent photograph, covers a steep underwater cliff.

an exceptionally capable sea-captain who lived in the Falklands, had been sent by Lafone in Montevideo to look for Gardiner's party. Smyley, having found the painted rocks on Picton Island and Gardiner's buried letter, had crossed under full sail to Spaniard Harbor.

From the deck of the *John E. Davidson* Smyley caught sight of a beached sailboat ashore.

With difficulty in the rough weather Smyley landed in a long-boat near the *Speedwell* and he found a grave with a rough marking, a dead man inside the boat, and, washed by the surf, a partly disintegrated corpse on which the birds had been feeding. The grave was that of Badcock; the dead man inside the *Speedwell* was identified by the name on his jacket as Pearce; and the body in the water was thought to be Williams. Smyley hurriedly buried the remains of Williams, then had to return to his ship which was slipping its anchorage. He promptly took the ship to sea to ride out the storm. He did not return.

Smyley brought away with him some of the missionaries' papers which he found on the sailboat. Upon reflection, while he read the papers at sea, he could not understand why Gardiner had not tried for the Falklands because Smyley thought he could have made it.

On the following January 19, 1852, a ship of the Royal Navy, the *Dido*, under Captain Morshead, visited Spaniard Harbor. The *Dido*, en route from England to the Pacific, had been instructed to look for the missionary camp in the cove on Picton; the messages painted on the boulders there had directed them to Spaniard Harbor where the British sailors found what remained: Gardiner's body beside the wrecked *Pioneer*, the two bodies in a shallow grave, and the body of the catechist in the cave.

Captain Morshead had the bodies buried and prepared a detailed report of the tragedy. His report was duly delivered to the British admiral stationed aboard a flagship in Valparaiso. The admiral in turn reported to London.

In this way the news of the end of Gardiner's mission reached home.

OFFICIAL REACTION
AND PUBLIC RESPONSE

In ENGLAND, when the news of the death of Allen Gardiner and his followers became known, the reaction from authoritative quarters was of violent disgust.

"Folly!"

"The waste of the lives of seven virtuous men!"

"Foredoomed—to try to penetrate such a tempestuous region so pitifully equipped!"

"Appalling!"

From experienced seamen, from editorial writers, from those determined to extend British influence and dominion, and from those who favored concentration upon social problems at home, condemnation exploded.

On April 29, 1852, *The Times* editorialized:

Neither reverence for the cause in which they were engaged nor admiration of the lofty qualities of the leader of the party, can blind our eyes to the unutterable folly of the enterprise as it was conducted or smother the expression of natural indignation against those who could wantonly risk so many valuable lives on so hopeless an expedition.

From many veteran sea-captains, especially from officers of the Royal Navy, came angry criticism of the foolishness of this attempt in small sailboats to penetrate a region where the natives were known to be difficult and the climate fearsome.

The whole expedition was deplored as the waste of seven lives beneath banners of piety and bravery.

In much of the commentary was the demand that the Patagonian Mission should be terminated.

Only the Reverend Despard dissented.

In a letter to *The Times* in response to the outcry, Despard as Secretary of the Patagonian Mission wrote:

"With God's help the Mission shall be continued."

Then money gushed into the Patagonian Mission. From all over England came checks, drafts, cash, pledges of all sorts. Despard had had very small success in obtaining donations for Patagonia; the Church Missionary Society in London had openly opposed him. But after accounts of the martyrdom of Gardiner and his six followers appeared in the newspapers, Despard no longer had to make calls to appeal for money; donations came in the mail from people in every county, from people Despard had never heard of. "Patagonia" now had a romantic ring to it, even better than "Mandalay" or "Zululand."

Left suddenly in command, Despard underwent a kind of character transformation. By nature he was and had been patriarchal. He and his wife had three daughters and a son and had adopted two boys, to make a formidable family with three offspring of each sex, but their manner before the world was modest. While Despard's income had been low and his positions inconspicuous, the family had no choice but to be penurious and self-effacing. Now, however, with the infusion of money for the Patagonian Mission, with the treasury in fact overflowing, Despard fulfilled his innate character. While Gardiner dazzlingly had held center stage, Despard had to be self-effacing. Now, startled into authority, Despard became a forthright, demanding leader, still bound by his middle-class values and customs but decisive and determined to be unquestioning of himself.

Promptly Despard adopted the plan Gardiner had left as his bequest: that facilities should be established in the Falklands for the education and religious training of the Fuegian Indians; that a brigantine should be obtained to serve as an offshore base in the Fuegian islands; and that very cautiously a land base should be established along the Beagle Channel from which a few Fuegians at a time could be brought for training to the Falklands and returned, until a civilizing effect was achieved among the Indians at large.

Despard publicized his plan—and even more money came in. More than enough to provide the brigantine and the support facilities and to maintain the efforts of a fast-growing staff. Despard bought a piano to facilitate his daughters' musical instruction.

Central to Despard's plan was his own personal conviction that Jemmy Button was alive. This conviction came to him intuitively, with the force of a revelation, and, as head of the Patagonian Mission, he felt entitled to hold firm to his conviction. Despard proclaimed not only that Jemmy was alive but that Jemmy would prove to be the vital link that was needed to bridge the gap between savagery and civilization, between abject darkness and divine light. The foremost aim of the Patagonian Mission must be to find Jemmy.

That no European had seen or heard about Jemmy since 1834 did not deflect Despard. That it was reasonable to presume at least the probability that Jemmy had died was a consideration Despard refused even to recognize. That Jemmy, if he were alive, might no longer be in the area where FitzRoy had left him nearly twenty years before was deemed to be of no consequence.

The vision in Despard's mind was that Jemmy was there, where he was expected to be; the missionaries would find him; and he would serve.

Despard's confidence was unshakable. And no one opposed him.

The construction of a brigantine was commissioned and the ship was finished by the fall of 1854—a full twenty years after the last sighting of Jemmy.

Proudly the brigantine was named the *Allen Gardiner.*

THE MOOD OF ENGLAND

During these mid-century years, England was undergoing a profound change of mood.

Having vanquished Napoleon, England was at the very peak of its power, consciously empire-bent, succeeding as if destined to do so, expanding its domain in Africa, in India, throughout the East, cementing its hold in Canada and Australia. At sea the superiority of the Royal Navy was unquestioned. On land England's armies were feared and formidable. In Europe it was recognized that England held the balance of power. All over the world English traders were doing business and were unrivaled in their enterprise and acumen. Profit was accumulating in

England, piling up, and the pound sterling was acknowledged to be the world's monetary unit.

By every measure, England at mid-century was entitled to let loose, to abandon itself in exultation.

Historically, among the empire-builders, Rome and England have held power the longest. Rome's sway lasted for more than five hundred years, England's for about three hundred fifty.

At its peak Rome was riotous and dissolute.

With a short and brilliant period of dominion Alexander the Great, while leading his army overland from Macedonia to India in an onrush of victory, had joined with his men in being fierce, plundering, drunk and quarrelsome.

With a span of power nearly as long as England's, the Spanish emperors (although yielding to England in Europe but reigning supreme in South America, Central America and North America from Mexico up through what are now Texas, New Mexico, Arizona and California) had been austere and fanatical in their religious zealotry.

But the mood that came over England in these climactic years of its national self-assertion was characterized by the assumption of a code of manners and morality which the nation put on like a heavy black shawl of good English wool.

Rigid decorum came to be expected within English society and was the style that England set for the world and expected the world to emulate. England was intrinsically individualistic, and the caricatures that England accepted as self-portraits were drawings by Hogarth and Gillray; the character-sketches were by Dickens; and there were always plenty of rakes, drunkards and debauchees to enliven the drawing rooms and the landscapes. But Queen Victoria during her long reign, both while she was married to Prince Albert and after his death, stabilized the hitherto-reeling monarchy; she set an example of quiet and restrained behavior and insisted upon such behavior from others; and, though some waggish and flamboyant free-spirits behind their hands called her *bourgeoise,* the English people as a whole subscribed to her sentiment.

So broad, in fact, was this adoption in mid-Victorian times of an increased emphasis on decency/propriety/conformity that England's chosen posture at the peak of its power may reasonably be viewed as the inclination of the nation at large, as a demonstration of the natural bent of the English people at a time when they were able to do whatever they wished.

The style of these times came on inexorably, without imposition, as the preferred style of a people who had every reason to be self-satisfied.

Why was this England's mood at the very apex of its parabola of power—this mood which inclined the British people to be constrained and insistent upon decorum when other peoples at their peaks had behaved so differently? This is an intriguing question.

And the answer may be that England was straitlaced in its glory because its drive to world-wide dominance, although championed by aristocrats in the old-fashioned way of conquerors, was really effectuated by middle-class traders who were neither aristocrats nor plutocrats, by tens of thousands of bustling middle-class and lower middle-class businessmen. The tried-and-untrue old saying is that trade follows the flag, but for England at the time of its greatest expansion, business actually came first (as in Zululand) and the aristocrats who controlled England's military forces eventually were caused against their will to extend the scope of their responsibility. In this sense England was essentially a commercial empire.

The middle-class men of commerce who were trading all over the world and were filling the orders while keeping the fires burning at home, these business people, the great majority of them, were not interested in the grand gestures, the extravagances and self-indulgences of the nobility before Victoria. They were middle-class people and, even in the glory of their success, they did not want to let loose, to abandon themselves in heady triumph. They did not want to abandon themselves in any way. They wanted things to be nice, to be decent, and their tendency toward strictness gathered momentum on the basis of broad public demand.

In religion, which became an ever more important aspect of propriety, the new manners required an ever more devout profession of profound piety. But this intensified religiosity was not accompanied as in Italy by extensive pageantry. Nor did it have a Spanish edge with a van of fiery clerics. England's embracing of religion during the mid-nineteenth century was given its character by leaders like George Despard, firm in their faith, unshakable in their conviction, insistent upon obedience, but definitely people of the middle class, counterparts of the English businessmen who were doing so well all over the world.

To a considerable degree, it was the new and popular emphasis on religious conformity, the upsurge of orthodoxy in the mid-nineteenth century that made Charles Darwin keep silent for so long.

For nearly twenty years following his return from the voyage of the *Beagle*, Darwin had been hard at work. He did not come home from the voyage to rest and while away his time as a gentleman farmer, well endowed by his share of the Wedgwood fortune that came to him from his mother as well as through his wife. Darwin during all these years worked just as he had worked alongside FitzRoy on the *Beagle*, diligently, ceaselessly, energetically, with inspiration and dedication. He used his wealth to give himself time, time without distracting obligations, without job or office, ample time to think, to classify all his specimens, to collate all his notes, to test and test again his great idea.

Much has been made of the fact that Darwin after his return from the voyage of the *Beagle* suffered for the rest of his life from a debilitating fever. But how debilitating this fever was is questionable. Andean fevers are strange and to this day have not been specifically diagnosed. They are a little like dengue and resemble the reactions to various insect bites. A typical bout comes on with pains in the hands, then with a roller-coaster alternation of high fever and rattling chills for about ten hours; then there is a day of tiredness, and a return to normalcy. At the beginning there may be four or five such bouts a year; after about ten years the bouts become less frequent and less severe. Such an ailment, though annoying, is not incapacitating.

The point is that Darwin's fever cannot explain the silence, as far as the English public was concerned, that Darwin imposed upon himself for more than twenty years.

Darwin did not keep his theory of evolution to himself. Again and again, through these years, he wrote outlines and abstracts of his theory. In 1842 he gave one of these outlines to his wife for safekeeping with instructions to publish it after his death. He showed these outlines and abstracts to his fellow-scientists, his old professors at Cambridge and Edinburgh.

Nor did Darwin keep to himself all the supporting evidence he was piling up. His old friends were kept steadily informed. Darwin was in constant correspondence with them and they came to visit him at Down House, the comfortable and large country home to which he retired to devote himself purely to concentration on the great idea that dominated his mind.

Darwin was recognized and respected in the academic community. He was an active member of the scientific societies. Even before his return from the voyage of the *Beagle* he had laid the foundation for his reputation with the steady stream of specimens he sent back to England from ports all over the world, along with notes that were clues to his emerging overview. (Before Darwin returned from the voyage, one of his professors visited Darwin's father, elaborately praised the work Darwin was doing and predicted a great future for him—to Dr. Darwin's amazement.)

Yet Darwin for more than twenty years would not put his theory into cohesive form and publish it.

That he would not make his theory public can be attributed in large part to his determination to accumulate and present substantial and overwhelming supporting evidence but also, I believe, to his reluctance to upset the English public in this period when religiosity was so respected and prized. Darwin knew that

Down House, from the rear lawn.

his theory would create an uproar, that his theory would be attacked by the religious leaders, and he knew that in the prevailing mood there would be broad public support for those who attacked him. Those who supported him, the scientific group within the academic community, were a small minority.

Darwin for himself did not like controversy. He had great affection for the society in which he lived, and he enjoyed its tranquillity. It is entirely likely that he would have preferred to have his theory published after his death. Nowadays we can't help wondering why.

How did Darwin know that the publication of his theory of evolution would create the ruckus that it did, that it would be denounced as blasphemy?

There were many precedents for the idea of evolution. The geologist, Charles Lyell, had in geological terms already described the evolution of the earth. Darwin's own grandfather, Erasmus Darwin, had given currency to the term "evolution." In France, Jean Baptiste Lamarck and others had proposed theories of the evolution of life. Darwin on his voyage had found a treasure-trove of the bones of extinct animals along the Patagonian coast, and it had long been known that such animals, dinosaurs and the like, had once existed and existed no longer, suggesting a pattern of development for living things. People had looked at fossils before.

Also, Darwin was unable to explain fully the mechanism of evolution. We aren't able to explain it fully today. Of course, Darwin could not have foreseen our discovery of DNA or our analysis of the gene-chain; he certainly could not have foreseen our present computerized mathematical study of probability as an alternative to mutation. When Darwin was pressed to explain the transmission of characteristics, he made some inaccurate guesses, which detracted from the soundness of his principles of natural and sexual selection.

(Had Darwin been aware of the genetic studies being conducted contemporaneously by Gregor Mendel in Austria, Darwin might have soundly extended his theory. But very few people knew of Mendel's work. And Mendel, an Augustinian monk, after only a few years in the study of genetics was promoted to abbot of his monastery and, as abbot, he was kept busy for the rest of his life in a struggle to avoid taxation of the monastery. Mendel's great innovative work in genetic transmission of dominant and recessive traits remained undiscovered until 1900.)

But Darwin's basic idea that life evolved over a long, long time from simple to more complex forms through a process of natural selection seems truistic to us now.

Yet Darwin knew that, once his theory was revealed in a fully developed form supported by all the evidence he had accumulated, he would be attacked not only by church leaders but by the majority of his countrymen who would tolerate no explanation of creation except the explanation that is in the first chapter of Genesis. And Darwin expected that one of his most assertive and most personal attackers would be FitzRoy.

So Darwin remained silent as long as he possibly could and did not, in fact, publish until 1859. Then, as is well known, the pressure on him to publish arose through a coincidence.

In 1858 a naturalist named Alfred Russel Wallace, who was in the East Indies at the time, sent to Darwin, who was an acknowledged authority within the academic community, a manuscript that without supporting evidence explicitly set forth a theory which was practically identical to Darwin's theory.

(It's interesting to note, as an example of the potency of an idea, that it was Thomas Malthus's *Essay on the Principle of Population* which struck the spark that for both Wallace and Darwin flared into their theories of evolution by natural selection. Malthus had pointed out that population growth was limited by famine, pestilence and war; Darwin and Wallace extended Malthus's idea to natural causes as the determinants in the origin of species of all living things.)

Darwin was shocked when he received the manuscript from Wallace and hastily alerted his friends who had read Darwin's abstracts and outlines over the years and knew of all the supporting evidence he had been accumulating. Darwin's friends insisted that he must at long last publish.

Then, with elegant gentlemanliness, Darwin and his friends sent Wallace's manuscript to the Secretary of the Linnaean Society and, along with it, an abstract of Darwin's nearly identical theory with reference to the supporting evidence which Darwin would subsequently present—and which Darwin did present in his famous book, *On the Origin of Species*, that appeared the following year.

THE MISSION CONTINUED

In 1852, while the *Allen Gardiner* was being built—and while Darwin continued to remain publicly silent—the Reverend Despard wrote to Captain FitzRoy and asked him to comment on the Patagonian Mission's new plan, which was the plan originally concocted by Allen Gardiner.

FitzRoy, who was known to be an authority on Tierra del Fuego, replied:

"It appears to me that your present plan is practicable and comparatively safe, that it offers a fairer prospect of success than most Missionary enterprises at their commencement, and that it would be difficult to suggest one less objectionable."

Despard, in his letter to FitzRoy, had not mentioned Jemmy Button, even though Despard's confidence that they would be able to find Jemmy was a fixation in Despard's mind.

FitzRoy in his own mind had in all likelihood concluded that, if Jemmy were not dead, he had wandered away and would never be found. Jemmy's fate was certainly not a matter on which FitzRoy chose to dwell.

FitzRoy during the twenty years since he had left Jemmy in the Fuegian islands had not enjoyed the kind of good fortune which enfolded his former cabinmate, Darwin.

Had Darwin not had a great revolutionary idea imbedded in his mind, obsessing his mind, his existence following the voyage of the *Beagle* might well have been vapid, like that of many independently wealthy English gentlemen. Darwin lived so comfortably, so peaceably, with nine live-in servants and three by the day, in a period when English workers were deferential. His wife, Emma, was devoted to him and, busy with her children and her staff, she did not concern herself with his work. She remained devout all her life, never questioning the account of creation in Genesis, and between Emma and her husband there was never any marital discord.

Charles's work, in fact, since through much of his life he made little money from it and he was not endowed with an office or a title of any sort, seemed more like a hobby or a preoccupation. Darwin was extremely fond of his children, whom Emma, beginning when she was thirty-one, produced in steady succession. Of their ten children two died in infancy and one in childhood (and the family and especially Darwin grieved deeply), but this was not unusual in Victorian times, and of the remaining children all were healthy and several were exceptional.

Darwin, focused intensely on his own thoughts, never intruded in the management of his finances and simply accepted his income and allotted it beneficently. His illness caused him to be very careful of himself, and Emma and all those around him cooperated wholeheartedly. Eventually Darwin was surprised and delighted when, as the years went on, the royalties from his books continued to increase, and in 1881 his income from the books exceeded 10,000 pounds.

FitzRoy, in contrast, was fractious and less lucky. A self-conscious aristocrat, FitzRoy had been raised with the assurance that he was independently wealthy, but already his gestures and flourishes had proved costly to him. Not only were his bankers difficult about honoring his drafts, but his file in the Admiralty contained several letters of reprimand for his unauthorized rental and purchase of auxiliary vessels.

After the return of the *Beagle,* FitzRoy was commended in Parliament. His extensive mapping was acclaimed by the Navy as exemplary. And he proceeded to spend a couple of years writing the very long *Narrative of the Surveying Voyages of His Majesty's Ships "Adventure" and "Beagle" between 1826 and 1836,* describing the two voyages of the *Beagle* and concluding with a chapter in which he confessed his occasional doubts but aggressively confirmed his fundamentalism and recommended it for the comfort of all young sailors.

A few months after his return FitzRoy married the daughter of a retired major general, and she quickly became pregnant.

FitzRoy did not go to sea again as a sailing officer. The Royal Navy's mapping of the world went on. The *Beagle* was sent out again, to Australia, with Wickham in command. Sulivan in charge of a surveying ketch returned to the Falklands. But FitzRoy, whether by choice or not, remained at home.

After the publication of his *Narrative,* he looked around for something to do, consulted with his relatives, and politics was picked out as the proper field for him to enter. A highly praised, relatively young Navy officer (he was thirty-six) with a globe-girdling voyage behind him, with a handsome family, and a religious conformist besides, was, as such a man would be today, a very attractive candidate.

FitzRoy's maternal uncle, Lord Londonderry (Castlereagh's brother), had just the place for him, a supposedly safe Tory seat in Parliament as the representative from Durham. In the eighteen-forties large landowners of noble blood were still effective in influencing the voting.

And FitzRoy was duly elected to Parliament, but not without a bit of trouble that left a stain upon him. It seems that another Tory candidate was proposed or proposed himself for the Durham seat, a younger man (twenty-six) named William Sheppard, who hotly denounced Lord Londonderry for political manipulation and attacked FitzRoy as an agent for the Londonderry interests.

FitzRoy wasn't used to the guff of politics or to tolerating insolence. A ridiculous go-around ensued, with bitter speeches by the two Tory candidates denouncing each other and with both distributing white papers in defense of their positions. Dueling wasn't quite out of style yet, and Sheppard challenged FitzRoy; they both named seconds; and their seconds negotiated various retractions and apologies, none of which satisfied Sheppard.

After weeks of wrangling, Sheppard finally withdrew his candidacy but could not calm the animosity he had worked up against FitzRoy.

After the election when FitzRoy was a Member of Parliament, Sheppard one afternoon waited for him in the Mall under the windows of the United Services Club where they were certain to be observed and, when FitzRoy came out, Sheppard went at him with a horsewhip.

FitzRoy's response was reflexive. Wrenching away the horsewhip, FitzRoy hit Sheppard twice, slammed him to the ground— and the confrontation was over.

But FitzRoy's behavior was not condoned in Parliament. He was criticized for being undignified. He served his term in Parliament but, perhaps in recognition that tact was difficult for him, he then sought an executive appointment which seemed to him more like command of a ship.

He was appointed Governor of New Zealand.

Had FitzRoy possessed stronger political instincts, he might have hesitated before accepting the appointment. But he far preferred the executive to the legislative role. He longed to be once again the one who could exercise authority—especially in a place he knew to be desperately in need of a firm hand.

FitzRoy had visited New Zealand before. On the return trip of the *Beagle* FitzRoy had stopped there for ten days. Then he and Darwin had traveled about, had observed the local conditions, and had formed firm judgments.

New Zealand in 1835, when FitzRoy and Darwin had visited, was a battleground of clashing corruptions. On one side were the native Maoris, tattooed Polynesians, belligerent and cannibalistic, already succumbing to whiskey and rum, already alerted to the usefulness of guns, quickly catching on to the meaning of money. On the other side was a motley mob of European adventurers (as well as some Americans), ex-whalers, ex-sealers, ex-convicts, eager to subvert the natives in every way they could. In between were a few missionaries who were frantically trying to implant English culture and morality.

England at the time of FitzRoy's first visit had not yet annexed New Zealand—so it was another situation where there was no law. A British representative lived in New Zealand, but he had no power and was disregarded, like Brisbane in the Falkland Islands or Gardiner in Zululand. Only FitzRoy, in the *Beagle* with the cannons exposed, offered any hope of justice, and during the ten days that the ship remained in harbor several disputes were brought to FitzRoy, who tried to make equitable decisions.

Most of the arguments between the Maoris and the Europeans concerned land. Just as there was a gap between the languages of primitive peoples and the Europeans, there was a gap between the tribal and the European concepts of land ownership. This was true with all the Indians in the Americas. But the Spaniards in South and Central America and in Mexico made no effort to trade for the Indians' land; the Spaniards took the land by force of arms and simply held it. The Romans, more than a millennium before, had imposed their own law in a world that vitally needed a rational system of law.

(It has always seemed to me that the Spanish *conquistadores* were the natural descendants of the Romans. Spain was conquered by the Fifth and Tenth Roman Legions. But after the Roman conquest of Spain was completed and the legionnaires wanted to return to Rome, the Roman Senate, panicked by the prospect of thousands of unemployed legionnaires in the streets, told the Roman soldiers in Spain to choose any place they liked, to build a city for themselves, and to stay there. So the Roman soldiers chose a site in Extremadura, a well-watered, fertile, healthy part of western Spain, and they built the city of Mérida, where to this day some of the finest Roman ruins outside Rome may be seen. Then, after a while, Rome and all Europe went to sleep for the thousand years of the Middle Ages—and, when Europe woke up again, it was Roman blood that was in the people of Extremadura. And from the towns and cities of Extremadura came the Spanish ironmen who conquered the New World: Hernán Cortés from Medellín, Francisco Pizarro from Trujillo, Pedro de Alvarado from Lobán, Hernando de Soto and Vasco Núñez de Balboa from Jerez de los Caballeros. All Roman descendants, by way of Extremadura.)

But the commercially minded English, armed with the fine

points of their eternally arguable Anglo-Saxon law, presumed that primitive peoples shared their concept of land ownership, which the Maoris certainly did not. The Maoris conceived only of tribal control of land, control which was occasionally lost and sometimes regained in the incessant intertribal warfare—but never individual ownership of land. When an Englishman would buy a vaguely defined tract of land by giving trade goods to a chief, he would prepare a contract which was beyond the understanding of the natives and then would insist that they abide by the contract.

Several Maori chiefs, catching on quickly, were adapting to these circumstances by selling to the Europeans highly desirable valleys that belonged to tribes other than their own.

Of the various factions in conflict in New Zealand, FitzRoy and Darwin in 1835 had definitely favored the missionaries. The missionaries, even granting the impracticality of some of them, were the only ones who, according to the standards of FitzRoy and Darwin, were trying to elevate the quality of life in New Zealand. The missionaries were the only ones who were conducting schools, teaching the Maoris to speak English, and making some attempt to work out dictionaries of the native languages so discussion and understanding would be facilitated. The missionaries were the only ones trying to discourage the trade in whiskey and rum, the only ones who cared about justice.

Consequently FitzRoy and Darwin—both young Englishmen trying to be fair and trying to see as clearly as they possibly could, trying above all else *to see*—stood up forthrightly for the missionaries and they expressed their strong feeling in an article which they wrote together and jointly signed (this was their sole collaboration, and it was later published in a Cape Town journal when the *Beagle* stopped there en route to England).

FitzRoy did not like all missionaries. He and Darwin did not like Richard Matthews, in spite of the courage Matthews had shown in trying to stay with the Yahgans in Tierra del Fuego, and they finally left Matthews in New Zealand in the care of his older brother, who was one of the missionaries there. On the whole, however, the New Zealand missionaries admired and applauded the effort FitzRoy had made for the Fuegian Indians in Tierra del Fuego, and FitzRoy felt that, as a scientist, he was sound in favoring the missionary effort in New Zealand since the causes of the missionaries were his causes: the civilizing of the natives, the Christianizing of them, for their own benefit and for the benefit of shipwrecked sailors.

Without doubt, when FitzRoy was offered and accepted the governorship of New Zealand in 1843 (the first governor having died after three years in office), he had ample reason to believe that he would be able to do a great deal of good there.

This was a grievous miscalculation on his part.

FitzRoy arrived in New Zealand (with his wife, his father-in-law and his three young children) aboard a commercial schooner, the Admiralty having ceased to provide ships of the Royal Navy for the delivery of colonial governors. So FitzRoy had no cannons to expose.

He landed and assumed the duties of his office at a moment when the attitudes of the rival factions had hardened into hatred; all were armed; and each faction had undeniable grievances for which vengeance was demanded.

FitzRoy landed in the north of New Zealand, where the Maoris and the foreigners were locked in a tense standoff. But in the south an English land development company had already brought ashore thousands of English immigrants to whom the company had promised land—land the aggressive managers of this company thought they had bought from Maori chiefs. This land development company had been nobly conceived for the benefit of selected immigrants who would become small land-holders; the concept was to be an alternative to colonization through the establishment of penal settlements as in Australia. But now the company was bent upon turning a profit and was obligated to the immigrants who trusted the company. The company managers wanted their contracts with the Maoris enforced.

FitzRoy had 156 British soldiers at his disposal, to impose his will on about 15,000 whites and perhaps 250,000 Maoris in a territory the size of the British Isles.

Determined to be firm, FitzRoy first made clear his sentiment: He was on the side of the Maoris on the theory that, even if they were in the wrong, it was the obligation of civilized people to treat the natives indulgently in an effort to train and to educate them.

Then FitzRoy forbade the transfer of any more land except by sale to the government. He wanted a moratorium on land-squabbling. Once the squabbling had died down, the government would resell the land. But the immediate response to his action was outrage: The managers of the land development company were outraged because they needed more land for their immigrants; and the Maori chiefs were outraged because they were dangling a bunch of valleys they did not control before the avid land developers.

FitzRoy had to attend to his exchequer. The government of New Zealand was broke; government salaries hadn't been paid in months. So FitzRoy, contrary to colonial policy which favored the raising of revenue locally, issued paper money in the form of interest-bearing notes and made these notes legal tender. As a result, the normally accepted kinds of currency began to be hoarded. Also, land transactions effectively ceased because the government had no appropriated funds with which to make purchases. Since the tax on land transactions partially sustained the government, the financial predicament worsened. So Fitz-Roy reversed himself on the prohibition of private land sales and increased the tax on such transactions.

Why should FitzRoy have been expected to be able to cope with problems such as these? From his experience as a sailing captain, he knew only that he had to be firm. His expertise as a navigator and surveyor was totally unrelated to civilian administration. During his single term in Parliament he had concentrated on river problems which were related to his area of competence.

FitzRoy as governor lasted for about a year and a half. He was recalled with regret by the Colonial Secretary, Lord Stanley, who had appointed him. Lord Stanley's chief complaint was not so much that he differed over any of the drastic steps FitzRoy had taken but that FitzRoy took these steps, knowing they were at variance with colonial policy, without asking the home office for permission and waiting for permission to be granted. FitzRoy, in fact, reported to the home office infrequently, thus causing Lord Stanley considerable embarrassment. Stanley had been continually importuned by the land developers and their friends who were fiercely critical of FitzRoy, and Stanley had been badgered by opposition members of Parliament who favored the land developers and who denounced FitzRoy over points about which FitzRoy had kept the home office ignorant.

Independence of action, of course, was a requirement of FitzRoy's nature.

Politically, FitzRoy was, as he said, "irreparably injured" by the recall.

When he returned to England, his wife, having in New Zealand delivered their fourth child with considerable difficulty, died. And her death seemed to FitzRoy a confirmation of his failure as a colonial governor.

In the course of his official duties FitzRoy again had spent a good deal of his own money. But he still had well-connected relatives and friends.

Through the influence of his relatives he was made superintendent of a government dockyard where he worked on the first screw-driven steamship used by the Royal Navy. Through the influence of his friends, who were aware of his dejection and sympathized with him, he was made a member of the Royal Society. Charles Darwin sponsored him.

But FitzRoy was at low ebb when he responded laconically to Reverend Despard's letter regarding the plans of the Patagonian Mission. We can only speculate whether FitzRoy's interest would have been aroused if Despard had mentioned his premonition that Jemmy Button would be found.

THE SEARCH

In 1854 the construction of the *Allen Gardiner* was completed. It was a very well-made, two-masted schooner with about one-third the displacement of the *Beagle;* it required a crew of only seven or eight. The ship was tried at sea and was then loaded, according to Despard's directions, in Bristol harbor.

Despard had three criteria: (1) his own notion of sensibleness; (2) single-minded devotion to the religious purpose of the Patagonian Mission; and (3) absolute faith that the efforts of the Mission, *his* efforts, would enjoy a divine blessing. The *Allen Gardiner* consequently carried a minimum of scientific equipment, not all the chronometers and barometers FitzRoy had taken or the pickling jars for specimens that Darwin had needed. What the *Allen Gardiner* did take was a complete, disassembled house plus other building materials and tools, plus trade goods and a very large quantity of nourishing biscuits as gifts for the Indians (no rum or whiskey).

Prior to the completion of the *Allen Gardiner,* Despard had obtained from the government the right for the Mission to acquire without competitive bid a tract in the Falklands, and the tract Despard had selected was Keppel Island, an uninhabited island of more than 5,000 acres which lay in a bay on the north side of West Falkland Island—far removed from the capital and trading town of Port Stanley which is on the east side of East Falkland. Despard had heard about the excesses of Stanley and wanted to keep his prospective training ground for the Fuegians uncontaminated. It was to Keppel that the *Allen Gardiner* was to go.

To command the ship, Despard accepted an offer from an experienced sea-captain who happened to be in England, a man named William Parker Snow who had a reputation for undertaking challenging assignments. Snow had been on one of the unsuccessful searches for Sir John Franklin, an English explorer who with his party was lost while seeking to discover a Northwest Passage in the Arctic reaches of Canada. Snow, upon reading a notice in *The Times* that a Mission ship was in need of a captain, offered to serve without pay. But Despard's policy for the now-well-endowed Mission was that all those who worked for it should be paid. So a contract was signed that gave Snow a small salary.

Parker Snow was an unstable man, or at least an opinionated, irascible man whose conflicting impulses created a tension within him that resulted in instability. He was without doubt a good navigator and a brave mariner, a competent sailor and a captain who knew that for safety's sake at sea he had to be obeyed without question. But it was excessively his nature to have his own way. Also, he was an adventurer who had seen so much and been through so much that religion as an alternative to reality appealed to him and he saw himself as a likely religious leader.

In his agreement with the Patagonian Mission, Snow specified that his wife was to accompany him and live aboard ship. Mrs. Snow was a pious woman, and the notion of her presence on the *Allen Gardiner* pleased Despard.

Trouble started when Snow began to hire a crew. He had explicitly stated that he must be allowed to choose his own crew, although he agreed to seek out experienced sailors who were devout and were amenable to religious routine. He had done so. Yet some of the missionaries subordinate to Despard—especially a young catechist named Garland Phillips—took issue with the religiosity of the men Snow was hiring. The routine for the *Allen Gardiner* to which Snow had agreed was that prayers should be read aloud to the entire crew three times a day, but some of the missionaries thought three times was not enough.

On this initial voyage Snow was to take out an advance party consisting of Garland Phillips, a doctor named Ellis, a carpenter and a mason. Phillips saw himself as the religious leader of the group, acting for Reverend Despard. Captain Snow chose to regard the doctor, who was a mild, indecisive man, as the leader.

Furthermore, in Snow's view the entire advance party was subordinate to himself because he, as captain of the ship, was the Mission's representative abroad until a missionary leader should be sent from England with orders to succeed him. Thus Snow interpreted his contract.

Despard himself would not go on the first voyage. Despard believed in thoroughness, and he had not yet perfected his organization of the Patagonian Mission, with a board and book-keepers to oversee the incoming revenues, with clerks to administer the collection routine, and with dependable English banks to act as custodians of the funds. After the Patagonian Mission in England was organized to his satisfaction, Despard himself would go out.

In October 1854 the *Allen Gardiner* sailed and after a voyage of three months reached the Falklands. Snow brought the ship first to Port Stanley.

There he met the Governor of the Falklands, a precise civil servant named George Rennie (the powers-that-be in England had finally, a quarter-century after Brisbane's murder, assigned a paid professional administrator to the Islands). Governor Rennie had his own plan for the Falklands: The Falklands were slowly and peacefully being settled by English people who were raising sheep (a few gentlemen farmers with their families were trying the Falklands, as they later tried Kenya and Rhodesia). Governor Rennie did not welcome the introduction of people who might prove troublesome. So the governor, being informed of the plans of the Patagonian Mission, warned Snow and Phillips that, if they were to bring over any Indians from Tierra del Fuego, the Indians must come willingly and the Patagonian Mission would be liable for whatever the Indians might do in the Falklands. The Mission would also be responsible for the health and welfare of the Indians. If an Indian were to be left destitute, the Mission would be fined under the Alien Ordinance; if an Indian were to die, the missionaries would be charged with manslaughter. Governor Rennie did not have an open-door policy.

With the governor's warning in mind, Snow went about taking

the Mission land party around to Keppel Island, which is not easy
to do by sail. He had to take the *Allen Gardiner* along the north
shore of East Falkland Island, across North Falkland Sound,
around Pebble Island and into Keppel Sound where there are
many islands. Like most of the Falklands, Keppel Island is low,
grassy, boggy, and it was utterly desolate.

It is not hard to anchor off Keppel Island but it's hard to land
comfortably. It was there that Snow disembarked Phillips, Ellis,
the carpenter and the mason, and offloaded their supplies. The
ship had been densely packed; Despard had not stinted on
equipment and had overlooked nothing. Not only was the disassembled house unloaded, but there were materials sufficient
for a larger house, including bricks, all kinds of tools, and more
than ample food supplies for the coming winter, including live
pigs, sheep and poultry. Some of the crew helped the missionaries put the house together and stow their supplies.

Snow did not like Keppel Island with its difficult shoreline.
And he distrusted the practical ability of those in the land party,
especially after they accidentally started a grass fire. He questioned Phillips and Ellis as to whether they wanted to be left by
themselves on an uninhabited island 75 miles by sea from the
capital, whether it was good judgment for them to remain. They
could go back to Stanley and await the arrival of the missionary
leader and more supporters. But Phillips had his orders from the
Reverend Despard: On Keppel Island he was to establish the
Mission. So he stayed.

And Snow, too, had his orders from the Reverend Despard:
After unloading the missionaries and seeing to their safe settlement, he was to sail the *Allen Gardiner* from Keppel Island
directly to the Beagle Channel, find Jemmy Button, and try to
bring Jemmy back to the Falklands.

This was Despard's command—in spite of the fact that Jemmy
hadn't been seen in nearly twenty-two years.

It's a close reach against the prevailing wind to sail from the
Falklands to the Beagle Channel, a chancy, sometimes difficult
sail. The *Allen Gardiner* went through the Strait of Le Maire,

passing between Staten Island and the hook of Tierra del Fuego, and Captain Snow set his first anchorage in Spaniard Harbor.

In fair weather he and his wife were taken ashore. Snow's irritation with the missionaries had subsided; he had become used to the religious routine aboard ship; and he was deeply touched when he and his wife found the martyrs' graves and prayed before them.

One headstone was in place, although the painting on it had been washed away by the raging water that overflowed the land during storms. Other headstones lay about the beach. And there appeared to be the weathered remains of wooden crosses stuck amid piles of rocks. Captain Snow and his wife could not tell which was Gardiner's grave. Mrs. Snow wept for all of them.

From Spaniard Harbor Snow sailed to Picton Island, anchored in Banner Cove and went ashore. There he was able to read the fading messages Gardiner had painted on the rocks four years before; the words had not been washed away because the cove, in the shelter of the islet, is never flooded by the sea. And he encountered the first Yahgans he had ever seen.

A few Yahgans were living on Picton, and they came to him. Others were approaching in their bark-canoes. Signal-fires were rising on all the shores.

After saying prayers before the painted rocks, Snow returned to the *Allen Gardiner*. It was his impression that the Yahgans who had gathered understood what he was doing because they ceased their begging while he prayed.

From the deck of the *Allen Gardiner* Snow studied the assembling Yahgans in their bark-boats as they circled around. They did not seem to him to be threatening. The *Allen Gardiner* carried two small cannons (Snow had told the missionaries the cannons were needed for signaling) and the crew carried small-arms. But the Yahgans were awed by any ship that was much larger than their own boats (the *Allen Gardiner* was big enough) and Snow hoisted anchor and left before they became bothersome.

From Picton, the first island at the eastern end of the Beagle Channel, Snow set out to see if he could find Jemmy.

Banner Cove on Picton Island, *by Capt. William Parker Snow.*

The Beagle Channel is over 100 miles long. The forested mountains of Tierra del Fuego are on the right as you go westward; Navarin Island and Hoste Island, with the broken bits of many islands diminishing to Cape Horn, are on the left. The Beagle Channel for most of its length is remarkably straight if viewed from one of the heights (undoubtedly FitzRoy and Darwin climbed to the tops of the mountains); it looks like the cut made by a cleaver across the tail of the continent. But from the water the throughway is obscured by headlands and islands close to the shore on both sides. Only the continuous westerly flow from the Pacific is the giveaway (and this was what made FitzRoy persist in his discovery). At the Pacific end the Beagle Channel divides into two arms, north and south, amid many small islands.

All along the shores of these islands people were scattered (Tierra del Fuego itself to the north is an island, even though from the Channel it seems like the mainland). Neither Snow nor any other Englishman or European could speak a Fuegian language, and FitzRoy had perceived that there were many different Fuegian languages and dialects.

By now Snow had seen the Indians, and they all looked alike to him—naked, painted and grimy, with long mops of matted hair, stunted.

How should he go about looking for one particular Fuegian?

His only guide was FitzRoy's *Narrative*. Snow had the two volumes in his cabin and had spent months poring over them. And his key, he had decided, was—English.

So Captain Snow ran up the British flag, sailed the *Allen Gardiner* into a cove, and at the top of his lungs hollered:

"Jem-mee Button!"

No answer. And at a distance only the usual guttural begging-talk of the Yahgans.

Signal-fires were all around him now, on the beaches, on the heights. Snow was persistent—and patient. He went past the pleasant stretch of coast where Harberton (a large sheep ranch) now lies on the Fuegian side, past Gable Island, and along the north shore of Navarin.

Again and again he went into coves—and called out Jemmy's English name. Only to hear his voice fade in the silence of this near-frozen bottom of the world.

He rounded the northwestern corner of Navarin Island and took the *Allen Gardiner* southward through the Murray Narrows between forbidding, tree-capped cliffs and into the bay where on the level land behind the beach on Navarin, according to FitzRoy's *Narrative*, the original camp for Jemmy, York Minster and Fuegia Basket had been built.

From the deck of the ship he called out again—and, though there were a few bark-boats in the bay, no one answered, except with the familiar Yahgan begging-talk.

There was nothing that Snow could see except grass on the level land behind the beach. He went into bays and inlets along the coast of Hoste Island to the west. In the middle of a scattering of small islands, Snow slowed the *Allen Gardiner* and once again hollered:

"*Jem-mee Button!*"

Fuegian Indians, fishing from several bark-boats nearby, were gaping at him and at his silently gliding ship. Then one of these Fuegians replied:

"Jam-mus Button, he here."

And from Indians in the other bark-boats came confirmation:

"Yes, yes. Jam-mus Button."

"Here."

There was a flurry as the Indians in their bark-boats came toward the *Allen Gardiner,* other boats filled with Indians coming from the outlets of creeks on the islands, others emerging from kelp beds near the shore.

When the Indians shifted from their usual guttural sounds to the sounds and inflections of English, the difference was instantly clear to Snow and to his goggling crew.

Quickly Snow brought his ship about and further shortened sail, effectively stopping in the water close under some high mountains.

From a bark-boat filled with Indians that pulled alongside, one of the men shouted:

"*Jam-mus Button, me! Where's the ladder?*"

At that moment Captain Snow nearly became a complete believer. Despard had been right.

There was no ladder because Snow had hauled aboard everything up which the Yahgans could climb, so a rope was thrown and up the rope climbed, as Snow later wrote in his own account of this voyage, "Jemmy Button—the very man himself—the protégé of Captain FitzRoy—the one upon whom the Mission rests so much of its hopes."

Jemmy was on deck, grinning and shaking hands with the crew. Snow, admittedly "unable to prevent a momentary confusion," gathered himself together, imposed his will on a couple of his sailors, and had the anchor dropped.

The man on deck undoubtedly was Jemmy, recognizable not

only by the broken English tumbling from him but from his likeness to the sketches FitzRoy had made of him twenty-two years before.

Jemmy was naked, grimy, his face stained from colored sludge. His eyes were smoke-bleared. His hair was long, matted on the sides, cropped (with sharp-edged mussel shells) over his eyes.

But Jemmy now, at about forty years of age, was stout, muscular, self-assured, with an air of authority, a middle-aged man in the prime of his competence, the natural leader of the Indians who were climbing up the rope after him. He showed no signs of the shy, vain, sometimes petulant boy that, according to Fitz-Roy, he had been. And the warmth and geniality that had always characterized him flowed from him—to Captain Snow, to the sailors.

Snow's impression at first sight was of a "stout, wild and shaggy-looking man."

When told that a lady was in the captain's cabin, "Ingliss lady?" Jemmy said and asked for "clothes to put on." When a pink-striped shirt and a pair of pants were found for him (pants large in the waist, cuffs turned up), Jemmy said, "Need braces." Jemmy seemed delighted each time he would grope for a needed English word and the word would come to him.

There were bark-boats all around the *Allen Gardiner* now and Snow was apprehensive. But he allowed aboard only those Indians for whom Jemmy vouched, and the others did not try to board. Jemmy did not approve of all those who were circling the ship. He said some of them were "not of his conetree" and warned Snow against those he pointed out in several of the boats. Jemmy described them as "bad" and used a Fuegian word that apparently had no precise English equivalent: When Jemmy identified a person he felt might be threatening or blameworthy, he used the word phonetically rendered as *oens*. There were a number of such *oens* men in the convention of bark-boats that surrounded the *Allen Gardiner.*

In one of the bark-boats, Jemmy acknowledged, was his wife, who to Snow's amazement and delight was calling to Jemmy using a few words of English. Jemmy had taught all these Indians a little English. But Jemmy did not choose to bring his wife aboard.

(In all the contemporary records, nineteenth-century propriety is observed: Jemmy's woman is called his "wife" and sometimes is referred to as "Mrs. Jemmy Button." Even these Indians who spoke a little English used the word "wife" for a man's woman. But the Yahgans had no dowry, no bridal gift, no marriage ritual of any sort. And each capable man had several women. The woman who was Jemmy's "wife" when the *Allen Gardiner* appeared was obviously a new one because Snow and his men noticed that she was very young, with a baby, and Jemmy had grown sons by other women.)

Snow took Jemmy below to his cabin where the table had been set for tea and Mrs. Snow was present. But both Jemmy and Snow were so affected they could not eat. Jemmy was delighted by the tea set, the circumstances. Snow took down the volumes of FitzRoy's *Narrative* and showed Jemmy the portraits FitzRoy had drawn of young Jemmy wearing a starched collar and coat and of Jemmy later in his wild state. As Snow reported, the portraits "made him laugh and look sad alternately, as the two characters he was represented in, savage and civilized, came before his eye. Perhaps he was calling to mind his combed hair, washed face and dandy dress, with the polished boots it is said he so much delighted in: perhaps he was asking himself which, after all, was the best—the prim and starch, or the rough and shaggy?"

Snow turned to the Appendix of FitzRoy's *Narrative* in which FitzRoy had phonetically transcribed, with their English equivalents, words in the Alikhoolip dialect (now more commonly Alacaluf, the westernmost Yahgans) spoken by York Minster and Fuegia Basket and in Jemmy's dialect which FitzRoy called Tekeenica. And Jemmy confirmed the words from his own language, so that Snow now had a small vocabulary of words he could use with the Yahgans who lived in this part of the Beagle Channel.

(FitzRoy's use of the word "Tekeenica" to denote Jemmy's

No. 15.

In the following fragment of a Vocabulary the vowels should be sounded as in the English syllables, bah, băt, eel, bĕt, I, bĭt, no, tŏp, rule, bŭt, hay ; and the consonants as in English, but giving to kh a very guttural sound. One Fuegian expression, something like the cluck of a hen, can scarcely be represented by our letters ; its meaning is " no."

FRAGMENT OF A VOCABULARY OF THE ALIKHOOLIP AND THE TEKEENICA LANGUAGES.

Also some Words of those spoken by the PATAGONIAN (TEHUEL-HET) and CHONOS INDIANS.

ENGLISH.	ALIKHOOLIP.	TEKEENICA.
York Minster's name	ĕl'lĕpăru	
Jemmy Button's name		o'rŭndĕl'lĭcŏ.
Fuegia Basket's name	yŏk'cŭshlu	
Ankle	acŭl'lăbe	tŭppallă.
Arm	tŏ'quĭm'be	car'mĭnĕ.
Arm (fore)	yŭc'căbă	dow'ĕlă.
Arrow	an'năquă	te'ăcu.
Beads (necklace)		ăcon'ăsh.
Back	tŭccăler'khĭtĕ	am'mŭckă.
Bark (as a dog)	stŭck'stă	wo'onă.
Basket	kă'ĕkhu (or) kha'ĭŏ	kă'ekhĕm (or) kŭsh.
Beads	ca'ĕcŏl	ah'khĭnnă.
Belly	kŭppŭdde	
Birch apple		a'fĭsh-khă.
Bird (little)	tŏw'quă	be'ghe.
Bite	ĕck'hănĭsh	e'tăŭm.
Black	fcal	
Blood	shŭb'bā	shŭb'bă.
Baby	cos'hĕ	yărŭmăte'ă.
Boat	ăth'lĕ	watch.
Bone	osh'kiă	ah'tŭsh
Bow	kĕrĕc-căna	whў-ăn'nă.
Boy	a'ĭl-walkh	yăr'ămuă.

FitzRoy, in the Appendix of his Narrative, prepared the first phonetic vocabulary comparing a word in English with the same word in Alikhoolip, or Alacaluf (York's language), and the same word in Tekeenica, or Yahgan (Jemmy's language). Fuegia could speak both Alacaluf and Yahgan; Jemmy could understand Alacaluf.

dialect is an example of the way colonizers often invented identi-fications. According to a man a generation later who was raised with Yahgans, "Teke uneka" in the Yahgan language meant "I don't understand what you're talking about." So, when FitzRoy or another Englishman had tried to convey a question to some perplexed Yahgan, the Indian must have replied in this manner, and FitzRoy duly used "Tekeenica" to refer to this part of the Beagle Channel, to the people of this part, and to their language. Actually no one knew then nor has it ever been determined just how many tribes and clans there were along the Beagle Channel or how many languages and dialects these people spoke. Since the Yahgans had no social organization and no cohesion except that of the little family group, there was no way to determine the difference between a clan and a tribe, a language and a dialect.)

Jemmy told Snow that no ship had been seen here since the *Beagle*.

Snow did all he could to revive Jemmy's memories—and Jemmy seemed to remember everything. When shown pictures of England, he said, "Yes, me know—Ingliss conetree. Vary good. You flag, me know, yes. All good in Ingliss conetree." But he also remembered his voyage to get there. "Long way—me sick in hammock—vary bad—big water sea." And he added, touching FitzRoy's *Narrative,* "Me know Cappen Fitzoy—Byno—Bennet—Walamstow."

Then Snow, according to his own testimony, asked Jemmy to return with them to the Falklands. And Jemmy refused. He would not go to the Falklands. Nor to England. Ever again.

JEMMY went ashore for the night and, when he came back in the morning, Snow noticed that on the back of his pink-striped shirt was the red clay soil on which he had slept. With Jemmy came a boatload of his relatives, and Snow gave him many presents and distributed presents to the Indians who were with him.

Mrs. Snow induced Jemmy's wife to come aboard with her baby and gave them presents.

Then, after Jemmy and his wife with their load of gifts had returned to their canoe and the *Allen Gardiner* was being prepared for departure, several Indians still on deck became restless, agitated. The wildness was rising in them and they were straining against the restrictions that Jemmy had imposed. For these primitive men more than enough time had passed for them to scheme.

The last two aboard suddenly seized Snow and tried to strip off his coat. Snow was a strong man and a violent wrestling match ensued.

The crew were coming on with belaying pins when the *Allen Gardiner* began to move in the water. And the Indians, frightened, released Snow and went over the side and down to their boats.

Without Jemmy, Captain Snow in the *Allen Gardiner* returned to the Falklands.

CHANGE OF COMMAND

S AILING back and forth between Port Stanley and the missionary settlement on Keppel Island, Snow became involved with the circle of leaders at Stanley. The men in this little group were chiefly traders, and the traders acted as bankers in the absence of any proper banking facilities. Snow, without adequate financing from the Patagonian Mission at home, had to draw funds from these traders to pay his crew and to replenish his supplies, and he pledged the *Allen Gardiner* as collateral.

Governor Rennie was succeeded by Governor Moore, who had been a captain in the Royal Navy and had achieved some renown in the Arctic, and Snow found Moore to be hospitable and compatible.

The Falkland Islands, by Conrad Martens.

At Stanley there was already forming the monopolistic economic arrangement that was to endure. The Falkland Island
Company with headquarters in London had extensive land interests which were jealously guarded (the wild cattle that still
roamed could not be captured on the company's land). Most
of the businessmen of Stanley were magistrates duly appointed
by the governor, so economic interest and legal jurisdic-
tion coincided.

These businessmen of Stanley did not welcome the Patagonian
Mission. They did not want Indians of any kind brought into the
Falklands; they did not allow Argentines in the Falklands; and
they disapproved of the Mission's plan to teach the Indians
farming and cattle-raising because this would impinge on their
own economic activities. Had the Mission's settlement been
closer than Keppel, the empowered men at Stanley would have
interfered more promptly and vigorously.

Snow became influenced by them. In connection with his

financial difficulties in obtaining funds to pay his crew, Snow discovered that in the employment contracts for himself and his crew there was no provision for return passage to England unless the full term of the contract was fulfilled. When Snow discussed this with his crewmen, they became upset, and dissension spread among those who worked for the Mission.

At one point Snow decided, unilaterally and precipitously, that the settlement on Keppel should be closed down on humanitarian grounds. He had brought the carpenter and the mason to Stanley to ask the authorities what they could do about their contracts, and in Snow's opinion it wasn't safe to leave the catechist and the doctor by themselves on Keppel.

Garland Phillips, speaking for himself and the doctor, told Snow they would never leave Keppel.

So Snow on one of his trips tried a ruse. When Phillips and Ellis came out to the *Allen Gardiner* in their little sailboat, Snow had his men cable the sailboat fore and aft and haul it out of the water and onto the deck of his ship.

But Phillips fought so fiercely, throwing a couple of the crewmen out of the sailboat, that Snow was obliged to relent and have the sailboat lowered again into the water, whereupon Phillips and Ellis returned to shore.

As time went on, and the carpenter and the mason returned to Keppel, Snow induced Ellis, whom Snow regarded as the superintendent of the Mission, to come with him and visit Stanley to listen to the businessmen there. But Snow was shocked when the doctor, apparently in accord with orders he had been given by Despard, had no general discussions with the men at Stanley but directly went about pricing captured cattle and seeing how many cattle would be available for transport to Keppel.

At Phillips' insistence Snow had to make frequent trips to Montevideo where ships from England called. The arrival was expected of a duly authorized missionary leader who would assume control; the eventual dispatch of such a leader had been promised. But no such leader arrived. A few working people were sent by the Mission—gardeners and cooks—along with farming equipment and more material for housing, and Snow transported them and their gear to Keppel where the Mission's installation was expanding. The original small house was now used as a storehouse and a larger house had been built, with corrals for the cattle the Mission did not yet have.

Finally, after two years had passed, into the harbor at Stanley sailed a ship called the *Hydaspes* eighty-seven days at sea from England—and on it was the awaited missionary leader. It was the Reverend G. Pakenham Despard himself with a party of eighteen people, including his wife and children, eighty tons of goods, furniture for the house he intended to occupy, and his piano.

Snow dutifully began to shuttle Despard, his party, their baggage and supplies, from Stanley to Keppel.

While conducting this shuttle operation, Snow described to Despard his meeting with Jemmy, which he had previously reported by letter. Despard simply would not believe that Jemmy had refused to come to the Falklands. It was fixed in his mind that Jemmy should come—and that Jemmy would begin the whole process of the conversion and education of the Yahgans. Despard was disappointed and disgusted with Snow—and surely said so.

While in Port Stanley, Despard straightened out the Mission's financial arrangements and confirmed that there were 130 penned-up wild cattle that could be bought. Despard wanted to buy them and have Snow in the *Allen Gardiner* transport the cattle, twenty at a time, to Keppel, where the corrals were waiting.

Snow thought this idea was absurd. The *Allen Gardiner* was a small ship with a narrow beam. To have twenty wild cattle on deck in some kind of improvised pen from which the cattle might break loose in rough weather was impracticable and dangerous.

Despard fired Snow. Despard fired him and refused to pay his passage back to England. In those days the English usually traveled with their mattresses and bedding and, when Snow asked if he could at least take from the *Allen Gardiner* the bedding from his cabin, Despard charged him two pounds for it.

So Snow had to pay for the passage of himself and his wife

from the Falklands back to England. As soon as they were home, Snow sued for wrongful dismissal. And he eventually lost the case, perhaps on the facts or perhaps because the tide of the times was running so strongly in the missionaries' favor.

Despard hired a new captain named Robert Fell, a more compliant sort, and Fell had to hire a new crew (actually Despard hired the new crew) because the crew Snow had hired quit when Snow was discharged.

Despard sent Fell in the *Allen Gardiner* to Rio and to Montevideo to buy and bring back lumber for further enlarging the facilities on Keppel Island where everything was bustling.

Despard fit into his schedule a trip to Spaniard Harbor. He had Captain Fell take him and his wife and the foremost members of his staff to the place where the martyrs were buried, and they all prayed at the gravesite.

On Keppel a school routine was set up for the children. More space was needed both for living and for warehousing.

THEN an odd thing happened, an oddity among so many oddities.

In the party Despard had brought with him from England was Allen Weare Gardiner, the grown son of the martyred, hyperenergetic missionary who had set this whole crusade in motion. Young Gardiner had completed his studies at Oxford and was awaiting ordination. He was determined to follow in his father's footsteps — and he was a hard-muscled young Englishman, as hard as he could be, rock-hard in his determination to emulate his father, hard from the playing fields of his schools, born hard as the son of a Royal Navy captain-turned-missionary whose frenetic efforts had led him to seek to serve in the most dangerous spots on earth.

As soon as Despard had the functioning of the installation on Keppel Island in hand, Despard sent Gardiner to bring back Jemmy.

This young Englishman, in the ship named for his father, went with Captain Fell and his crew south and through the Strait of Le Maire past Picton Island and into the Beagle Channel.

From Captain Snow they had learned just where to look for Jemmy. And they found him. Gardiner's report of the meeting, in the version prepared by the Patagonian Mission, sheds little light on the emotions of the men.

According to Gardiner, Jemmy, having been summoned from a nearby island by one of his daughters, simply agreed to come to the Falklands. Jemmy was pleased by the presents Gardiner gave him. Jemmy seems not to have been curious about who this young Englishman was.

This is the Mission's version of the meeting, and the Mission frequently edited or interpreted actual notes to improve the impression for popular consumption. So some reading between the lines may be called for.

When he met Jemmy, young Gardiner must have had pulling within him two violent cross-currents: He was pulled one way by his determination to convert these people, as his father had wanted to convert them, to bring them from the darkness of savagery into divine light; and he was pulled another way by his hatred of these people who had hounded his father to death on the lonely beach he had recently visited, and he must have loathed these little Indians and been unable to deny his repugnance for them.

So they had a face-off: Jemmy, genial, with the easy self-assurance of a competent middle-aged man who was sure of his situation in life, and young Gardiner, fresh from the playing fields of Oxford, with his father's cause and the vision of his father's death at odds in his mind.

Gardiner's purpose was to bring Jemmy to Keppel Island. And, according to Gardiner, Jemmy consented to come with him.

In the Mission's version, Jemmy's *willing* consent is stressed. Jemmy, after agreeing, spent a night ashore when he could have changed his mind but he didn't and reboarded the next morning. Then the ship, after leaving, encountered shifting winds, had to return and anchor again, and Jemmy had a second chance to change his mind but didn't.

Finally, on June 16, 1857, the *Allen Gardiner*, with Jemmy aboard, sailed for the Falklands.

Why did Jemmy consent to come to the Falklands, after he had firmly refused Captain Snow?

Maybe Jemmy simply changed his mind. He may have missed the excitement of his contact with the English. His life at home may have bored or displeased him.

Maybe Jemmy decided to come because it was midwinter in the southern hemisphere and the living was difficult. Or maybe Jemmy consented because Gardiner made him elaborate promises.

Maybe Gardiner gave Jemmy more presents than even Jemmy expected, although there were no goods available that had not been given before.

But maybe, in that face-off of two men who could be mortal enemies and might be spiritual companions, Gardiner prevailed in some fundamental way. Jemmy had long ago learned to recognize and admire the taut and heroic qualities that had been FitzRoy's.

Possibly, of course, Captain Snow, having been admonished by Governor Rennie, had never asked Jemmy to come to the Falklands.

In any case, the historical fact is that Jemmy consented to come with young Gardiner—and there is no evidence or intimation of physical coercion. Jemmy's subsequent behavior in the Falklands belies any possibility that he was forced.

In making the best of it, Jemmy brought along with him his current wife and three small children. According to Gardiner, Jemmy agreed to stay in the Falklands for six months.

There is no tone of triumph in Gardiner's report of his retrieval of Jemmy. It seems this was nothing less than the Reverend Despard expected.

START-UP TIME

THUS the process, at last, was systematically begun—the execution of the idea that had been oncoming for years. FitzRoy had tried to initiate the process when he had brought Fuegian Indians to England for education and religious training, then to return them to their homeland. Now the Fuegians were brought only to the nearby Falklands, so a routine for bringing them over and taking them back would be easier and the desired result could be attained more quickly: the civilizing of these poorest people on earth for their own benefit and for the benefit of all sailors who risked shipwreck when they had to round the stormy cape.

Jemmy, as the first of Despard's students, proved to be lazy. He had no patience with the catechism Phillips offered to go over with him and he showed little interest in the practical skills Despard thought he should acquire: farming, construction. Jemmy still liked to please, and whenever Mrs. Despard favored him in some way he would pick wildflowers or catch some fish for her, although in Jemmy's opinion, later expressed, the fishing around Keppel Island was no good.

The truth probably is that Jemmy, while on Keppel Island among the missionaries, felt useless. He knew what his situation among his own people had been and was. He was sure of his own competence in that most difficult environment. He did not see the need for the skills Despard had decided he should acquire. He had seen crops trampled and houses destroyed. And he had an unexpressed inner pride based upon his ability to endure and prevail in his own circumstances. To most competent Yahgans this confidence in their own ability came unself-consciously and was never reexamined. But Jemmy had had cause to doubt himself after the time he had spent in the advanced atmosphere of England—and that he had now successfully established himself on his own terrain must have been a matter of conscious gratification to him.

So he loafed about on Keppel Island and watched the missionaries as they labored to expand their settlement. Jemmy and his "wife" and children became accustomed to the ringing of the bells that marked the routine of prayers and hymns with which each day was punctuated. And although Jemmy's wife and children would whisper in Yahgan when they talked among themselves, all of them, including Jemmy, improved their knowledge of English.

The English language, in and of itself, was undeniably a winning commodity. All the Yahgans liked to use it and readily learned it. Whether it was the sound of English or the flexibility of English or the brain-pleasing sensibleness of English that was the essential attraction, may be pondered. But English definitely caught on.

It was part of Despard's plan that, in reverse, the missionaries should learn Yahgan so that their eventual communication with the Indians could, if necessary, be in the Indians' own tongue. But this was difficult to accomplish because, although Jemmy would sometimes put himself out to go over a few Yahgan words with Despard or Phillips, Jemmy and his family did not like to speak aloud in their own language before the missionaries.

The only one of the English to penetrate Jemmy's family circle and to be included in their talk in Yahgan was an adopted son of Despard, a boy of thirteen or fourteen named Thomas Bridges. The boy had a good ear for language, was fascinated by it, and was at an age when he could still pick up a new language without translating into his own. So before long Bridges was the acknowledged interpreter whenever some explanation proved difficult, either for the Indians to the English or for the English to the Indians.

The strange thing is that—in spite of all the problems and delays, and in spite of the intensely devout, stifling way the missionaries talked and wrote and acted in the mid-nineteenth

century, in spite of England's distractedness and the absence in
the missionary movement of formidable intellects like FitzRoy's
and Darwin's—progress was being made. The spider's thread of a
link was being established between the Yahgans and the English.

AFTER four months Despard had had enough of Jemmy.

According to Jemmy's own testimony, later given, Despard
said, "Go back, Jemmy. You're old." Despard recognized the
adaptability of the young and he intended to bring over another
batch of Yahgans of a generation more receptive to learning.

Despard and Jemmy reached an understanding that, when
Jemmy was brought back to his home, Jemmy would talk to his
people and arrange for other Yahgans to come and stay on Keppel
Island. Whether or not Despard made clear to Jemmy that
Jemmy's own return home was contingent upon his arranging for
replacements is a matter for conjecture. But it seems highly
unlikely that Despard would have dispensed with Jemmy had
Despard not been assured that the vital process of bringing over
and taking back the Yahgans would continue.

This time Despard and some of his associates went to the
Beagle Channel in the *Allen Gardiner*, with Jemmy and Jemmy's
family aboard. They deposited Jemmy, his wife and children
amid their own people and, in accord with the understanding
Despard had reached with him, Jemmy talked to his people, and
Despard peaceably took on board nine Yahgans destined for
Keppel Island. The nine comprised three family groups—three
men, three women and three children—and among the nine was
one of Jemmy's grown sons whom the English began to call Billy.

Phillips had come on this trip, and beneath the dour exterior of
this obstinate, hard-knuckled young missionary was an enthusiast, a passionate Puritan. He had designed and hand-sewn a flag
that he wanted to raise over Tierra del Fuego—not the British
flag but the Church's flag—red with a white cross and in white
letters the words "Tierra del Fuego" which he had painstakingly
embroidered on the red.

With a couple of the younger sailors Phillips went ashore and clambered up a hill to a spot where a lone tree stood. They climbed the tree, stripped off the branches and at the top attached the flag, which fluttered in the steady wind.

The watching Yahgans were amused. Jemmy's presence no doubt contributed to the congenial atmosphere.

Despard had Captain Fell take him around Ponsonby Sound and along the west coast of Navarin Island, and Despard concluded that the best site for a mission house would be the place FitzRoy had originally selected on Navarin, just south of the Murray Narrows on a sheltered bay where there was a nice stretch of flat grassy land behind the stony beach, the place Jemmy called Wulaia. Despard went ashore and staked out the precise area where a mission house would be built.

While Jemmy had been with them, Despard, Phillips and others had landed from time to time on the small islands and, while the nine new Yahgans were aboard, they had gone ashore at Wulaia. But the missionaries had not stayed ashore for long. While Indians were aboard, those circling about in the bark-canoes were subdued. Also, Despard probably did not comprehend the degree of protection that the size of the schooner afforded him.

Returning to Keppel Island, Despard retained the second group of Yahgans for ten months. They responded better than had Jemmy and his family. They liked singing and joined in the hymns. They were all baptized and seemed to understand what that meant. And, like all the Yahgans, they eagerly took to English.

A F T E R ten months, Despard was ready for another changeover.

This time Despard did not choose to go back to the Beagle Channel himself; he was busy supervising what had become a substantial missionary installation on Keppel Island. Young Gardiner had returned to England to be ordained. So Despard put Phillips in charge. Phillips had just been married to a girl who had been sent out by the Mission, but his trip to the Beagle Channel was to be only a short one and his bride would remain on Keppel with Captain Fell's wife.

At Despard's direction, sections of a framed house were put aboard the *Allen Gardiner,* along with additional building materials. With Phillips and the nine Yahgans as passengers, plus Captain Fell and his crew of seven, the ship was fairly well filled. Among the crew were several competent carpenters, led by the bo'sun—a tall strong Swede named August Petersen, called Agusto.

Despard's instructions to Phillips were that he was to erect the mission house on the grassy land where Despard had staked out the site; that "should there be a friendly spirit" he was to hold a Sunday service in the house to inaugurate it and to demonstrate its purpose for the Yahgans; and that he was then to bring back another group of Yahgans for religious training and education. Despard was certain Jemmy would arrange for the replacements.

When the time came to embark, word passed among the missionary workers on Keppel that the departing Yahgans had stolen a lot of little things—including some of the personal belongings of the English workers. The Yahgans were now clothed and had been clothed ever since the missionaries had taken them in charge; in addition, the Yahgans carried bundles which they were taking home with them.

Despard had to make a decision. Some of the things the Yahgans may have taken were the kinds of things he would readily have given them, though he could not condone the taking of the mission workers' personal belongings. Despard did not want to seem overly indulgent toward the Yahgans before his devout English staff who were working so hard for him. Also, it was the sentiment among the missionaries, especially on the laboring level, that these Indians should be grateful for what was being done for them, and it was gross ingratitude for them to steal.

So Despard ordered that the bundles of the Yahgans should be undone and searched. Phillips, who was going to be traveling with these Indians, objected, but Despard overruled him.

The Yahgans objected vociferously. They regarded these bundles as theirs to take home. They gesticulated wildly and sputtered in both Yahgan and broken English. But the more they objected, the more they obliged the Reverend Despard to remain firm before his onlooking English staff.

And some things were discovered that had not been given to the Yahgans, particularly personal mementos. The Yahgans could not distinguish between things that belonged to the establishment and the workers' personal belongings.

So the English staff, with its ornaments retrieved, was assuaged. And the Yahgans, in Phillips' charge, departed, upset and disgruntled.

The *Allen Gardiner* made the 70-mile run to Port Stanley and went into harbor there for a day and a night before leaving for Tierra del Fuego. Various people at Port Stanley—English sheep-ranchers, farmers and their wives, not the magistrates—picked up from the Yahgans that the Yahgans were furious because they had been searched and things they regarded as theirs were taken from them. These people at Stanley duly spoke to Captain Fell and Phillips and warned them of the situation.

The rough crossing to Tierra del Fuego kept everyone occupied, but once the shelter of the Beagle Channel was reached, the *Allen Gardiner* smoothly and quickly made its way around Navarin Island to the bay by the designated site for the mission house. Then the anchor was dropped.

Bark-boats filled with Yahgans soon gathered around the *Allen Gardiner.* The Yahgans on board complained to those in the bark-boats. Towers of smoke were rising from the islands all around. More bark-boats were coming. The clamor became intense.

Jemmy was allowed to come on board.

Jemmy felt responsible for the nine Yahgans, including his son Billy, who had been kept on Keppel for the past ten months, and he took their side in objecting to Phillips over what the Yahgans regarded as the niggardliness of the missionaries. To emphasize the less-than-generous way the Yahgans were being treated, Jemmy demanded from Phillips some presents for himself.

A Cove on the Beagle Channel, *by Conrad Martens.*

The fact was that no presents had been sent for Jemmy. Despard had been concentrating on the house that had been loaded in sections onto the *Allen Gardiner* and on all the necessary building materials that had to be included. Deck space on the ship was limited. Despard had simply forgotten to include presents for Jemmy. Besides, Despard presumed that Jemmy would have kept the presents he had already been given. And Despard thought that Jemmy had already received enough in the way of presents to last a lifetime.

Jemmy didn't think so.

Phillips gathered together some food and a few tools for

Jemmy, who obviously did not regard these gifts as adequate. To show his displeasure, especially while his own countrymen were watching him just as appraisingly as Despard's English staff had been watching Despard, Jemmy threw his gifts over the side into his canoe and left the ship.

Then a sailor on the *Allen Gardiner* told Captain Fell that some of his personal things were missing.

Fell ordered that the nine Yahgans be searched again; this time their clothing as well as their bundles should be gone through.

The Yahgans were close to hysterical, which was their mode when wildness came over them. Billy Button was frothing. Another of the Yahgan men about the same age as Billy, named Okokko, was clinging to his bundle. The women and children were screaming. And the third Yahgan man, who had been a particular favorite while on Keppel Island and was nicknamed Squire Muggins (his Yahgan name was Schwaiamugunjiz), leapt at Captain Fell, who threw him off.

The crewmen pulled away the Yahgans' bundles and found in them the trinkets the sailor was missing.

This so enraged all the returning Indians that they tore off the clothes the missionaries had given them and, naked, went over the side into the waiting bark-canoes.

Armed and resolute, Captain Fell and his crewmen stationed themselves around the deck of the *Allen Gardiner,* with the two small cannons exposed. Nothing more happened then.

Phillips had heard from people in the Falklands who were familiar with the Fuegians that he could expect a flagging of the Indians' spirit when they were confronted with firmness.

Captain Fell and his sailors took turns on guard all night, and the Indians eventually calmed down. Their shrieking subsided and even the guttural begging-talk died out.

FLASH-POINT

IN THE morning it was misty and a chilly spring rain was falling, off and on. The Yahgans preferred to stay close to the fires in their wigwams. The situation appeared peaceful, and Phillips was determined to obey the orders he had been given.

In the mist and rain the crew of the *Allen Gardiner* began to ferry ashore the sections of the mission house. It was hard work—to balance the sections in the longboat, then to guard the material left on shore, while two or three sailors would return for another piece of the house. But Phillips took the lead in the work and inspired the others. The big Swede, Agusto, could handle a whole section by himself.

On the site which Despard had staked for the mission house the building proceeded, even though the crew had to guard their unloaded materials both day and night.

After a couple of days the weather improved. Then crowds of curious Yahgans began to assemble. They thronged around the house, and other Yahgans could be seen on the heights. Bark-canoes loaded with Yahgans kept coming into the bay from all directions.

The mission house was, in Despard's words, "in the English fashion," and he expected that it would impress the Indians who had never before seen such a house.

Also, many of the Yahgans who hadn't seen the *Allen Gardiner* before were impressed by the size of the ship anchored in the bay.

Both Phillips and the Reverend Despard hoped that the purpose for which this house was being erected would finally be understood by the Yahgans; perhaps Jemmy would explain to his countrymen, or else the Indians would just be able to see, that this was a House of God, a place for singing hymns, a place of Christian worship. Phillips, as he worked, assured the others that eventually these Indians would come to see the light.

While the sailors guarded the partly built house at night, Phillips would lead them in the singing of hymns—and Yahgans could be heard in the rustling darkness, joining in.

As the construction neared completion, the restlessness of the Yahgans increased and they became more of a nuisance, trying to snatch away nails and the jackets the sailors had taken off—shouting, screaming, threatening, yet gleeful as the Yahgans always were when they were hunting. But each man from the *Allen Gardiner* had a hammer in hand most of the time, as well as a pistol tucked at his waist, and they kept off the Yahgans.

When the mission house was nearly done, Phillips decided to make a fence around it. So two of the sailors cut down beech saplings and began to set them in the ground around the mission.

And then it was Sunday, the sixth of November, 1859.

The mission house was not quite finished, nor was the fence. Nor had Phillips even begun to discuss with Jemmy the matter of the next group of Yahgans who were to go to Keppel Island.

But Phillips, being an enthusiast, decided that this was his opportunity—on this first Sunday—to reveal to the Yahgans why this house had been built and why it should be left alone and respected and revered. Despard's instructions were to hold a Sunday service in the house "should there be a friendly spirit"—and the best way Phillips could imagine to encourage a friendly spirit would be to gather together with the Yahgans in the mission house to pray and to join in prayerful song.

Early on Sunday morning Phillips brought those who had slept aboard the ship to join those who had stood guard through the night and they cleaned up the site around the mission. Then in the longboat they all returned to the *Allen Gardiner*. Aboard ship, the men stored their tools, put away their guns, and put on clean shirts. Captain Fell and all his crew had been carefully chosen by Despard for their piety.

Unarmed, and with only the cook left on the ship, they returned to shore in the longboat, beached it, and proudly marched up to their new mission house—Phillips leading, with Captain

Fell, Agusto, the other sailors following him. Phillips carried a Bible in his hand.

On the beach several hundred Yahgans were milling about, watching, and the Indians made way for the missionary and the men from the ship.

After Phillips and the others had entered the mission house, as many Yahgans as could crowded in after them.

FROM the deck of the *Allen Gardiner*, the cook—an uneducated, lower-class English kid named Alfred Coles, twenty-three years old—watched and remembered what he saw because what he saw was indelibly etched upon his mind.

As soon as Phillips, Captain Fell and the sailors were inside the mission house, Yahgans who had not gone in and who remained on the beach ran to the longboat, took away the oars, and pushed the longboat out into the water.

Coles heard a hymn struck up inside the mission house—then the outcry of many voices, all the packed-in Yahgans shrieking at once—and out from the mission house came running, stumbling, running again, the white men who had gone ashore. Chasing them, beating them with clubs, stoning them with accurately thrown fist-sized rocks, were the Yahgans, men and women.

It was a massacre.

Only Phillips and Agusto made it to the water's edge. Coles saw Phillips, bleeding, wade into the water after the drifting longboat—and he saw Billy Button hurl the stone that struck the missionary on the temple and felled him, to float face-down and drown in the water.

Agusto was killed on the beach. Towering over the little Yahgans, the Swede made an easy target and was hit in the face and about the head by a barrage of the fist-sized stones that the Yahgans threw with such force until he went to his knees and fell on his back. Then the Yahgans stood directly over him and smashed down their stones until they cracked open his skull.

Captain Fell and all the other sailors except one were murdered around the mission house, as more Yahgans came running with their bone-tipped spears that they drove into the fallen bodies. One sailor, a favorite among the crew, Hugh MacDowell of Devonport, called Hughsey, was killed inside the house.

By himself, staring in terror from the deck of the *Allen Gardiner,* Coles listened as the shrieking of the Yahgans rent the Sabbath air that had been intended for church-bells, hymns and carols.

THIS was the crime, the horrendous crime, of gargantuan proportion. It was a bloody spree of killing, the massacre of unarmed men who were led by a missionary with a Bible in his hand, the brutal murder of men who were trying to bring a message of peace and gentleness.

The atrocity was carried out by natives, some of whom had been Christianized. By natives, some of whom had had prolonged contact with civilization. By natives, many of whom had learned to speak a little English.

These missionaries and these natives had been in the process of bridging two worlds—the civilized Christian world and the elemental savage world—and the bridge had been made! Only to be broken in a spasm of slaughter.

WHEN Coles saw the Yahgans in their bark-canoes coming toward the *Allen Gardiner,* he panicked and jumped into the dinghy—disregarding the cannons, not even taking a pistol—and he rowed as fast as he could for the tip of the bay furthest from the site of the massacre.

The Yahgans pursued him but their bark-boats were slow, cumbersome and overcrowded. So Coles was able to reach shore in the dinghy and escape into the woods.

AFTERMATH

O N KEPPEL ISLAND, month after month passed
and the *Allen Gardiner* did not return. The wives of Phillips
and Fell were anxious, and Despard became more and more
concerned. Finally in a small mission boat aptly named the
Perseverance Despard went to Port Stanley.

The authorities at Stanley knew nothing. So Despard sought
out Captain Smyley, who had been the first to find the remains of
Gardiner's party in Spaniard Harbor.

Smyley, an American from Newport, Rhode Island, was not
exactly ostracized at Stanley, but he was not included in the
controlling circle. He had been officially appointed U.S. Commercial Agent for the Falkland Islands, but this designation was
peculiar since the U.S. did not recognize British sovereignty in
the Falklands. In his official capacity Smyley mainly defended
American sealers who got into trouble with the British authorities, which did not endear him to the British. Smyley owned two
ships, the *John E. Davidson* and the *Nancy*, and as a goad to the
British on the Falklands he employed as his first mate a young
Argentine, Luis Piedrabuena (who later planted the Argentine
flag on many islands in the Fuegian archipelago and is reported to
have refused a British offer of 10,000 pounds to remove the
Argentine flag from Staten Island).

Smyley was a serious, scientific-minded sea-captain who regularly reported on the winds and currents of the South Atlantic to
the U.S. Hydrographic Office where a lieutenant in the U.S. Navy,
Matthew Maury, was compiling statistics for a guide to navigation.

When bringing the *John E. Davidson* down from Newport in
1846, Smyley had been confronted with a mutiny that had been
planned by some crewmen he had hired in New York who wanted
to steal the ship. Smyley, though he was shot, put down the
mutiny and had the mutineers jailed in Brazil.

Smyley was a cool, extremely level-headed captain whose

Button Sound, *by Capt. W. Parker Snow.*

competence and thorough knowledge of the South Atlantic made him the choice for the English and all others whenever a rescue had to be made.

Despard hired Smyley to go and look for the *Allen Gardiner.* Smyley acknowledged the urgency and without delay set sail in the *Nancy,* with a crew of only six.

Smyley did not need and would not have accepted from Despard any instructions regarding the Indians, among whom Smyley had sailed before at the eastern and western ends of the Beagle Channel. So Despard withheld the restrictions he had placed on Captain Snow and the advice he had imposed on Captain Fell. Smyley did not share the Patagonian Mission's hopes for these Indians, nor had he any of FitzRoy's feeling. Smyley had no feeling about the Indians, one way or the other. He did have a feeling, even a passion, about saving the survivors of shipwrecks.

Smyley sailed directly to Wulaia. And there, in the bay, he found the stripped hull of the *Allen Gardiner*, afloat and adrift. The brigantine still had the masts intact but obviously had been ransacked.

Smyley saw the empty mission house ashore. No Yahgans were about. The few who had been on the beach or fishing near the shore in their bark-boats had hidden themselves in the woods.

Taking advantage of the Indian inactivity as long as their surprise lasted, Smyley with four of his men, all armed, went in their longboat and boarded the *Allen Gardiner*.

The brigantine was empty, utterly and eerily empty, with cabins and holds as cleaned out as the deck. Smyley and his men heard the echoing of their own footsteps as they walked about and inspected what had been a well-equipped ship. Every removable object had been taken from her. There was not a dangling line, not a bit of sail; every piece of iron had been pried off.

Smyley knew the eyes of Fuegian Indians were fixed upon him when he stood at the rail of the *Allen Gardiner* and looked over the shore. The Indians were watching from the forest, from the heights, from the islands all around.

In the longboat Smyley with his men went ashore for a closer look at the mission house. On the *Nancy* anchored in the bay, two crewmen were standing beside the exposed signaling cannons.

As soon as Smyley and his men beached their boat, Alfred Coles came running from the forest like a crazy man having a fit and he collapsed into the arms of the sailors.

Coles was frightful to look at. He was totally naked. His white skin had red splotches and was raw and cracked on his nose, on his shoulders. His lips were swollen and cracked—and his face was so strange: His eyebrows and his beard had been plucked out and stubble was regrowing; only the long, reddish blond hair on his head remained in a dirty matted mass. In his red-and-white face his eyes were dark, bleared from smoke. He was covered with boils, some burst, some ready to burst. He was emaciated and shaking.

Coles babbled out his story of the massacre.

Smyley saw a few Indians edging out from the trees. So he had his men put Coles into the longboat and they returned to the *Nancy*.

They carried Coles up the ladder and tried to restore him with food and drink, slowly provided, a small mouthful at a time. The boy had difficulty controlling his shaking, his twitching. He scratched at the boils that afflicted him. The crewman who functioned in a medical capacity applied salves and tried to calm him.

Then another sailor called out because a Yahgan canoe was alongside—and up the ladder, which the sailors had failed to draw in, without permission to board came Jemmy Button, who leapt upon the deck.

Smyley had never seen Jemmy before.

Jemmy, with a half-smile, perhaps of apology, perhaps of shame, identified himself in English.

That did it for Captain Smyley.

Smyley ordered the Indians who had come with Jemmy in the canoe to cast off—in a tone they could not misunderstand. He forbade Jemmy to leave the ship and assigned two sailors to make sure he didn't. Within seconds Smyley had the anchor up and the ship under sail for the Falklands

Part Three

THE TRIAL OF
JEMMY BUTTON

PROCEEDING
UNDER PRESSURE

AFTER Smyley had left for Tierra del Fuego, the anxiety had spread from Despard through the community of Port Stanley, and after Smyley's return the horror had to be faced.

Rumors and fears were sweeping like tiderips even among those on the land. To the English in the Falklands, Tierra del Fuego did not seem far away, and several prominent gentlemen farmers were talking of returning to England or of settling elsewhere.

Governor Moore, genuinely shocked by Smyley's report of the massacre, was concerned as well by the fact that this trouble had occurred during his administration. Though the atrocity had been committed outside the area for which he was responsible, the Patagonian Mission, based in his area, was involved. His attitude had subtle ramifications.

The official plan for the Falklands, which he and his predecessor had advanced, was for the peaceful economic development of these islands by English immigrants chiefly engaged in sheep-raising, for the perpetuation of British sovereignty, and the maintenance of a naval station. Moore did not feel that the activities of the Patagonian Mission were in harmony with this plan. And he most definitely did not want the Mission to benefit from publicity which might result from this massacre, as the Mission had benefited from the publicity which had followed the martyrdom of Gardiner's party.

So Moore's intention was to go slow—to be precise, not to

make himself vulnerable to criticism, and not to hurry into a presentation that might work to the advantage of the Patagonian Mission.

Resisting the pressure of the unrest, Moore settled upon his procedure. He would make a prompt report of the massacre to the Duke of Newcastle, who headed the Colonial Office in London, and he would append depositions from the sole broken survivor of the tragedy (Coles) and from the one Fuegian Indian he had on hand (Jemmy). The Governor could assure his superior that a thorough inquiry would be made in due course and a subsequent report of the inquiry submitted.

It would take six to eight weeks for his initial report to reach London. The report would be taken by schooner to Montevideo, there to be held by the British consul until he found a ship bound for England, and the ship in all likelihood would, at the least, stop at Rio and the Azores. During this time of transit, Governor Moore would conduct his thorough inquiry and make a final report.

Moore hoped that the slow pace of this procedure would act as a kind of reduction chamber, squeezing out illusions, fears, hopes and dreams, and reducing perceptions to the bleak realities— even though in the illusions, fears, hopes and dreams were the human motivations.

The Governor assembled a board before which the depositions would be given and assigned clerks who would do the recording by hand with pen and ink. The board, which he chaired, included the Colonial chaplain and the trader/banker, the representative of the Falkland Island Company, and other magistrates.

Many citizens of Stanley attended the hearing.

THE TRUTH, UNDER OATH,
THE SWORN TRUTH

ALFRED COLES was the first witness to be called. He swore before God that his testimony would be true.

His name was Alfred Coles. He had been hired by Captain Fell in Montevideo, where he had been stranded, in September 1858, more than a year before the massacre, to work aboard the *Allen Gardiner* as cook and seaman. In order to get the job, he had told Captain Fell he was pious, although Fell hadn't much choice because the pay was very low.

Coles confirmed to the board—in his awful, lower-class English which the clerk who recorded the deposition para-phrased—that he had observed the massacre from the deck of the *Allen Gardiner* and, terrified, had escaped to shore in the dinghy. While hiding in the woods, he had seen the Yahgans who had pursued him in their bark-boats take the dinghy away with them and go back to join with many others in the looting of the ship.

(Like all the other dinghies, longboats and whaleboats stolen by the Yahgans over the years, this dinghy was never found.)

Coles testified that he had hidden in the woods for days, he thought for two weeks or so. He had been very hungry and thirsty. He quenched his thirst by sneaking over to a creek in the woods and drinking there. For his hunger he would go down to the shore at night and, hoping for moonlight, search for mussels and limpets which he would eat raw when he found them. He lost weight rapidly; his clothes began to bag on him; and he cut and bruised himself scrambling about the rocks in the dark.

Eventually he was sighted by some Yahgans—he was so hun-gry that he had stayed at the shore for the first flush of light before sunup because he hadn't been able to find any mussels or limpets in the dark. The Yahgans chased him; in his weakness he could not run fast; and they caught him. There were five or six Indians, both men and women, he thought. They knocked him down, sat on him in their nakedness, pressed him to the ground with their own stinking bodies, and they stripped him until he was as naked as they were. He was scared almost out of his wits—and humiliated and mortified.

The Yahgans were intrigued by the whiteness of his skin and, while several of them continued to hold him down, others looked him over very carefully. Then, with a pair of sharp-edged mussel shells, the oldest man among them plucked out his eyebrows and his facial hair. Like most of the sailors, Coles had both a mustache and full beard, so it hurt to have his facial hair pulled out. But he was too frightened to scream. And who would hear him screaming? Only other Yahgans, and if many of them were to gather together, the atmosphere, as he had seen before, would only worsen for him.

As it was, the task of plucking out all the hair from his face seemed to take longer than the Yahgans expected; some of them lost interest and became restless; and when the older man was done, they allowed Coles to sit up. (The Yahgans, of course, removed their own facial hair with mussel shells in this way, but the Indian men had only a few hairs on their chins and around the corners of their mouths.)

These Yahgans were hungry themselves; it was early morning and they were about to gather food. This was not a group that had worked itself up to a fighting fury or a stealing frenzy, and their spontaneous energy had been used up when they chased him through the woods.

Now they let him come with them, for which he was grateful because in the daylight, along with them, he was able to find a lot of mussels that he gulped down. On the surface of the water he saw the reflection of his own weird, hairless, bleeding face. But, at least, he wasn't so hungry.

In the bay in the daylight he saw clearly the floating hulk of the *Allen Gardiner* and saw that the ship had been ransacked. In the nightlight he had not been able to see how thoroughly the Indians had looted the ship.

For several weeks he stayed with the family group of Indians who had caught him, stripped him, and made him like themselves.

The Indians really did very little. They didn't work. They fished and hunted only sporadically. It was springtime and there were wild berries to eat in the woods. These Yaghans had a wigwam and he would huddle with them around the fire in the shelter of the wigwam at night.

These Yahgans knew a few words of English—they knew the name "Jam-mus Button"—but mostly Coles and these Indians communicated through gestures. He asked them about the ship, pointing at the ship and indicating in gesture and tone his questioning. And they mimed for him how they had killed the other men. Indians from islands all around had gathered for the killing, summoned by "Jam-mus Button," and they threw stones, struck with their clubs, thrust with their bone-tipped sticks, angry, *oens* (whether this use of *oens* referred to Phillips and the crew of the *Allen Gardiner* or whether this referred to Indians from other islands was unclear). Then, after the killing, all the Indians had stolen—the clothing from the corpses, everything they could take from the ship—and had run around with the stolen things. What a splash there had been when what was apparently a cannon was dumped overboard!

From what these Yahgans said and conveyed to him, Coles concluded that clearly Jemmy had instigated the massacre. While the Indians were enacting for him their attack, it was "Jam-mus" this and "Jam-mus" that, as if Jemmy had been in charge—even though Coles from the deck of the *Allen Gardiner* had not seen Jemmy, had not caught sight of Jemmy a single time, during the massacre.

Coles was certain it was Billy Button, Jemmy's son, whom he had seen throw the stone that had killed Phillips. Even at a distance of 300 to 400 yards (from the ship to the shore) he had recognized Billy, and Coles knew Billy well, having had Billy on board the ship for the trip from Keppel.

Coles had also seen Okokko and his family during the massacre, running aimlessly about the beach in terror. But Coles, who at close hand had watched Jemmy and Phillips arguing aboard the ship, had not on the morning of the massacre actually seen Jemmy.

Yet what the Yahgans did convey to Coles—and Coles thought he understood them—was that Jemmy had directed the looting of the ship, had told the others what to take, had showed them how to loosen the equipment to dismantle the ship, and it was Jemmy who had directed that the cannons should be dumped overboard.

And the Yahgans, Coles further testified, conveyed to him, acted out for him, using their few words of English, what had happened at the end of the day of the massacre after the *Allen Gardiner* had been substantially looted.

As night came on, the Yahgans were fearful of staying on the ship, and the last of them, with a final load of loot, were preparing to follow the others ashore to their wigwams.

But Jemmy stayed them—the fiercest of the Indian men and women, the most loot-laden. Jemmy wanted to show them what he was going to do.

He was not afraid to stay aboard the ship at night. He led them down the short flight of stairs to a cabin. The Yahgans did not comprehend that this was the captain's cabin. To them it was only the most ornate of the many chambers on this strange ship.

During the day Jemmy had kept the other Yahgans away from this room, and the captain's bed was undisturbed, made up with sheets and a blanket and a pillow in a pillowslip. It was wide for a bed aboard ship; Captain Fell had often slept in it with his wife.

There, Jemmy told his countrymen, was where he was going to sleep, there in the captain's bed.

Then the other Yahgans abandoned the *Allen Gardiner* and went ashore.

FROM one family group of Yahgans Coles wandered to another. He seemed not to arouse their anger, now that he was naked and without facial hair and was pitiably thin. There was general amusement over his whiteness and, because he aroused smiles and laughter, he was often welcomed into the wigwams. Sometimes a child or a woman or occasionally a man would come and beckon for him.

There was even some sympathy for him when his boils came on. The Yahgan women showed him how to apply mud and wet weeds to the boils, though the treatment did him no good.

Jemmy himself did not live on this island. Jemmy's wigwam was on a nearby island. But Jemmy came over from time to time and would throw together a wigwam for himself and his family and would stay for a few days.

When Coles first approached Jemmy, who had been told about him, Jemmy seemed to Coles to be a little shamefaced, although not much interested in Coles, in fact less interested in him than were the others.

Jemmy had allowed Coles to sit by his fire at night. On a chilly rainy night when Coles was trembling, Jemmy had given him an otter skin to put around his shoulders to keep warm.

This was the sworn testimony of Alfred Coles. After the deposition was read to him, Coles made his mark on the document.

THE TESTIMONY of Jemmy Button followed.

Jemmy moved slowly when he took his place in a wooden chair set before the table behind which sat the members of the board. Jemmy seemed to show his years; in his mid-forties he was old for a Yahgan. He was heavy-bodied. And he moved with the care of an experienced man who was aware of the importance of the situation he was in—"this travelled Fuegian," as Captain Snow had described him when Snow was favorably inclined toward him, "this partly civilized Fuegian," as Snow had later called him.

Jemmy was dressed in clothes that had been given him, sailor's garb, a shirt and turned-up pants with braces; no shoes had been found that would fit him.

Jemmy took his oath before God to tell the truth and seemed to understand the meaning of the oath; Jemmy had been catechized many, many times. Then Jemmy gave his account of what had happened on Navarin Island—and it differed from Coles' account.

Jemmy's English was poorer than usual. He had to grope for words, and his pidgin outpouring was often hard to understand.

Jemmy acknowledged that he had had harsh words with Phillips when the *Allen Gardiner* arrived, bearing the nine Yahgans who were being returned from Keppel. This, Jemmy said, was because these Yahgans had not wanted to go to Keppel. Jemmy himself, he told the board, had not wanted to go to Keppel when he had gone. None of the Indians wanted to go to Keppel. This is why the nine Yahgans objected so much when their bundles were taken from them and searched. This is why they tore off the clothes the missionaries had given them and jumped over the side into the Yahgan canoes. They were afraid they might be taken back to Keppel.

Then Jemmy's testimony became wandering, his broken English becoming unclear. He seemed to be complaining that the fishing was so bad at Keppel. There were no seals (although there are plenty of seals around the Falklands, there may then have been none where Jemmy was on Keppel Island). He was never able to spear a big fish. Never even saw a big fish.

When called upon by Governor Moore to give his account of the massacre, Jemmy denied he had been there. He had not gone to the mission house. Having received no satisfaction from Phillips, he had intentionally stayed away. He'd had nothing to do with the killing.

Oens men had done it. *Oens* men had come from distant islands and they were the ones who had murdered the men from the *Allen Gardiner*. Jemmy tried to explain which groups on which islands were the bad people; some were worse than others;

his people were the best. But *oens* people—Jemmy had no control over *oens* people.

Jemmy said he had never gone aboard the *Allen Gardiner* following the massacre. He had watched from the shore of a small island close by while the *oens* people had looted the ship. He had seen the splashes when they had thrown heavy things overboard into the water.

Jemmy said he had never slept in the captain's bed. Wouldn't have slept in the bed. Jemmy said he was so upset after the killing he had "run about, no more sleep, run about."

Jemmy acknowledged that he knew Alfred Coles. Many days after the massacre, when Jemmy went to Navarin Island, he had seen Coles and had tried to help him.

Jemmy wanted to go home. If he was taken back home, he promised he would show the captain (Smyley) where the graves of the murdered men were.

Jemmy implied—or it was thought by members of the board that he implied, because his English was so broken—that he and his sons had buried four of the bodies.

(Here is another oddity, because the Yahgans did not bury the dead. They had no ritual for burial, no rituals at all. They had no shovels or other implements with which to dig graves. They were known sometimes to burn a wigwam with a corpse in it. Sometimes they left bodies at distant spots in the woods. They never put dead bodies into the water because the bodies would float. The Yahgans were made uneasy by death and, whenever someone died, the family group would move on. Yet Jemmy—from his time in England and from all his contacts with English people—undoubtedly had become familiar with the ritual of burial and the respect the English paid to it.)

THESE depositions, with Captain Smyley's report, were all the testimony the board of inquiry had to go on.

The impression the board members had formed of twenty-three-year-old Coles was surely a poor one. Apart from his deplorable use of his own language, Coles still bore the signs of his ordeal. His skinny neck stuck up like the stem of a tulip from the overly large opening of his collar. He still had boils on his face and neck, even on the backs of his hands. He still twitched. Coles was a lost English kid, orphaned or abandoned, flotsam of the sea. He was not a type who inspired confidence.

Jemmy, on the other hand, the Governor and the magistrates found agreeable, as did many observers of the inquiry. Jemmy's manner was appealing. His pidgin English and the way he looked in his ill-fitting English clothes amused many of the citizens of Stanley. And Jemmy's grin was infectious. He was not a disgrace to his race but, rather, was the member of his race who had gone furthest to bridge the gap between the races.

Governor Moore, in his report to which the depositions were attached, set forth his own conclusions, in spite of the fact that this was to be a preliminary report.

Moore informed the home office that the Indians who had been brought to Keppel Island by the Patagonian Mission had been brought against their will.

On Keppel the Indians were treated as slaves and were made to tend the gardens and the livestock without pay, which was unfair to the Indians and to the farmers and ranchers on the Falklands who paid their workers.

The nine Indians who were being returned to their home had been provoked by the missionaries who had repeatedly gone through the Indians' bundles. This was attested to by many people at Stanley.

Furthermore, the missionaries had been foolhardy when among the Fuegian islands with a native population known to be unfriendly they had left their ship inadequately guarded and had gone ashore unarmed.

ALTHOUGH it was popularly perceived in the Falklands that the Governor and the magistrates were critical of the missionaries, and although in the course of the inquiry a fondness toward

Jemmy had developed among some of the citizens, many other English people there were appalled and outraged by the massacre—and a public argument was carried on in the streets of Stanley.

The militia officer in command of the garrison loudly announced that he wanted to organize a punitive expedition to sail to the Fuegian islands and teach the Indians a lesson.

Governor Moore forbade any such adventure. No warship of the Royal Navy was in the area at this time. Nor were there funds in the Falklands treasury to pay for a punitive expedition (and Moore had enough experience as a civil administrator to know with what disfavor the home office would view a request for funds for such a purpose).

Besides, Moore argued openly, a military expedition sent among the Indians would punish the innocent as well as the guilty. How could it be determined who were the guilty ones among a native population that couldn't speak English and whose language was not spoken by those sent to administer the punishment? A volley at a fleeing crowd of Indians would slaughter children who were totally innocent as well as men and women who may have had nothing to do with the massacre.

Another point the Governor made, warming to his subject, was that the nine Indians who had been kept on Keppel were provoked by the intrusive searches conducted by the missionaries. These nine, when brought back to the Fuegian islands, had passed on their feeling to the others. Indians knew no law and they knew no God. When provoked, these simple people killed. Killing to them was their natural response to a variety of provocations, to almost any provocation, and the retaliatory killing of some of them would accomplish nothing.

Thus the fact of the massacre dissolved in a welter of conflicting attitudes. A few missionary workers who had come from Keppel and were staying in Stanley expressed the opinion that, if a military expedition were mounted to punish the Indians, the effort to Christianize them would be set back perhaps irreparably. This sentiment, coming from those who had been most deeply hurt, neutralized even the bombast of the garrison commander.

In an effort at a final word, the Governor announced positively that immigration or importation of Fuegian Indians would cease.

DESPARD

T HE ONE who participated least in the public debate in the Falklands was the Reverend George Pakenham Despard, who had a reputation for being vociferous and outspoken.

Despard was waiting at Port Stanley when the *Nancy* returned. He learned the facts quickly from Captain Smyley. Perfunctorily, since he was responsible for Mission property, he asked Smyley to retrieve the ransacked ship, which Despard had commissioned and outfitted, whenever it seemed safe and feasible to do so. Also, Despard, in accord with the Mission's purpose and policy, asked Smyley, when he brought back the ship, to bring another group of Fuegian natives.

Despard exchanged a few words with Coles.

And he looked at Jemmy.

Then, heart-sickened, Despard returned to Keppel Island. He did not remain at Stanley for the duration of the inquiry.

At Keppel, the missionary contingent mourned for Garland Phillips and for Captain Fell and his pious crew, and condolences were lavished upon the widows. But the faith of the missionary workers was strong as ever; they raised up hymns of dedication; they accepted this tragedy as a hurdle that God in his wisdom had placed before them to test their mettle in this battle for such a good cause.

Despard resigned his position with the Patagonian Mission.

He wrote a letter addressed to the board of the Mission in England and requested that someone should be found and sent out to replace him. As far as he was concerned, his service in this crusade to convert the Fuegians was at an end. The light had gone out for him.

Why?

Men had been martyred before. Allen Gardiner and his devout followers had died of starvation. It was the martyrdom of Gardiner and his party that had thrust Despard into a position of leadership and had created his opportunity to serve. Then Despard had responded powerfully, enthusiastically, energetically. It was Despard's vigor that had brought the Patagonian Mission to prominence; it was under his leadership that the Mission had come so far—until now it was more than adequately financed and had a training installation on the Falklands according to plan, and the routine of religious training and education of a few Fuegians at a time had begun.

Why was Despard so disheartened by this setback?

Governor Moore's prohibition against further importation of Fuegian Indians, when Despard became aware of it, was only the kind of challenge to which Despard had responded many times. Despard never hesitated to pit himself against secular authority. The mood of religiosity in England was known to be intense and all missionary efforts were assured of broad popular support. In a dispute with the Governor, Despard almost surely would have prevailed. This was the kind of battle Despard had won again and again.

But Despard had not the heart for another battle. His resignation was unqualified and unequivocal.

What may be said of Despard's reaction is that it was profoundly sincere. If he did not truly feel the elation of the crusader, he would not lead the crusade. His reaction was quintessentially honest.

I think it was only Jemmy who could have so affected him. Despard would not have been devastated by a few names added to the long list of Christian martyrs. On the Mission's path of progress there were bound to be occasional setbacks. Despard was not the kind of man to be overly fond of Phillips or any of the others or to be emotionally overcome by their deaths. Also, this setback in its way was a glorious one: Phillips and the others had died after erecting a mission house in a heathen land; unarmed, they were about to conduct a Sunday service; Phillips had had a Bible in his hand. The picture of this band of true-believers marching on to glory would be the flag under which many more supporters of the Patagonian Mission in the future would rally and march.

But George Despard would march no further. Jemmy was the light that went out for him. Not Jemmy in and of himself as Despard had known him during the lassitudinous months Jemmy had spent on Keppel Island. But Despard had thought about Jemmy long before he ever saw or met him. Like Gardiner, Snow and many others, Despard had read about Jemmy in FitzRoy's *Narrative.* So before they ever met, he had a vision of Jemmy in his mind, a vision that for Despard was a brilliant revelation, a vision which assured him that Jemmy would be the bridge for Christian benevolence, that Jemmy would be the connection between savagery and civilized kindness. This is why Despard had never doubted that Jemmy would be found. Despard's vision of Jemmy was fundamental in his mind; his vision of Jemmy was the foundation for his sureness that what he foresaw would come true. Despard, before assuming the leadership of the Patagonian Mission, had never in his life had such a feeling of sureness; he didn't know where this sureness came from, only that he had it; and his vision of Jemmy was his unquestioned basis for it.

And so much had happened to prove that Despard's premonition was true. Jemmy had been found, alive and well, decades after FitzRoy and Darwin had left him. Jemmy had come to Despard on Keppel Island. After Snow had failed to induce Jemmy to come to Keppel, Jemmy had come at the request or command, which may have been inspired, of the martyr's son. And Jemmy had been key to the Mission's progress: Jemmy had arranged for the second group of Yahgans to come to Keppel. Jemmy blessedly had sent his own son to Keppel.

But now that was over. Now Despard faced bleak reality. When he looked at Jemmy, he saw the rudiments of humanity—

and nothing more. Despard was heartsick. Perhaps he now had a feeling similar to the feeling that Charles Darwin dispassionately was trying to introduce to a world that wanted to believe otherwise: that change could be accomplished and was accomplished only by the passage of almost incalculable time, by the passage of millions of life spans, by a factor of time so nearly infinite that the efforts of individuals limited to their own life spans shrank into insignificance. And this feeling ruled out the glorious rewards sought by martyrs and by the dedicated leaders of crusades.

Despard set his family to packing for their return to England.

EVEN Despard's patriarchal nature within his own family seemed to fade. He had always been the unquestioned and unself-questioning head of his family, especially so since he had succeeded to the leadership of the Mission. But now, after his letter requesting replacement had been dispatched, Despard let his adopted son, Thomas Bridges, who was then about seventeen, choose for himself the course he would follow.

Despard asked the young man whether he would prefer to return with the family to England or whether he would rather stay with the Mission installation in the Falklands. Despard had never asked his son such a question before, had never before allowed his son such use of his own judgment.

Bridges was by far the best Yahgan-speaker of all the missionaries. And he had been raised in the religious atmosphere in which almost every expression bore evidence of piety. Recalling England and their modest, commonplace life there, Bridges foresaw for himself in England nothing more than the resumption of that modesty. So he elected to stay and to dedicate himself to the continuation of the effort to Christianize the Yahgans.

FROM Port Stanley Governor Moore sent a message to Despard on Keppel Island, requesting him to come again to Stanley and add his testimony for submission to the Duke of Newcastle. Moore wanted from Despard a description of the circumstances under which the Indians had lived on Keppel and an account of the search they had undergone before the return to their home.

Despard refused to cooperate. He sent back to the Governor a curt note to the effect that this board of inquiry was authorized to investigate solely a maritime disaster (the looting of the *Allen Gardiner*) and the massacre of the missionary party had occurred on shore. Therefore the board's extension of its investigation to the onshore tragedy and any circumstances which some might associate with it was unauthorized.

So, without Despard's testimony, under date of March 15, 1860, Moore sent off to London his report with the depositions attached. And two and a half months later Moore made a final report after a supposedly thorough investigation, only to the effect that no further evidence had been discovered.

JEMMY

I N STANLEY HARBOR Captain Smyley methodically went about preparing the *Nancy* for return to the Fuegian islands to bring back the *Allen Gardiner*. He loaded aboard spare sails and tackle. He reinforced his own crew and hired an additional crew to sail the *Allen Gardiner;* in fact, Smyley hired all the available able-bodied seamen who were willing to go, and included several of the militiamen whose commanding officer had advocated a punitive expedition.

There was no popular dissension over the purpose of this trip. It was to retrieve British property. Both those who supported the missionaries and those who opposed them were in agreement not to stand for the abuse and abandonment of a British-owned ship.

Although Smyley always carried arms aboard the *Nancy*, the Governor loaned him additional carbines and ball cartridges.

Smyley took Jemmy along to point out the graves of the murdered men.

WHEN the *Nancy*, thus staffed and equipped, sailed into the bay of Wulaia, there were no Indians about, either on the beach or in their fishing boats. The ship had been sighted from one of the hilltops; all the Indians had retreated into the woods.

After other fights the Yahgans had remained wary for a while, especially after a raid by the Ona and most especially if they had killed an Ona. Now they knew that the token of their mischief was there in clear sight—the hulk of the *Allen Gardiner* adrift in the bay. And on the grassy land behind the beach was the wreckage of the mission house.

Smyley allowed some time for the Indians to reappear, for their begging instinct to overcome their fear.

After dropping anchor near the *Allen Gardiner*, he and his men had a meal aboard the *Nancy*. When the Indians still did not appear, even though there were wigwams all around the beach, Smyley had his longboat lowered and with rope and a spare anchor went to the *Allen Gardiner* and secured the hulk.

There were no smoke signals on the headlands, either summoning or warning other Yahgans.

Aboard the *Allen Gardiner*, Smyley found that the Indians apparently had not come again; the ship was as he had last seen it—a dismal, ransacked shell. But the masts were sound.

So Smyley—with his own ship heavily guarded, the crew in the longboat heavily armed, and the additional crew, also heavily armed, aboard the *Allen Gardiner*—began to ferry from the *Nancy* to the *Allen Gardiner* the necessary sails, spars, lines, supplies and equipment for the return voyage to the Falklands.

While the men worked through the afternoon, some Indians appeared on the beach. Then a few got into their bark-canoes and cautiously approached the *Nancy*.

Neither Smyley nor any of his men could say anything intelligible in the Indian tongue. The militiamen were tense in their readiness to shoulder their guns and fire. But Jemmy at the rail called out to his countrymen—not in urgency but in a gentle tone. And the Indians, who were tense with fear, responded. Then a discourse between Jemmy and those in the boats was carried on that defused the pervasive air of menace.

Jemmy knew that Smyley needed water and firewood, so he told the captain that his people would fill the casks and bring wood. Reluctantly Smyley decided to take the chance. He allowed two of the bark-canoes to come alongside and lowered to them empty casks for filling. The Indians in the boats quickly paddled back to shore. And soon they returned with the water-casks full, with bundles of firewood—and on their spears they offered up fresh fish.

Barter was such an ancient human activity—for both the Indians and the white men—that reflexively the sailors and even the militiamen tossed back nails and small hand-tools in exchange for the fish.

Jemmy, who had been uncertain and quiet on the trip from Stanley, not knowing what was in store for him, now became more animated and sent some of the Indians back with more empty casks. The Indian women with their children were coming out from the kelp in their canoes, and a playful atmosphere was irresistibly developing.

The night passed peacefully, with strong guards maintained on both ships, with the longboat lifted onto the deck of the *Nancy,* with all ladders pulled in, and with Jemmy who was the sole connection between the Yahgans and the white men held as a hostage.

Shortly after dawn, while the *Allen Gardiner* was being readied to sail, Smyley with a contingent of militiamen and sailors went ashore with Jemmy who promised to show them the graves.

The Indians were shy of the armed party on the beach and were not forthcoming as they had been from their boats the preceding day. Smyley saw the heads peeking from the wigwams and the shoulders of those who were hiding behind trees in the woods. He left four men on guard with the longboat.

Jemmy led Smyley and the others past the remains of the mission house and a short way up the bank of a creek to a small natural clearing in the woods. Jemmy looked around the clearing, as did Smyley and his men. There were no mounds, no signs that the spongy evergreen matting that covers the forest floor had ever been disturbed. So Jemmy led them back and went along the forest edge of the grassy land behind the beach.

Smyley with several men walked over to the mission house. The ground around it had been trampled by many feet; it was churned and ruffled. But there were no signs of gravedigging.

Smyley looked inside the house which had been built "in the English fashion." The windows were broken or completely knocked out by thrown stones which had also made holes in the walls. A few stones were still lying about. Part of the floor had caved in. Part of the roof was missing.

Jemmy led Smyley and his men to a ravine where Jemmy peered among the rocks. Jemmy kept mumbling to himself in English, knowing he was understood—about graves, hard work, heavy rocks, his sons to help him. He said he was sure the graves were here. Or here. Or maybe over there.

From the beach and the forest, Indian eyes were watching the men from the ships as they stumbled along on their fruitless search.

When it became clear that there were no graves, Smyley reached out, turned Jemmy about and confronted him.

IN THE planes of Smyley's hard face and in Smyley's cold eyes Jemmy saw—nothing. No hope. No concession. No inclination to have things other than they were.

Smyley was not like FitzRoy, whose eyes had shone. Nor like Darwin, whose clear-sightedness was always cloaked by his good manners. Nor like Snow and his wife, who had been easy to charm. Nor like Despard (excepting that last moment) and the Mission workers, who were pledged to be hopeful.

In Smyley's face Jemmy saw nothing, not even anger, only the recognition of reality.

SMYLEY, when he looked into Jemmy's face, which was no longer a blank primitive face but a face with comprehensible expression, saw cupidity. Smyley saw wiliness. And willfulness with hardly any restraint.

Smyley dismissed whatever incipient conscience there might be in Jemmy. Smyley did not grant that conscience would be fostered by kindness. Smyley allowed Jemmy nothing for having once been received—in a palace chamber with a high jeweled ceiling, amid harpoon-bearing, gorgeously liveried men—by demigods whose faces were flushed from wine.

Smyley did not look for any trace of the conscience that many presume to be inherent in the human soul.

WITH a sharp command to his men Smyley had them shoulder their arms and march off to the longboat.

Smyley left Jemmy there, among his own people, at the edge of the forest on Navarin Island.

But when Smyley and his men came to the longboat, they found Okokko and his family excitedly beseeching the guards.

Okokko identified himself to Smyley in English, and Smyley was made to understand that this young Indian and his family, now naked and indistinguishable from the other Yahgans, were one of the three Indian families who had been on Keppel Island.

Okokko conveyed to Smyley—with almost wild desperation, by gestures and in broken English—that they wanted to return to Keppel, that he was afraid to remain among his own people, that he and his wife and child would be killed.

So Smyley took Okokko and his family with them in the longboat and they returned to the *Nancy*.

Smyley called to the *Allen Gardiner* to raise sail. And soon both ships were on their way home.

When they reached the Falklands, Smyley sent the *Allen Gardiner* into Stanley harbor while he in the *Nancy,* with Okokko and his family aboard, went on to Keppel Island.

In defiance of Governor Moore's prohibition against further importation of Fuegian Indians, Smyley delivered Okokko and his wife and child to Despard on Keppel, and Despard without hesitation took them in. Then the *Nancy* returned to Stanley, where Smyley maintained his home.

No fine was ever imposed on Smyley or Despard, nor were they reprimanded. (Actually there was no legal basis for a fine or reprimand. Under the Alien Ordinance a fine of 20 pounds was to be paid by anyone who imported Indians and *left them without means of subsistence.*) Despard immediately merged Okokko and his family into the missionary establishment, where the Indians were housed and fed and where they worked and resumed their training and their religious education. So Smyley and Despard, as suited both of them, while disregarding the Governor's proclamation, did not break the letter of the law.

Okokko and his family remained among the missionaries. They were the first Fuegian Indians to stick, as if they were pollen on the Antarctic wind, pollen that until now had been lost on the water; these were the first Indians to stick to the civilized routine of work and worship.

Part Four

THE TRUE ENDING—
AND THE ENDING OF
TWO OF THE MEN

ENGLAND DISTRACTED

W HEN Governor Moore's report of the massacre (his initial report) reached the Colonial Office in London—it was received on May 8, 1860—a notice digesting the news was posted for the public and the press.

But popular attention in England at this time was focused elsewhere, and only a few short articles appeared in the newspapers. Some of these articles postponed discussion by stating that a fuller report based on thorough investigation was to follow. In a few articles it was incorrectly implied that a trial, rather than an inquiry, had been conducted.

The editors of the newspapers were unable to find a handle for this story; they seemed unsure of reader reaction; and the editors themselves were diverted.

A missionary party had been lost, true. But this sort of thing was happening from time to time all over the world where missionaries were making inroads into uncivilized regions. And Governor Moore's comments neutralized whatever indignation might have been aroused against the natives by criticizing the missionaries.

That these Fuegian Indians, or some of them, were to a degree Christianized gave the story some piquancy. But if much were made of this point, the effect the missionaries were having on the savages would be denigrated—and all the missionary societies and their supporters would be offended.

Jemmy, of course, had once been widely written up in the English press and in the newspapers on the Continent as well. But that was twenty-five to thirty years ago. And Jemmy in this report from the Falkland Islands was not clearly portrayed: He was not positively identified as the instigator of the massacre, nor as the leader of the looters. In the report it was stated that the only survivor from the *Allen Gardiner*, the cook Coles, had never seen Jemmy either in the melee around the mission house where the murders were committed or on the ship during the looting. So Coles' testimony—as it appeared to the legalistic newspaper readers of England where the national pride reposed in the thousand-year-long development of English justice—seemed like the most far-fetched kind of hearsay: Coles hadn't even heard the story he recounted of Jemmy's involvement; he had acquired his belief from Indians who knew only a few words of English and who acted out for him the supposed sequence of events.

And Jemmy hadn't been convicted. The report did not say what had happened to Jemmy; it did not say that he had been taken back to his island home and had been left there by Captain Smyley.

Lacking a catchy lead, and without much interest in such material at this time, the editors downplayed the story. In 1831 when Jemmy with York and Fuegia had been presented to the King and Queen, that had been news. In 1834 when Jemmy, though starving in the Fuegian islands where he had been left by FitzRoy and Darwin, had declined FitzRoy's invitation to return to England, that had been a story to wring all English hearts. Besides, that news had become known only when the *Beagle* returned to England after her round-the-world, five-year voyage, and everyone was interested then in FitzRoy's mapmaking, in Darwin's research, in the full story of the wonderful adventure. The poignant incidental item about Jemmy was a part of that whole outburst of publicity.

In 1852 when the death of Gardiner and his party by starvation had been reported, there were thunderbolts to be hurled at those who were to blame. The English as the leaders of the Industrial Revolution expected efficiency from themselves, and a tragedy of inefficiency had taken place.

But in 1860 the newspapermen of England were not inclined to devote much space to this story of a massacre in Tierra del Fuego. A few tears were to be shed for the slain missionaries, but similar stories were coming in from Africa, from the East.

FITZROY AND DARWIN

Whatever England in 1860, what was almost literally making those isles from which the waves were ruled rock like ships in a storm at sea, was the battle royal following the publication of Darwin's *Origin of Species*.

FitzRoy fit himself into this battle.

Since his recall from New Zealand and the death of his wife, FitzRoy had been working to rebuild his life and his career. He married again, taking for his second wife the daughter of a cousin within his own family circle (so FitzRoy and Darwin both married cousins and had with them remarkably companionable marriages that allowed these men of scientific bent to concentrate intensely on their work). With his second wife FitzRoy had three more children, daughters.

A new career opportunity for him arose in 1853. An international conference was held in Brussels on the problems of navigation at sea; the focus of the conference was on the uncertainty of the weather. The initiative for the conference had come from the director of the U.S. Hydrographic Office, Lieutenant Matthew Maury, to whom Captain Smyley and many other Yankee sea-captains around the world reported. For years Maury had been distributing logbooks and using the information the captains returned to him to compile statistics on the winds and currents.

This kind of work was of great interest to England, since England had the world's largest navy and merchant marine, and in the aftermath of the conference the British government actually allocated some money to the Board of Trade for the setting up of a small office to pursue the study of weather as it affected navigation.

The Board of Trade asked the Royal Society to recommend someone to head the new office, and the Royal Society, into which FitzRoy had recently been admitted, recommended FitzRoy. (It's likely that Darwin, after arranging for FitzRoy's admission to the Royal Society, was also influential in nominating him for the new post.) In due course FitzRoy was named Meteorological Statist, which in the terminology of the times meant statistician.

DURING these years of their middle age, prior to the publication of *The Origin of Species*, FitzRoy and Darwin corresponded and met occasionally and FitzRoy would visit Darwin at Down House.

As friends since their youth, they were oversensitive and vulnerable to each other to a degree that would not apply to more recently made acquaintances and friendships. FitzRoy and Darwin knew each other so well that each of them could see histories of motivations in their most casual remarks and implications which may not have been consciously intended.

They were still to each other the shining young men they had been when they had gone round the world together in search of Truth. Then they had not been the authoritative figures they were expected now to be, but green and pliable aspirants. Even FitzRoy, though at twenty-six he had been encased in his role as responsible sea-captain and had been born to his sense of entitlement as an aristocrat, had been uncertain, and he had shared with Darwin his doubts and fears. And Darwin, at twenty-two without a vocation, not even sure that he was rich, had had in his mind his semi-commitment to be a clergyman. These were the selves that FitzRoy and Darwin saw in each other, the young selves that had sat over the cabin table and over the oars in a dinghy for endless hours of intimate discussion. It is often unpleasant to be known in such depth.

Darwin for relaxation during his middle years used to like to have novels read to him in the afternoon (he ceased to have patience for them as he grew older and his grand ideas took over all of his mind). When FitzRoy tossed off the comment that the works of Jane Austen were "on everyone's table" (by which he meant on the tables of everyone in the Londonderry circle) Darwin was offended. FitzRoy instinctively had taken advantage of his knowledge that Darwin favored stories more than did he, the practical man of the sea—with a further little hint that Darwin's fondness for Jane Austen was really plebeian because all of FitzRoy's kin took her for granted.

FitzRoy, on the other hand, had to envy the respect Darwin was accorded by so many leaders of the scientific community. FitzRoy may even have been hurt by Darwin's kindness in sponsoring him for membership in the Royal Society; FitzRoy's proud nature could not easily accept that it was Darwin's prerogative to help him, when, according to FitzRoy's lights, it should have been his prerogative to help his younger and less wellborn cabinmate.

Rivalry between those who have been close friends from youth is nearly inescapable. And FitzRoy had to envy the way Darwin was able to arrange his life so that he could devote himself with a clear mind to his experiments and his thinking. FitzRoy may also have envied Darwin's ability to concentrate. Once, at a flower show, Darwin became so absorbed in a yellow flower that he was transfixed for about ten minutes staring at the flower, trying to fathom the function of its parts (which caused a workman to comment that the poor fellow would be better off if he had a job). FitzRoy, too, was obsessional by nature, but he could not afford and may not have been capable of this degree of absorption. The details of living forever nagged at him.

Of course FitzRoy envied Darwin's wealth and the way Darwin used it. At Down House—with its horde of servants, its stables and private park amid the lovely fields of Kent—FitzRoy had thrust before him the fact of England's changing nature: that factory profits now exceeded the land rents and honoraria of the aristocracy.

On intimate matters the old friends conjoined without reservation. When FitzRoy's daughter died at the age of sixteen or seventeen (his oldest child by his first wife), Darwin with touching sincerity commiserated with him, mourning the loss of such a beautiful young girl. Darwin likewise had lost a child past infancy, and they were both men who adored children.

When Darwin was piqued by FitzRoy, Darwin made no retort. His contentment was like a mattress that softened the blow.

But FitzRoy had no such mattress. When he was piqued by Darwin—by the slightest implication from Darwin that the academic community was superior in intellect or by Darwin's not caring about the cost of some item that would have been of importance to FitzRoy—FitzRoy snapped back. And his touchiness was irksome to Darwin.

Sometimes they clashed over politics, even though they both had a distaste for political argument. It was FitzRoy's firm conviction, not without support, that the Whigs had frequently sandbagged him (the Darwins and all the Wedgwoods were Whigs). When the Ministry had changed from Tory to Whig, the second voyage of the *Beagle* had been canceled. (To these friends from youth, old resentments remained forever fresh.) FitzRoy had often smelt Whig while his troubles in New Zealand were mounting. Worst of all, there seemed to be a preponderance of Whigs in the scientific circle surrounding Darwin, and it was this circle that threatened the sanctity of orthodox belief.

So FitzRoy and Darwin had to avoid broad areas of discussion because such discussion led to sharp disagreement.

FitzRoy was plagued by money troubles, just as persistently as Darwin was bothered by his fever. And it was incompatible with FitzRoy's aristocratic posture to have to worry about money.

FitzRoy never doubted that he was entitled to be in charge. He never questioned his own propriety when he gave orders. He felt instinctively that it was his obligation to be firm in whatever he did—because what he did was right and good, for England and for humanity.

Yet he couldn't quite get by with this aristocratic stance. It was a stance that worked for most of his relatives. They had succeeded and were succeeding to positions of ever-greater power, to knighthoods, to lordships, while he was still untitled.

When FitzRoy, affecting noble disdain, opted for what he considered necessary and worthwhile regardless of cost—as when he had hired auxiliary vessels while he was in command of the *Beagle* or when in New Zealand he had paid official expenses without waiting for authorization—he had suffered heavy financial losses that his bankers pointed out to him were serious, losses that limited the scope of his living and imposed burdens on those he loved.

Darwin knew of FitzRoy's straitened circumstances and sympathized with him. Darwin knew FitzRoy had many times paid out of his own pocket when the government (Whig or Tory) should have paid. And Darwin treasured his old friend because he knew, perhaps better than anyone, that, when FitzRoy had laid out those sums, he had done so for universal betterment. It stung FitzRoy to have to realize that in any sense he was a subject for Darwin's sympathy.

What may perhaps be said most fundamentally about this relationship of Darwin and FitzRoy—this deep-founded friendship and rivalry—is this: that each of them to the other stood for a diametrically opposed viewpoint and, since they were both men of powerful intellect and great capacity, the coincidence of their association served in each of their lives as a vital stimulus.

To Darwin, all through his life, there was FitzRoy, the once-adulated friend from his youth, standing for a kind of fixed mentality. This was the mentality that obstructed the advances of scientific skepticism to which Darwin was devoted. And that FitzRoy was associated with this mentality inspired Darwin.

To FitzRoy, all through his life, there was Darwin, whom he had once patronized and protected, whom he had tried to lead onto the path he thought was right, with whom in their youth he had been frank and open, there was Darwin trying to undermine the society FitzRoy felt it his duty to protect at the cost of anything—his fortune, his life.

For each of them, always there was the other—as a worthy antagonist, as a beloved friend. They personified for each other the conflicting poles of thought of their times. That for each of them there was always such a friend with whom to contest may account in part for their prodigious efforts.

As Meteorological Statist, FitzRoy immediately took an approach far in advance of Maury's. Maury was intent upon accumulating statistics on the winds and currents so that, on the basis of these statistics, probabilities could be established as a guide for navigation. Maury's system undeniably produced valuable results: Acting upon a suggestion from Smyley, Maury altered the route from the ports of New England to Rio, and as a result the sailing time was shortened by several weeks.

But FitzRoy, instead of relying on the experience of the past, focused upon weather forecasting. It was FitzRoy, in fact, who gave that word—*forecasting*—its currency.

FitzRoy passionately believed that lives of sailors and ships' passengers all over the world could be saved if only sea-captains could be forewarned of bad weather. Ever since his youth, FitzRoy had had faith in the barometer. When he had been captain of the *Beagle,* he had closely watched the barometer in his cabin and, forewarned, had been able to have his ship ready, with sails trimmed and headed into the wind, when the storm would hit.

Once, when FitzRoy had been in command of the *Beagle* for only a few days, he had not taken instant action in response to the falling barometer and, in the ensuing storm, he had lost two men. FitzRoy never forgot this lesson (or forgave himself for his own negligence).

On another occasion, on the trip homeward bound from New

Zealand, FitzRoy had pointed out to the captain of the ship that the barometer was falling. The captain had observed the fine weather and done nothing. So FitzRoy without the captain's permission had induced a few crewmen to trim the sails, drop another anchor, tighten the cables—and the ship with a full load of passengers (including FitzRoy's family) had been ready for the sudden squall.

The limitation in connection with barometer readings had always been that a significant reading was available only at the port where the barometer was located or on the ship that was carrying the barometer. But now the telegraph was coming into use all over the world—and significant barometer readings could be sent ahead, from port to port, and the path of a storm could be foretold and charted.

FitzRoy, like Darwin, had a tremendous capacity for work. When dedicated to a worthy project, FitzRoy became single-minded: His intensity would dominate him. And he became obsessed with weather forecasting.

FitzRoy was especially concerned for the welfare of English fishermen, the men who went out in small boats and who were often lost in the frequent storms around the British Isles. For them he had small, durable, inexpensive barometers manufactured, called FitzRoy barometers, and he issued a manual that in simple terms provided instructions on their use.

He set up a network of twenty-four stations (eighteen in the British Isles, six along the coast of Europe) from which barometer readings and weather reports were telegraphed to him in London.

Before long, the sedate *Times* for the first time in its history was printing a "weather forecast." At ports in England and on the coast of Europe, signals warning of storms were run up in accord with FitzRoy's predictions.

FitzRoy designed new forms for ship's logs, placing greater emphasis on barometric readings. Since FitzRoy's logs were different from those distributed by Maury, the Board of Trade, which was responsible for the Meteorological Statist, asked the

Royal Society for its opinion on the proper form to be used. The Royal Society in turn had its appropriate committee study the matter, and the judgment of the committee, on which Darwin sat, was crystal clear: Let FitzRoy make the decision.

CROSSCURRENTS

O F COURSE, weather forecasting then, as now, was a chancy game. And FitzRoy's predictions were sometimes wrong.

Both encouragements and discouragements came his way. He was promoted to rear admiral. But the Board of Trade wanted to know why he was not concentrating on the compilation of statistics; that's what he was hired to do, what a statistician was expected to do; that's what the renowned Maury was doing, compiling impressive masses of statistics. (Maury in the United States had a staff of twenty; FitzRoy had a staff of three.)

But FitzRoy, instead of compiling the record of the weather of the past, was intent upon solving the mystery of the weather that was coming. His standard predictions were for the next two days, and he would not be diverted—because he knew that if a sea-captain could be warned of an approaching storm, if a captain could have even an hour or two of advance notice, lives would be saved.

Once, Queen Victoria paid FitzRoy the compliment of sending her footman to the Admiral's house in London to inquire if the weather would be suitable for her to make the crossing to the Continent.

Yet FitzRoy was passed over for promotion to head the Maritime Department of the Board of Trade, which would have included the meteorological office. Instead, Sulivan, FitzRoy's old lieutenant from the *Beagle*, was named to the higher post (though the meteorological office was exempted) and Sulivan, who was an agreeable man, was knighted.

FitzRoy had old enemies who never ceased to deprecate him with members of Parliament. The Wakefield family was very active politically, and they were the organizers of the New Zealand land development company whose plans FitzRoy had impeded when he was governor.

From many people in various places FitzRoy received letters of thanks for his accurate weather predictions—a letter from a harbor master who on receipt of FitzRoy's report had run up a storm-warning just in time; a letter from a couple who had to cross the Irish Sea and who on FitzRoy's advice had waited, even though the weather was fine, until a predicted storm had come and gone.

On the Continent FitzRoy's methods were being emulated. Actually the system FitzRoy created for weather forecasting was in embryonic form the same system that is employed today. In his headquarters in London he collated all the information telegraphed to him and drew lines (isobars) where the same barometric reading prevailed and other lines (isotherms) where the temperature was the same. Then he prepared charts (he coined the expression *synoptic charts*) that clearly showed the weather fronts, with the wind speeds and an estimate of the time when the weather-change and disturbance along a front would arrive. But FitzRoy was unable to measure the high-altitude air currents and he was totally unaware of jet streams.

When the owner of a fishing boat, ignoring FitzRoy's prediction of a storm, sent out his boat because the herring were running and the owner didn't want to miss a catch and the boat was then lost in the storm, FitzRoy publicly damned all those whose economic interests overcame concern for the lives of the seamen who worked for them. In response, the shipowning families complained about the occasional inaccuracy of FitzRoy's predictions.

In public recognition of the fact that weather forecasting was not a perfect science, FitzRoy was gently lampooned in *The Times*.

But FitzRoy never claimed he would always be accurate. His advice, he maintained, was cautionary. He knew he was working with a science that would be advanced and refined in future years. But he never budged from his position that by foretelling the weather the lives of people at sea could be saved—and this meant to him that meteorology was worthy of continuing investment and effort.

FitzRoy wrote a book called the *Weather Book* which was an explanation of meteorology. It filled an important need, and repeated printings sold out. Unlike Darwin, however, who without need for ready cash was able to make favorable arrangements for the publication of his books so that most of the money from eventual sales came to him, FitzRoy, ever in need of ready cash, sold the copyright to his publisher for the lump sum of two hundred pounds.

FitzRoy was promoted to vice admiral. As always, though, he assumed the favorable tidings—while criticism dismayed him.

THE GREAT HULLABALLOO

M OST VEXING of all to FitzRoy was the hullaballoo when Darwin's *Origin of Species* appeared.

Having long ago chosen his position in this fundamental contention, FitzRoy was nevertheless taken by surprise as if caught out at sea in a storm that hadn't been predicted.

Oddly there had been little reaction in scientific circles when Wallace's and Darwin's papers had been presented at the Linnaean Society and there had been practically no popular reaction (which had suited the advocates of orthodoxy, who were eager to dismiss all radical notions). The original papers were viewed as unsupported theories of evolution like others that had been circulated before; they were regarded as mere speculation and did not demand serious attention. Darwin had not kept secret from his friends his basic position; others had read his various digests, as they had read Lamarck and others.

Yet the publication of Darwin's *Origin of Species* in 1859 had the effect of a bombshell. This marked the first time when a theory of evolution was supported by detailed evidence, by example after example, and when there was a unifying principle: the principle of natural selection.

By natural selection Darwin explained that he meant evolution which was clearly *reasonable,* which was necessitated by nature, evolution that obviously made sense. When the environment changed (usually as a result of a change in rainfall) or when animals wandered into a new environment, and the changed or new environment made advantageous the possession of a particular characteristic which previously had been of no importance, those members of the species that happened to possess the now-advantageous characteristic would endure and propagate and would soon make general the possession of the advantageous characteristic, while the members of the species lacking that characteristic would die out.

If, for example, there were some animals with necks of varying lengths and these animals that had been feeding on low shrubs were to wander into an area where the foliage was on high trees, then the members of the species that had long necks would be able to reach the foliage on the high trees and would endure, while the short-necked members would die out, until eventually the entire species that remained would have long necks.

Or, if the climate turned cold, the animals with heavier pelts would endure and propagate until heavy pelts became characteristic of the species.

Or, if a species that had lived on land was forced by predators to live in the water, those members of the species that happened to have very large lungs and a thick layer of fat would survive — and by propagation their characteristics would become the characteristics of the species.

Within each species there was great variability that could produce many slight but important variations. In addition, occasionally there were mutations (drastic variations, chance births) which, if better suited to the environment, could produce rapid change.

Given time enough, Darwin argued, given millions of generations with the natural environment forever changing as geology showed the environment had been changing, and given that new adaptations would prove successful in response to new conditions, then the evolution of all living forms could be reasonably explained.

In *The Origin of Species,* in densely reasoned form, was the outpouring of all Darwin's thought, study and research over the preceding twenty-odd years. Here was a book that could not be dismissed as speculation. Here was a cogent argument based upon elaborated evidence that, unless refuted, would require a fundamental change in scientific thinking and a severe reconsideration of religious dogma.

Darwin himself, though personally disinclined toward controversy, did everything he could to see to it that his theory was vigorously advanced. He had complimentary copies of the book sent to almost everyone who might be regarded as an authority, and he wrote extensively to these scientists begging them to try to see, even a little, his point of view. Diplomatically Darwin did not solicit agreement, only the slightest kind of nod.

And, like wildfire, the news of his book spread all about. The copies offered for sale were bought up in a day, and the initial publication was followed by reprint after reprint.

This nettled FitzRoy. So much of Darwin's argument was based on evidence Darwin had accumulated while on the voyage of the *Beagle.* FitzRoy did not have to remind people that he, too, had been on that voyage. He had seen what Darwin had seen. And it was on that voyage that FitzRoy had become a devout believer.

FitzRoy was not the product of a pious upbringing. On the

contrary, the aristocrats from whom he was descended were a flamboyant, freely sinning lot disdainful of restraint.

It was while FitzRoy as a young man had read his Bible over and over when he was at sea that he had come to his belief. (While on the *Beagle*, he had attributed his occasional doubts and lapses to the followers of Voltaire, but now he blamed them on Darwin.) It was while he was on that five-year voyage that he had come to the firmness of his faith, which he in turn recommended to all young sailors as a course of comfort they should follow.

FitzRoy was an outstanding example of the degree to which the ubiquitous middle-class religiosity of these times altered the conduct of aristocrats. The religious upsurgence of the nineteenth century in England had its roots in the Puritan movements. Professions of piety came easily and often from the bustling businessmen who were in the vanguard of England's rapidly expanding commercial empire. Religionists like George Despard were the leaders, and their cause was emphatically approved by the long-reigning Queen. It was a riptide of middle-class fundamentalist religion that in nineteenth-century England was overwhelming the rationalist tide of the eighteenth century. And in the pell-mell mixture of adherents were not only the middle-class clergymen but aristocrats and many scientists.

To himself FitzRoy was, first and foremost, a scientist—and a scientist dedicated to practical applications that would save lives, not a speculative theorist like Darwin whose ideas wouldn't save anybody and wouldn't have any practical effect in the world. As a scientist, FitzRoy had concluded that the Bible was the Word of God—and it was damnable blasphemy for anyone to doubt it.

Furthermore, FitzRoy recommended his belief to young sailors because FitzRoy knew the need for the comfort of belief when you began your service at sea at the age of fourteen. Could Darwin know of such need? Darwin had never been away from home except to go to school until he had come to the *Beagle* where he had been under FitzRoy's wing.

In exasperation FitzRoy wrote letters to the newspapers expounding his anti-evolutionary views and signed them "Senex." Darwin recognized FitzRoy's style and his sentiments, yet with his customary benevolence he seemed to be amused. Actually FitzRoy when he wrote as "Senex" served Darwin's purpose because Darwin wanted to maximize the public controversy over evolution. Controversy in itself attracted attention to Darwin's theory.

IN JUNE 1860 at Oxford there was a meeting of the British Association for the Advancement of Science. FitzRoy, as Meteorological Statist, was there to read a paper on British storms. The storms his paper referred to were the famous storms described in British history, with an attempt to explain how these storms might have been predicted.

On the day following the delivery of FitzRoy's paper on storms the broadly ballyhooed and long-awaited debate was scheduled to take place between the zoologist Thomas Huxley, speaking for Darwin, and Bishop Wilberforce, speaking for God. FitzRoy stayed over for it.

In *The Origin of Species* Darwin, in fact, did not argue against a divine First Cause of life (to himself, in that sense, Darwin was a self-proclaimed theist). When people of a religious bent read his book, however, and when they comprehended Darwin's argument that evolution by natural selection was more *reasonable* than any other explanation regarding the development of living forms, they took this as an assault upon the Biblical explanation that the whole universe and all species in their present forms (including mankind, starting from Adam and Eve) were created by God in six days (and the English clerics had already demolished the verbal dodge that six days may have meant six epochs; to the clerics, each word of the Bible had to be taken literally, and six days meant six *days*).

By the time of the scheduled debate, seven months after the first appearance of *The Origin of Species*, simplifications and

Darwin as an orangutan, as portrayed in the March 22, 1871, issue of Hornet, *a British publication.*

distortions of Darwin's theory predominated. Caricatures and cartoons were used in place of complicated, sophisticated ideas. And reasoned discussion, with the terms carefully couched, was impossible to achieve.

(I wonder if this doesn't reveal an inadequacy perhaps in our own language, in modern honed English, or else in our ability to think, to reason, to apply logic with precision. Certainly there existed in 1860—and there exists ineradicably today—a gap, a chasm that separates those for whom Darwinian theory leaves an unbearable void, an unfulfilled need, and those who espouse Darwinism but refuse to address, as Darwin refused to address, the need for more than a biological explanation. This gap ought to be bridgeable by perfected definitions, by limits placed on over-assertions; maybe fresh concepts are needed. But no rope of words or chain of thought has ever been able to link the two sides of this chasm. Perhaps a link might have been made if the religious focus of the anti-Darwinians had been upon some amorphous, interpretable philosophy, like Virgil's notion of the *anima mundi*. It was Virgil's suggestion that, apart from the material reality of the world, there was a great living force—a soul of the universe, the *anima mundi*—and each living thing bore some of that soul which upon death returned to the whole. To such a philosophy a bridge might have been established by scientists willing to grant a limitation to Darwinian theory. But the requirement in 1860 was that the specific creation myth of Judeo-Christianity must be accommodated: that God created the world, that God created Adam and Eve, that all existence is the result of a single slashing stroke of divine creation. It was this myth, as set forth in precise detail by the priests and preachers of England, that Darwin and his followers could not accommodate.)

Well in advance of the anticipated debate it was known that Bishop Wilberforce would make elaborate fun of monkey-ancestry, to which Darwin's theory had been reduced. Huxley had tried to avoid the confrontation, knowing it would be a circus. Darwin, of course, was not even present in Oxford. Other scientists inclined toward Darwin preferred not to attend the debate. But the Bishop, who would have made a great television evangelist, forced the meeting at which he and Huxley had it out.

Most of the scientists who were present (no verbatim records were made) acclaimed Huxley the victor because the Bishop's heavy-handed thrusts seemed to them to have been wittily par-ried by Huxley's effective pedantic counterthrusts. Yet the fact is that Bishop Wilberforce, who had more popular support at the meeting, kept his support and the confrontation really amounted to very little.

In the discussion period after the debate FitzRoy, terribly disturbed, loudly maintained that he had tried to dissuade his former shipmate from the drift of his ideas, knowing that this drift was bound to take him away from the comfort of belief.

Even as FitzRoy was talking amid the hubbub, he was outraged to find himself aligned with the clergymen. These religionists were not the company of his choice. FitzRoy counted himself among the scientists, and he wanted to win over the scientists to his point of view. But he couldn't make himself heard.

THE VARYING VIEWPOINTS

I T I S significant that Darwin's theory was rejected, or rejected at least in part, by many of the leading scientists of the time, even by those whom we now presume to have been Darwin's adherents. Huxley himself had his reservations. And Sir Charles Lyell was never completely won over.

Lyell, a Scot, was the greatest geologist of the nineteenth century. The first volume of his book, *The Principles of Geology,* had come out shortly before the *Beagle* sailed and was given to Darwin by one of Darwin's mentors with the warning that it was interesting but radical. Lyell's book, which Darwin read and re-read on the voyage while FitzRoy was reading his Bible, had begun to open Darwin's mind, because in his book Lyell argued for a long, long development of the earth—far longer than the 6,000 years the religionists declared to be the truth—and Lyell had in part dated his geological strata by the kinds of fossils that appeared in the rock. Thus Lyell, from a geological standpoint, had intimated the biological evolution that became Darwin's view.

Darwin deeply respected Lyell and hoped that Lyell would include himself in Darwin's camp. But Lyell held himself apart because there was a certain aspect of Darwinism that Lyell found repugnant—not illogical but distasteful and emotionally or spiritually unacceptable. Lyell granted the fossil evidence that clearly showed the development of living forms; he accepted as obvious the increasing complexity of these forms, progressing from simple forms up through animals, perhaps specifically through various kinds of monkeylike animals to human beings. What Lyell objected to and found repugnant was that no line was drawn in Darwin's theory to distinguish between animals for whom instinct was the dominant motivator and human beings who uniquely were self-conscious, capable of reflection and self-examination, and whose self-consciousness was the basis of man's moral nature which might be called the human soul.

Darwin argued—he argued directly with Lyell, and Darwin's firmer adherents also argued with Lyell and declared publicly and to one another—that the theory of evolution according to the principle of natural selection had nothing to do with man's spiritual nature. Darwin's theory was simply a biological reading of the development of all living forms and proposed no explanation or analysis of man's unique abilities and propensities—to believe in God, to accept moral discipline, to be aware of one's moral nature.

But Lyell felt that—granting this limitation on the scope of Darwin's assertion (and indisputably there was nothing in *The Origin of Species* to the contrary)—then still there was a missing factor, something unsupplied by a theory which promised to be all-encompassing.

But the theory of evolution, Darwin and his adherents argued, was not intended to be all-encompassing. The theory had nothing to do with man's self-consciousness or with his moral nature or with a First Cause.

Then, Lyell reiterated, there was something missing.

Within the past century there have been a number of serious, unflamboyant thinkers who have tried in various ways to draw a kind of line between animals driven by instinct and self-conscious man who creates a pressure upon himself to behave morally. A line of this sort cannot be drawn biologically; there are no biological facts to point to. Yet such a line seemed to Lyell to be needed. Or perhaps it is fairer to say that Lyell for himself, for his own inner comfort, needed such a line.

D A R W I N has been overdrawn to accord with his caricature in *Vanity Fair* as a bemused silent figure (like a Cheshire cat) aloof from the turbulent discussion. Actually he was a vigorous, articulate participant in the scientific societies, a prolific correspondent with fellow-scientists, and, whenever his friends would visit him at Down House, a voluble host. He and Lyell must often have talked over and tried to resolve Lyell's objection.

As gentlemen of their time well acquainted with the domestication of animals, Darwin and Lyell must have analyzed the effects of animal-training, the way house dogs slink away after tearing apart a slipper or a sofa pillow, the way bears are trained to dance; even seals and dolphins can be trained. Of course the restraints upon animals are simple, and the rewards and punishments for the animals are immediate. Whereas our expectation from ourselves is that there is inherent in mankind a comprehensive conscience which exerts a steady pressure that affects and hopefully dominates our animalistic impulses.

Certainly Darwin, in responding to Lyell, must have thought of the savage men he had seen on the voyage of the *Beagle*. He knew that mankind in the form of these savages endured at a level almost indistinguishable from that of animals.

If it occurred to Darwin and Lyell, Jemmy would have been a very interesting specimen for them to ponder. In Jemmy, under the powerful microscope of their minds, they would see a human being in simple form, a basic organism like a single-celled paramecium. But then Jemmy, as a result of his manifold experiences

Darwin, caricatured with the smile of a Cheshire cat, in
Vanity Fair, *September 30, 1871.*

with civilized people of advanced culture, had been given a drop of stain so that the parts of his human nature stood out, as would the parts of a paramecium. In Jemmy they would be able to see not only the impulsiveness that Jemmy and his people had in common with the animals but also whatever potential there may be for sensibility, reason and conscience to distinguish Jemmy both from the animals and from his own savage kind.

This is what Jemmy would have meant to Darwin, who was personally inclined to be kindly but whose intellect propelled him continuously toward reasoned conclusions unaffected by sentiment. Viewing Jemmy, he would not have been hopeful. He would have been skeptical about Jemmy's moral nature.

Lyell might have been hopeful. In spite of everything he knew, in spite of the truth he had found in the rocks, he wanted to see in every human being a kind of nature that made mankind different from the animals.

FitzRoy, on the other hand, though he never to our knowledge sat in with Darwin and Lyell, would have been sure—and his response would have been resounding. FitzRoy had seen as many and more aborigines than had Darwin. And he liked them all—the more primitive and less corrupted, the better. Without doubt or hesitation he granted the goodness in primitive men and their capacity for conscience.

From the viewpoints of these three scientists—Darwin, Lyell, FitzRoy—would have come three different interpretations of Jemmy, as well as three differing views of life.

Darwin's view of life was that it was evolving reasonably, mechanistically, without divine guidance or intervention. He hoped that in this continuing process of evolution mankind might further improve and that eventually a better human state might be achieved. Yet, as he aged, his hope diminished for a plan in which human improvement could be considered an aim. In spite of the warmth of his family environment and his personal contentment and comfort, he became more and more gloomy. In his old age he was far less hesitant to reveal the atheistic inclination to which his intellect propelled him—that there was no plan or moral principle in the morass of living.

Lyell, while agreeing with much of Darwin's argument, objected to the diminution of mankind that Darwin's theory proposed. Lyell would not agree, could not agree that mankind had no moral direction. As a scientist, he believed that in the evolution toward increasingly complex forms of life there was evidence of betterment or, at least, of the potential for betterment.

FitzRoy, for his part, had an emotional response that overwhelmed and denied the logic of Darwin's theory: FitzRoy simply could not bear to look at a world not organized around his fixed beliefs—in the Royal Navy, in England, in God. For him Darwin's view was a vision of utter desolation.

THE STRESS, THE STRAIN

FITZROY WAS picked at from all quarters. An economy-minded Member of Parliament named Augustus Smith repeatedly attacked the appropriations for FitzRoy's office and played to the crowd by pointing out all of FitzRoy's mistaken weather forecasts. Smith found such carping to be politically rewarding, so he never relented.

THOUGHTS came to FitzRoy that were self-defensive but useless to him. For example, when he was resentful of what he considered unfair criticism of his weather forecasting, he would recall that for the second voyage of the *Beagle* he had installed Franklin's lightning rods on the masts and cabled them to ground in the sea. At that time he had been severely criticized; his expenditure for the rods had been questioned. But FitzRoy, ever protective of the lives of his men, had persevered. Now lightning rods were routinely installed on all the ships in the Royal Navy.

But had there ever been a word of apology offered to FitzRoy for those attacks upon him in the distant past?

DARWIN and Jemmy were the two men who in an intimate, personal sense meant most to FitzRoy in the course of his life. And it is from the deep wells of such relationships that the emotions which mold us come.

FitzRoy had always felt a fondness for Indians. After his encounter with the Patagonian Indians, he had recorded in his diary that, disagreeable though it was even to look at these savages and to realize that we ourselves descend from human beings in such a state, still we must remember that to Caesar the Britons who painted themselves blue and wore only the hides of animals were similarly disagreeable. FitzRoy, speaking for himself, was pleased and excited to observe these men at the dawn of their development in "their healthy, independent state of existence."

This was what FitzRoy admired: that, naked and with only the crudest weapons and tools, these primitive men were able to endure and to keep themselves strong and free. FitzRoy never turned from them in disgust, as did Darwin and so many others. FitzRoy always saw the health and the strength in primitive men and he respected their ability to cope with their environment by using their hands and their heads when they had very little else to help them. It was FitzRoy's sympathy for primitive men that had brought upon him the enmity of modern exploiters.

When FitzRoy had first fished from the sea the naked Indian boy of fourteen, this was how Jemmy had seemed to him— healthy, strong, independent, and admirable for being able to endure amid these cracked, storm-wracked islands at the bottom of the world.

When FitzRoy would recall himself as a youth, he would remember himself as healthy, untroubled, strong and independent—eager and ready to fulfill his destiny.

WHILE the *Beagle* was in Chile and FitzRoy broke down, he expressed to Darwin his concern about the insanity in his family. (Darwin shared this concern because there was also insanity in Darwin's family.) FitzRoy was worried that he might have inherited a tendency toward suicide from his uncle, Lord Castlereagh. It is not unreasonable to presume that FitzRoy must also have worried about the possible inheritance of a homosexual inclination.

FitzRoy had such a tightly constricted life—a life so rigidly bound by rules, when as a boy he was sent to the Royal Naval College and then to sea, when in his youth as a midshipman he was placed in charge of grown men, when as a young captain he bore such a backbreaking load of responsibility, when so much was expected of him and he expected so much from himself. All this pressure was intensified by the rigidity of the Victorian era, by the imposition of the monarch's conventionality, by the dominant influence of the clergy. It was a cruel irony that FitzRoy, by choosing to subscribe to the popular religiosity, further increased the pressure upon himself.

Bound by that iron corset of rules and expectations, FitzRoy inevitably must have looked with some longing at the freedom of the Indians—with the air flowing round their bodies, with no afterthought for their actions, with no code of sexual conduct.

When the Yahgan boy he had befriended and carried to England and back as his ward came again on board the *Beagle* as a starveling, FitzRoy may have wanted to comfort those bones of the boy he had abandoned. All sailors fear shipwreck and being abandoned on a desolate shore, and here was Jemmy whom he had willfully abandoned. The depth of FitzRoy's regret was infinite and lasting.

YEAR after year more scientists were coming to agree with Darwin—not in total agreement usually, but in basic agreement. The scientific community throughout England and throughout the world was clearly and steadily drifting toward Darwin's point of view, disregarding Darwin's inaccuracies (while so few would disregard FitzRoy's mistakes in forecasting the weather).

FitzRoy could not deny that Darwin's theory was catching on. And honors were being awarded to Darwin. It was not FitzRoy's envy of Darwin that determined his feeling, even though Darwin who needed so little was receiving so much. FitzRoy's pride kept his envy in check. And always between Darwin and FitzRoy there was the bond of affection from their youth.

FitzRoy's reaction to Darwin's success was more profound than his personal feelings. The horror was that Darwin's vision was winning—Darwin's awful vision, devoid of righteousness, devoid of goodness, devoid of God. FitzRoy could not bear the triumph of that vision which in the core of his soul he felt was repulsive and hateful.

M A U R Y was in England—Matthew Maury, the American naval officer who was FitzRoy's forerunner in meteorology—and Maury's words were being used by FitzRoy's enemies to deprecate FitzRoy's procedure in the Meteorological Office.

Maury was a talkative, gregarious man with a strong and sensuous face. Having been raised, like FitzRoy, with the expectation of being in command at sea, he had been one of America's most promising naval officers until in his early thirties he was crippled in an accident when a coach in which he was riding overturned. The accident left him severely lamed, and the U.S. Navy, retiring him from sea duty, had created for him the job of hydrographer. So Maury and FitzRoy both were once-young naval officers for whom brilliant careers were foreseen and were now, as middle-aged men, in positions that many viewed as personal accommodations for them.

Maury was a Virginian and, like many American southerners, was a graceful man whom the English, especially those who imported American cotton, found charming.

Actually Maury and FitzRoy got along well; both were professional seamen trying, in the face of a lot of sneering comment on both sides of the Atlantic, by scientific means to make life at sea a little safer. But Maury was often erratic and intemperate and said things that caused trouble for FitzRoy (it served the purpose of FitzRoy's enemies to treat Maury with exaggerated respect).

FitzRoy particularly sympathized with Maury because, when civil war broke out in America, Maury sided with the South. Now, not only was Maury's side losing, but Maury financially was being ruined. So it was little wonder that Maury was intemperate.

FITZROY's own financial problems worsened—with all his children by two marriages, with his continued habit of paying for things he wanted to do in his office whenever appropriations were denied him.

It was partly financial consideration which caused FitzRoy to leave his house in London and move his family to the suburb of Upper Norwood.

As in Chile when he was young, FitzRoy had trouble sleeping. He would sleep in snatches that didn't refresh him. He became unable to do his work, to bear his work. He would take the ten o'clock train from Norwood to London, only to reach his office and find that he could not concentrate. It was the habit of a lifetime for him to work hard, and he had a tremendous capacity for work. But now his compulsion to work—his sense of obligation that he should work—drove him toward a breakdown.

FitzRoy was fifty-nine years old. The healthiness of his body was not reasserting itself. The outline of the taut aristocrat he had been in his youth was diffused in weariness and sagging flesh.

His wife worried about him and consulted doctors. Sometimes FitzRoy seemed unable to talk. It was his habit and his expectation of himself to wind up whatever he had to say so that his words—whether an order or the expression of an opinion or just a casual observation—would come out with firm meaning and justification. Now he would often begin to speak—and stop before he was intelligible. And begin again. And stop again.

The doctors prescribed rest. And he tried to rest. He tried not to go to his office. Then he felt he had to go to his office—but he couldn't bear to stay there.

Besides, what reason had he to rest? He wasn't wounded. He wasn't waiting for a physical hurt to heal. How could he justify his need to rest when his solicitous wife wanted him to play whist with her in the evenings? Was that man playing cards in need of rest?

Yet it was only when he was lying in bed that he felt that his whole world was not rocking.

O N Saturday, April 29, 1865, he had a bad day.

In the morning after breakfast he declared that he had to see Maury again. Maury was in London. Mrs. FitzRoy, in light of his firmness, readily agreed that he should go.

But he couldn't make it out of the house. In exhaustion, only a few hours after rising from his bed, he had to return to his bed. His wife consoled him.

He rose and dressed again for lunch. He did not eat much.

After lunch his wife was scheduled to go out in the carriage and asked him if he would come with her, but he said it would do him more good if he took a walk with two of his daughters. There was an effort by everyone in the family to allow for any kind of behavior from him, however inconsistent, and to maintain around him the normal functioning of the family in the hope that he would be drawn back into the family's routine.

When his wife returned in the late afternoon, she found he had not gone for a walk with the girls but had gone to London to see Maury.

He returned around eight in the evening, so upset that he was incoherent, and he was terribly tired. They all sat down, as usual, for dinner.

He said he had to see Maury again, even though he had just seen him. There was to be a soiree for Maury on Sunday and

FitzRoy thought he should go. At his instruction his wife had already written declining an invitation to the soiree. Hadn't he just seen Maury? He had, but . . .

After dinner, to relax him, Mrs. FitzRoy once again suggested whist. But he said no. He had had such exciting conversations with Maury and others in the afternoon that he couldn't apply himself to cards.

Usually he took a short nap after dinner. But that evening he couldn't lie still, he couldn't sit still on the couch. After his three daughters had gone up to bed, he again told his wife that he wanted to go to London to see Maury on Sunday. She asked him if he hadn't already said good-bye to Maury. He said that he had.

His wife went up to bed in the expectation that he would follow her. But he didn't. So she came down again.

FitzRoy was standing up—he couldn't bear to be still—by a table strewn with newspapers and with his papers. He told her he would come to bed soon. So she went upstairs again.

And he did come upstairs soon after that, undressed, kissed his wife, went around to his own side of the Victorian double bed and got in. It was midnight and she quickly fell asleep.

Around dawn, when the clock chimes struck six, she woke up. He was awake. When she asked him how he had slept, he said he had slept off and on but had not had the deep sleep he needed to restore himself. She said they must do something to keep out the morning light.

Both of them dozed until the chimes struck seven.

Then he asked her if the maid wasn't late in awakening them because he had to make the train to London. She told him it was Sunday and the maid wouldn't call them until half past seven because there was no need for him to make the train.

On the previous Sunday he had not accompanied his family to church. He had stayed home, with his Bible and his prayer book in his hands. His wife, after she and the girls returned from church, had asked him what he had read, and he had replied that he had read as much as his mind was able to take in.

She hoped he would come with them to church today.

After a few minutes he got up from the warm bed and went toward his dressing room. Each of them had a dressing room where there was a water basin and chamber pot.

He went into a little adjoining room where his youngest daughter named Laura was sleeping. His wife assumed he kissed the girl as she slept, because that was his habit. After that, he went into his dressing room.

He closed the door that separated his dressing room from the bedroom. A few minutes passed. Then his wife heard the bolt that he moved on the door to lock it. It was not his habit to lock the door, because no one would have disturbed him when his door was closed.

With the door bolted, FitzRoy took from his shaving case his straight razor. He looked at his image in the shaving mirror. His eyes in the mirror were looking back at him. And he was looking at the image of himself.

Then, with one decisive stroke, he cut his throat.

SETTLEMENT OF THE ESTATE

C HARLES D ARWIN probably understood Robert FitzRoy's suicide better than anyone else. Darwin had known FitzRoy at all the stages of FitzRoy's adult life. Darwin as a very young man had known FitzRoy when FitzRoy had been that most heroic of young captains leading an expedition around the world. Darwin had known him as an idealistic politician who was as hopelessly enmeshed by venal forces as Laocoön had been by the snakes. Darwin had known him as the most feeling of sea-captains, trying to advance an only partly effective science that promised to improve the safety of sailors and all those who traveled by sea.

It was Darwin, perhaps only Darwin, who had seen in FitzRoy all of FitzRoy's contrary qualities: his arrogance; his oversensitivity; his tactlessness; his extravagance for causes of his choice, not for personal indulgences.

Darwin mourned the passing of his old friend, and felt in his passing the ticking off of years for himself.

FitzRoy's enemies, even after his suicide, continued their attack on his work and on his office. The economy-minded Member of Parliament never let up. Neither did the Wakefields. A few people spoke out for FitzRoy, but the fact that they had to speak for him revealed the conflicting opinions of him. And his suicide implied his own negative judgment of himself. FitzRoy's widow emotionally maintained a valiant defense of her husband who had left her and her daughters, she said, only his reputation.

FitzRoy at the time of his death had many outstanding debts; he owed considerably more than there was cash to pay. His financial picture was not that of a gambler or a profligate; he had no disproportionate or questionable debts. It was simply the picture of a man who for years had fallen further and further behind financially. Long gone were the assets he had been born to, the assets of an aristocrat—landholdings that produced a steady income, cash that was managed for him.

Of FitzRoy's debts, Darwin later wrote that a subscription was raised to pay them. There can be little doubt that Darwin was foremost among the subscribers.

TWILIGHT IN
YAHGASHAGA

F ITZ ROY was unaware when he killed himself, as was Darwin at that time, that Jemmy had died about a year earlier.

Of Jemmy's last few years—after Captain Smyley in the *Nancy* had returned him to the Fuegian islands and left him—little is known.

Jemmy had no alternative but to take up again his old life—and for him it was undoubtedly flat. The fungi (bulbous clumps growing from the trees) on which the Indians often subsisted were tasteless in comparison with English food. Even when the Yahgans gorged on fish during the autumn run, Jemmy would not join in their glee. The adventure of a lifetime for a Yahgan man would be a trek to bring back iron pyrites or, if winter famine were worse than usual, a hike to recover buried blubber. But to Jemmy these adventures were pale in comparison with trips across the ocean, with his recollections of England and Brazil and even the Falklands.

After his abandonment by FitzRoy, Jemmy had become proud of himself for being able to survive and prevail where he had been born. But now the Yahgan life to him seemed listless. While the Indians would lie around the fires in their wigwams, naked, easily sated sexually, bored and quarrelsome, Jemmy's mind would wander.

Indians generally talk a lot. Since they aren't moved to do much, they talk. But their talk is limited by their tribal language and by the degree to which their minds have become elevated. The North American Indians were famous for being great talkers, endless orators who tried the patience of U.S. cavalry-men. In the talk of the Cherokee and Sioux and Cheyenne and Navajo the Indians' observations of nature would be inflated by their allusions to a spirit-world that was the ethereal phase of the nature on which they depended for life.

But the Yahgans, although they talked a great deal and passed their lives talking in their makeshift wigwams, had no elevated or fantastical or spiritual notions to talk about. Their language accordingly had no words that did not relate in a most direct way to realities. So the Yahgans talked endlessly about what was all around them—the rain, the snow, the wind, the water, fish, boats, seals, guanaco. They had neither thoughts nor words for much else.

But Jemmy must have had his own thoughts, and his own thoughts were not limited to the weather and the few practical facts of his existence. Nor was Jemmy inclined to dwell on old glories, because his visit to the King and Queen had been a long time ago.

What was vivid in Jemmy's mind was the massacre. Carnage would not have seemed unusual to Jemmy. He had fought Ona, Alacaluf, other Yahgans. Heads had been bashed, bodies speared. Jemmy's own people were forever fighting with one another. Bottled up, with the urge in their blood to move southward but at land's end with nowhere further to go, without a mythology to contemplate and improve upon, or music to charm them, or even a rhythmic drumbeat, the men would frequently fight with each other. Within the wigwam where there wasn't space to throw a fist-sized stone, they would kill one another by twisting back the head until the neck snapped.

Violence in itself was of little interest to Jemmy. Nor was it that the killing this time had been of white men. The Yahgans, like all Fuegian Indians, had killed white sailors who had been shipwrecked.

What made the massacre unique in Jemmy's mind was that those killed were hymn-singers. Jemmy knew them well. He had recited his lessons a thousand times with Garland Phillips.

Jemmy had disliked Despard (while he had loved FitzRoy) but nonetheless Jemmy had been affected by Despard's persistent

benevolence. The missionaries—even Matthews—always advocated kindness, which still seemed strange to Jemmy. All the
English resorted to kindness—the sailors, all those people in
Walthamstow who had brought gifts, the people who had kept him
and questioned him in the Falklands. And they had been repaid by
slaughter. FitzRoy's faith in Jemmy had been repaid by killing.

Never before in the life of a Yahgan had a Yahgan worried over
right and wrong. But Jemmy had so many times heard the
songs—hymns and carols—and he knew what they implied:
gentleness, goodness, thanksgiving.

This time, after the first few notes, the song had been drowned
out by a tidal wave of Yahgan shrieking. Afterthought was not the
habit of the Yahgans. Their language lacked adequate words for
afterthought. But Jemmy—the traveled Fuegian—engaged in it.
Without adequate words.

In the shelter of his tossed-together wigwam, inured to the
weather, Jemmy contemplated his own consciousness of crime.
And the pangs of conscience were exciting to him, startling, and
made his blood race not unpleasurably, faster than his blood had
ever raced before.

It was the quickening of civilization—and it made him tingle.

MALTHUS AT WORK

J EMMY died in the epidemic of 1864 that reduced by
half the Yahgan population.

A sealing schooner had come from the Falklands to the Beagle
Channel. The schooner's captain had one of FitzRoy's charts to
guide him (FitzRoy's charts of the Beagle Channel, the Patagonian coast, and especially the Strait of Magellan, were in common
use). The crossing from the Falklands to Tierra del Fuego against
the wind had been arduous. There had been a gale, and the trip

across 350 miles of open ocean, which often took only a few days, had taken a month and a half.

Safe within the channel, the sealers slowly worked their way through to the Pacific, slaughtering and skinning seals as they went.

The Fuegian Indians were startled and sickened as they always were when they watched the sealers work. The seal, like the buffalo for the Indians of North America, constituted for the Yahgans a great bounty. They would utilize every bit of a seal: They would eat even the hide if it was winter and they were hungry enough, or they would cut the hide into strips and tie the strips together to make a rope by which a man could be lowered from a cliff to look for birds' eggs in the nests on the ledges; the Yahgans would use a seal's bladder as a storage pot. But the sealers aboard the schooner were wasteful and left a bloody trail.

The sealers also left a disease that resembled measles. The Yahgans had no immunity to it. And half the native population died.

In the preceding year Thomas Bridges, Reverend Despard's adopted son who had elected to stay on Keppel Island in the Falklands, had come in the *Allen Gardiner* and, for the first time since the massacre, had resumed relations with the Yahgans. With Bridges in the *Allen Gardiner* had come Despard's replacement, an exceptionally brave and even-tempered man, the Reverend Whait H. Stirling, who, in the pattern of Despard before him, had been Secretary of the Patagonian Mission in England while Despard had spearheaded the missionary effort abroad.

The missionaries called this trip by Bridges and Stirling the "Trip of Pardon." From the missionaries' point of view, nearly four years after the massacre, this was the significance of the trip: They were pardoning these natives, most of whom they had yet to convert.

The missionaries assumed the Yahgans were in great fear they would be punished, that there would be a reprisal. Instead, the missionaries were forgiving them.

But it's highly doubtful that the missionaries were correct in assuming the Yahgan frame of mind. The Yahgans were not good rememberers; they had not yet begun to develop even their own oral history. And to people who lived in the present an act of fighting that took place nearly four years ago was apt to be forgotten or merged into a heap of similar memories.

What stupefied the Yahgans, what so surprised them that they behaved with the quietude of recalcitrant children, was that on board this ship was a white man who spoke to them in Yahgan.

Thomas Bridges spoke fluent Yahgan. When the Indians warily approached the ship in their bark-boats, he talked to them—he talked about their boats, he promised them presents, he told them not to be afraid, but, most astonishing of all, he talked!

The "Trip of Pardon" was judged by Reverend Stirling to be an outstanding success. Bridges went ashore in the dinghy and visited with the Yahgans in their wigwams (Stirling did not accompany him because they wanted the initial contacts to be very casual). Bridges distributed presents and promised more.

So a link was made, finally, at least a link of good will, by establishing a connection in the native language. Bridges and Stirling did more than repair the link that had been broken by the massacre. They established a new and better kind of link by which trust could be improved on both sides.

Bridges told the Yahgans he would come back often to help them. On the "Trip of Pardon" Bridges did not see Jemmy. Jemmy was not among those who came out to the *Allen Gardiner* nor did Bridges chance to visit Jemmy's wigwam. And the next year when Bridges returned, Jemmy was dead.

BY MAKING repeated trips to the Fuegian islands in the *Allen Gardiner*, Bridges and Stirling won the trust of the Yahgans to such an extent that in the next four years over fifty Yahgans willingly went to Keppel Island—a few at a time. On Keppel the missionary staff tried to teach them practical skills and to explain the basic tenets of Christianity.

In 1866 Reverend Stirling, to publicize the successful resumption of the Mission's work, booked passage for himself and four Yahgan boys (one of whom was another of Jemmy's sons) on a schooner bound for England. But Stirling and the Yahgan boys did not stay long in England. The English press showed little interest in them, and Queen Victoria showed none at all. So Stirling worked within his own Mission circle and then returned to the Falklands.

Stirling and Bridges prepared good-conduct certificates which they distributed to the Yahgans with instructions that the Yahgans were to show these certificates to any shipwrecked sailors they might come upon. The certificates were intended to calm the fears of the shipwrecked sailors and to give the Yahgans an opportunity to demonstrate their intention to be helpful.

Thus FitzRoy's original aim for the Fuegian Indians was effectuated. And a number of years later the Yahgans did try to help a shipwrecked party in an event that was publicized in England, though in detail the event was somewhat equivocal.

A schooner en route from Liverpool to Valparaiso with a load of coal burned up off False Cape Horn, and in a lifeboat the captain, his wife and eight crewmen after drifting for many days washed aground, smashing their lifeboat on the exposed, rocky southern shore of Hoste Island. An Indian man and woman in a bark-canoe sighted the survivors and summoned other Indians. The Yahgan men landed (which is very dangerous to do with the ocean swells pounding against those rocks) and they found that only two men in the shipwrecked party were still alive; these two were emaciated, dying, and too weak to stand; their limbs were already stiffening. The Yahgans brought fresh water and a killed sea-bird to eat, but the two dying men were beyond reviving. According to the Yahgans, one of the sailors was still able to communicate with them and gestured for them to take the clothing that was strewn around and he gave them an English sovereign. According to the Yahgans, they wept for the dead and the dying.

Leaving the shipwrecked party, the Yahgans in their canoes went directly to Thomas Bridges, reported their finding and told

Cormorants (shags) on an island in the Beagle Channel. These sea-birds were a convenient food source for the canoe Indians.

their story. Bridges, who was not a gullible man, believed the Yahgans, even though the Indians were all wearing pieces of English clothing. And he accepted from them the English sovereign they wanted to use in trade.

Then in the *Allen Gardiner* Bridges with some of the Yahgans on board went to the southern side of Hoste Island, anchoring the ship in the nearest cove. With several of the Yahgans and three English seamen he went in a longboat to the spot on the rocky coast where the shipwrecked party had been swept aground. There, while the oarsmen held the longboat from the rocks and rode the ocean swells, Bridges and the Yahgans jumped ashore.

Bridges found the bodies, neatly laid out as the Yahgans had left them, with water and the sea-bird at hand. The Yahgans had not stripped the corpses. On several of the bodies Bridges found notes, last testaments, written in despair and addressed to relatives in England.

When Bridges sent these death-notes to England along with a favorable report of the aid attempted by the Fuegian Indians, the Board of Trade, with the approval of the Queen, saw fit to send to Bridges presents for the Indians of one pound sterling to be given to each Yahgan man and woman who had helped, plus a sum of twenty pounds to be used by Bridges to purchase gifts for the tribe as a whole.

TO ADVANCE from their base in the Falklands, Stirling and Bridges had to choose a site for the establishment on a permanent basis of a mission house in the Fuegian area, and they finally chose the place where Ushuaia is now. This was a fortunate choice because this place, which is on the southern shore of the island of Tierra del Fuego along the Beagle Channel, was convenient to the many islands inhabited by the Yahgans yet the Yahgans avoided it because the Ona in the forests to the north were too close. Consequently the missionaries would be able to attract a few Yahgans to them, while not being overwhelmed by the Yahgans.

On Keppel Island a small house (about twenty feet by ten feet) was constructed in sections, brought over on the *Allen Gardiner,* and was set up atop a hill on a little peninsula west of the bay. From this vantage point Navarin Island across the channel to the southeast could be watched, as well as the opening of the Murray Narrows directly across the channel between Navarin and Hoste, and the channel itself eastward and westward was visible for quite a distance.

At which time, in 1868, Bridges was recalled to England for his ordination as a deacon—and Bridges' departure provided Whait Stirling with an opportunity to show the quality of his character.

Stirling lived all alone in the mission house atop the hill on the peninsula beside the bay of Ushuaia for six months—in spite of the ghosts of all the martyrs. In the night Stirling would listen and wonder whether he had heard the sound of a paddle in the water. During the days he would look at the towers of smoke that occasionally were sent up where some excited Yahgan was throwing beech boughs on his fire, to signal to others, to do what?

Stirling was the first white man ever to live among the Yahgans—and he survived. When Bridges was returning from England (with a wife) in 1869, he met Stirling in Montevideo. Stirling, having completed his stint among the Yahgans, was en route to England, where he was made a bishop. His bishopric was based in the Falkland Islands, and he later returned to Port Stanley, while Bridges took up residence in the mission house at Ushuaia.

I n 1 8 7 3 Bridges met Fuegia Basket. By this time it had become known among the Indians along the Beagle Channel that trading was to be done at Ushuaia and perhaps presents would be given; at the least a warm welcome could be expected. So one day some Indians in their canoes came to Ushuaia from the westernmost islands, and among these westerners was Fuegia.

She spoke to Bridges in English. She remembered many English words—*knife, fork, beads, little boy, little gal*—and she recalled Captain FitzRoy and the *Beagle* and her time in England. Bridges could talk to her in both Yahgan and Alacaluf.

Fuegia was then more than fifty years old. She was strong and healthy. As a child, according to all the English records, she had been sweet-natured and frolicsome, and so she seemed to be as an adult. She was then one of the women of a sturdy eighteen-year-old Alacaluf man. (This was not unusual among the Indians; men and women of all ages past puberty would form sexual alliances.)

Fuegia told Bridges that York Minster long ago had been killed by the relatives of a man York had killed. Fuegia had at least two grown children by York, and her children lived in the western islands.

Bridges tested her to see if she remembered anything she had been taught about Christianity; he used the ritualized questions of the catechism. But she remembered nothing of this sort.

These Indians from the western islands—both Yahgans and Alacaluf—knew how to use hides as sails on their canoes, and they lived a hardy, dangerous life, exposed to the open ocean. They looked down on the Yahgans who clung to the sheltered shores of the Beagle Channel.

After a week at Ushuaia Fuegia and the other westerners left for their home—and Bridges didn't see Fuegia for another decade.

But in 1883, when he was on a trip through the western islands, Bridges did see her once more around London Island. She was then old and sickly and was living again among Yahgans with whom she had a blood-tie. She was afraid of *tabacana,* that her relatives would strangle her or suffocate her to hasten her death. But there was nothing Bridges could do about that.

There is one other story (not told by the missionaries) that may or may not apply to Fuegia. In 1842, when Fuegia would have been in her early twenties, the captain of a sealing schooner in Port Stanley reported that, while he was cruising through the islands at the western end of the Beagle Channel, an Indian woman had come aboard who had spoken some English and that "she lived some days on board."

This may have been Fuegia. No other Indian woman in these parts was known to speak English.

The sailors on commercial schooners didn't use Indian women very much, as different from the English traders in Zululand who promptly acquired harems of black women. But these little Indian women, though naked, though plump, and though the sailors were often out on voyages that lasted years, did not generally attract the European men. This may have been because the Indian women were in some way repulsive, perhaps as a result of their diet which consisted so heavily of mussels and limpets. It was not because the Indian women never bathed; the Zulu women never bathed; and the Yahgan women swam daily. Maybe it was because the Yahgan men were so belligerent and the Yahgan women were kept close by from puberty on. Perhaps it was because the Yahgan women were physically so strong. We simply don't know.

What is remarkable in the sea-captain's report, though, is that the Indian woman was allowed to live aboard *for some days.* Even had the sailors all used her sexually, the episode might have been expected to be over quickly, and the woman returned to her bark-canoe. Only if the sailors had become genuinely fond of her would she have lived aboard.

AFTER the permanent mission at Ushuaia was established, further steps were taken that enmeshed the Fuegian Indians with the civilized world.

Sheep were introduced on Navarin Island, and a routine for shearing the sheep was developed. A work-party, including Yahgans, each season would come from Ushuaia to shear the sheep and take away the wool.

Some of the Indians, observing the ample harvest from the missionaries' garden plots and being encouraged by the mission-aries, became farmers.

Yahgans crewed on the *Allen Gardiner,* and later Yahgans crewed on the schooners that more frequently now came to and through the Beagle Channel. A few Yahgans remained in the Falklands, both on Keppel and in Port Stanley.

As the population of the civilized world was increasing and expanding even into the most remote regions like Tierra del Fuego, the contacts of the Fuegian Indians with all sorts of Europeans and Americans, Africans and Chinese, became more common. Eventually the Welsh from Patagonia filtered south-ward, and some Yugoslavs settled in Ushuaia. As a result of these contacts, contagions spread among the hitherto-isolated Fuegian Indians.

Back in England, the Reverend Despard, in an attempt to rationalize his personal withdrawal from the missionary effort, wrote a book entitled *Hope Deferred, Not Lost.* In it he pointed with pride to the progress that was clearly being made on the stepping-stones provided by FitzRoy, Gardiner, Phillips. Despard mentioned his own accomplishment in founding the mission on Keppel as a contribution in this brave, unstoppable, onward march.

And the Indians were rallying to the missionary banner. Undeniably they were responding to the incursion of civilization. The Indians were becoming more tractable, gentler even in their relations among themselves. Ideas for their own improvement were being embraced by them and even were occurring to them. The excitement of conscience was enlivening them.

But the onward march of the Christian missionaries and the beginning of a popular response from the Indians never achieved fruition because the Fuegian Indians were disappearing.

We like to think that mankind triumphs, that human superiority is asserted all over the world, that this is the human destiny. In fact, mankind has made starts in many places. Mostly mankind has prospered. But some of the human starts have been less successful and the people, unable to advance from primitive circumstances, are barely able to cling to life—as in central Africa, the outback of Australia, the jungles of the Philippines.

In a few places, like Tierra del Fuego and the Fuegian islands, indigenous mankind has been unable to survive and has died out. And no bomb was required for extermination.

T H O M A S B R I D G E S noted the steady reduction of the Indian population. Venturing along the channel from Ushuaia, he would go into cove after cove where previously there had been Indians and would find the beaches deserted. Whole islands that had previously been inhabited were depopulated.

In 1886 Bridges resigned from the Patagonian Mission; he sought and received from the Argentine government a grant of

50,000 acres on the south shore of Tierra del Fuego east of Ushuaia. There he founded and established the settlement called Harberton and spent the remainder of his life (about twelve years) in the business of raising sheep.

During the quarter-century Bridges had spent as a missionary, his parallel dedication had been to the preparation of a Yahgan-English dictionary which after many years he finally completed with loving care and with great admiration for the extensive vocabulary of the Indian tongue. Yet his final admission to himself, which he confessed in print, was that the Yahgan language was inadequate to transmit the concepts of Christianity. The Yahgan language, in which Bridges could think and was fluent, was, he concluded, inflexible and unadaptable for the expression of ideas that were not the ideas that naturally occurred to the Indian mind.

Bridges' acknowledgment of this inadequacy of the Yahgan language, as well as the continued thinning out of the Yahgans, ultimately brought his mission to an end.

F R O M an estimated population of six thousand the estimate of Fuegian Indians was lowered to three thousand and around the turn of the century to about a thousand. The estimate continued to fall.

No single disease overcame the Fuegian Indians. But contagions came to them on the ships from faraway places, fostered by the animals that were imported, abetted by the effects on the native food-chain.

During the decades in the first half of the twentieth century the Fuegians were counted in the hundreds—as the settlement of Europeans and Argentines at Ushuaia grew. After the construction of the Panama Canal the ship-traffic fell off, but a few local industries remained.

In the nineteen sixties the last of the Yahgans, and even the last of the few half-breeds, died.

The Yahgans are now extinct.

As extinct as the mylodon.

As extinct as the moa.

Part Five

DARWIN ENDURING

HE WHO LAUGHS LAST
HAS LITTLE
TO LAUGH ABOUT

D ARWIN lived seventeen years after Jemmy's death and eighteen years after the death of FitzRoy. So the confluence of these three lives did not apply to their entirety. But the significance of their lives in relation to one another remains remarkable: Darwin, like a generator of immense power, transmitting the bleak, cold light of pure reason; FitzRoy in convulsive, self-destroying fury opposing him; and Jemmy—with conscience just beginning to dawn in him—burning up like a sparrow that happened to flicker into the field between these two charged poles of intellect and feeling.

Darwin, in the years remaining to him after the deaths of Jemmy and FitzRoy, was swathed in comfort. The original foundation of Down House was probably laid in the late seventeenth century. From that foundation, extensions were made and, in Darwin's time, there were further changes—a handsome bay was added, a gracious drawing room, larger wings and outbuildings; the veranda at the back was rebuilt. The trees, the Sand Walk, the garden, all improved in beauty as the years went on.

Even Darwin's routine—which had always been a complete indulgence of his mind—was refined. For exercise, horseback-riding had been his lifelong habit, but one day his horse fell down with him on it. He was not hurt, but afterward he exercised only by walking. He said he preferred walking because he was not distracted from his thinking by having to control the horse.

He developed a ruthless but efficient procedure for reading books as, with his fame spreading, more and more volumes were sent to him. With a new book he would take a sharp knife, cut off the spine and throw away the whole cover, leaving himself with loose pages that were easy to turn. Then he would put the loose pages in a box until he decided whether to keep the book in the box or dispose of it.

Karl Marx, a profound admirer, wanted to dedicate *Das Kapital* to Darwin. And Darwin dutifully taught himself German in order to read it. He plowed through about 120 pages before giving up. Then he wrote a kindly and appreciative note to Marx that political economy was really not his field and he declined the honor of the dedication. But he kept that box.

He developed angina, and the pain in his left arm often forced him to be inactive. He wrote notes of advice to himself (only a very little lukewarm splashing for the morning wash, no tight clothing, and no straining for bowel movements) and directives for the servants (no spicy food to be served him, only fresh and well-cooked fish and meat, and half an ounce of brandy in water occasionally). Gradually he nearly abandoned the last meal of the day.

And all around him he always had his lively and loving family. He said he never wanted better company.

Darwin was such an affectionate man—only such an affectionate man would have held to his friendship with a character as prickly as FitzRoy—but the strength of his intellect always kept him from romanticizing. And hope is the product of the romantic inclination.

When Darwin was young, he was attracted by the hope of an afterlife with a reward in Heaven.

In middle age he could still see the possibility that perhaps evolution had a direction not only toward increasingly complex forms but also toward improvement for mankind, toward a better human state. At this stage he and Lyell might have come close to full agreement. But in old age he saw only evolvement—without aim or direction.

The key to Darwin's thinking was time—eons of time, an unbearable span of time—wearying, saddening, shrinking individual worth, with only natural causes in operation. For Darwin, the challenge was to understand the functioning of nature; as he solved one riddle after another, he was fascinated. But most people wanted and needed a more immediate and dramatic explanation than the slow working of nature: They yearned for Jovian thunderbolts, or explosive creation, or, at the best and most beautiful, divine intervention and Christianity.

They could not endure the idea of only action and reaction through time which began at a point dim and distant and went on without end. This endlessness of time may be granted for the rocks but not for life. Yet Darwin maintained that this was the most reasonable explanation.

FitzRoy could not live with it.

And Jemmy, moved by FitzRoy and caught up finally in the Christian conscience, would never have been touched by such a thought.

In Darwin's last years it was only time that he saw evolving, time which bore with it changing life-forms.

Darwin loved his life. He loved FitzRoy as his friend. He liked Jemmy for Jemmy's quaintness, kindness and innocence, and he pitied Jemmy for being a misused specimen. But, for Darwin, intellect overbore all.

AFTER the publication of *The Origin of Species* Darwin had more than twenty years during which he continually refined his theory, regarding it as only a step along a path on which many steps remained to be taken. He intended *The Origin of Species* to be considered a short work to be succeeded by a longer and fuller work in which the processes of evolution would be further explored. Since we are still trying to advance our knowledge of these processes, we can understand and sympathize with Darwin's feeling that his work was never finished.

In his remaining years after publishing *The Origin of Species*

Darwin's study in Down House. In the writing-chair he wrote
The Origin of Species. *Leaning against the chair is the cane he*
was fond of, a stout piece of wood around which a vine had
curled and the wood and vine had fused.

Darwin published ten more books, each of which advanced and extended his theory in some particular application, such as in cross-fertilization or with insectivorous plants.

In one of these books, *The Descent of Man,* Darwin clarified an idea he had previously introduced. In *The Origin of Species* he had mentioned a distinction between evolution by means of natural selection (*reasonable* evolution, with the changed environment requiring for survival longer necks or heavier pelts or bigger lungs) and evolution by means of sexual selection. In *The Descent of Man* Darwin more fully explained himself.

Darwin observed that propagation of a species and the consequent evolutionary direction of the species were influenced not only by the *reasonable* requirements of natural selection but also by the inclinations of sexual selection which were frequently *unreasonable.*

To be sure, sometimes the criteria of sexual selection were reasonable. When the strongest male members of a species, the best fighters, were the ones preferred or accepted by the females in mating, the species as a result became ever stronger with the males better and better equipped for fighting. This could be carried to disadvantageous extremes—as when the male elk developed such big horns they could hardly lift their heads or when the prehistoric mastodons developed such big tusks that the tusks dragged on the ground. In the short run, though, the advantage of effective fighting apparatus in the male was obvious.

But sometimes in a species there would be a characteristic that within the species would clearly be sexually attractive—and this characteristic would make no sense at all. For example, some male birds can puff up their throats to an extraordinary degree. Darwin could see no possible usefulness in this ability to puff up the throat, which the male birds did only at mating time. Yet the females tended to mate with those males that were best at puffing up their throats. Consequently the species became more and more characterized by males that could enormously puff up their throats.

Similarly, male elephant seals can inflate their noses, and the bigger-nosed male elephant seals are the ones accepted for mating by the females, though the inflatability of the male's nose, as far as Darwin could see, served no practical purpose except that the inflated nose was within the species clearly regarded as sexually attractive. And the species, of course, as the result of intensive breeding by the biggest-nosed males, produced males with an ever-greater ability to inflate their noses.

There are in the animal kingdom all kinds of displays by males to attract females (the great tail-display of the peacocks or the singing of the male songbirds) and the display-making ability of the males consequently becomes more and more marked within the species, even though the display-making in and of itself serves no useful purpose.

So Darwin concluded that, although *reasonable* natural selection generally guides the course of evolution, a role must be allowed for sexual selection, which also influences the course of evolution and which may be unsupported by any obvious reason.

Thus Darwin allowed within his theory for an irrational element (sexual selection) which together with all the reasonable requirements of natural selection moved along the process of evolution.

Applied to human beings, this idea seems to me unquestionably true and in its way appealing. George Santayana wrote: "It is not wisdom to be only wise." And I think it's nice to know that the reasonableness of evolution by natural selection has its exception in the occasional madness of sexual selection. Some may find this thought disturbing, but I find it consoling.

DARWIN liked to take snuff. He had a little collection of snuffboxes.

He was working at the utmost edge of his ability, trying to fathom what men had never fathomed before, trying to shed the light of intelligence where there had been ignorance. Each day he demanded from himself a little bit more than his still-sleepy mind after breakfast would easily provide for him. So he would take a pinch of snuff (powdered tobacco) for the slight stimulation that it gave him. He felt that this helped him to extend himself a little bit further.

More than once he tried to break this habit which his wife, Emma, found dirty and disgusting. He would put the snuffbox outside his study on the newel post. But when in the course of his morning's work (and he worked every morning of his life when he could) he knowingly would need an insight which was just beyond him, he would leave his study and retrieve the snuffbox.

Certainly no man in the nineteenth century—and few men in history—have worked more effectively, prodigiously and daringly.

QUEEN VICTORIA AND EMMA DARWIN

CHARLES DARWIN was not Queen Victoria's kind of man, and she was able to trump him because she was born a little later, lived a little longer, and because she was Queen.

Victoria was the embodiment of England's firm endorsement of conformity in the nineteenth century; she epitomized the nation's stance at the apogee of its power following the defeat of Napoleon. George Macaulay Trevelyan, England's greatest social historian, has pointed out this curious anomaly.

Viewed with the Queen in mind, it may have been the influence of Victoria that delayed Darwin in making public his theory. Queen Victoria did not approve of iconoclasts.

What Huxley said after reading Darwin's chapter on natural selection in *The Origin of Species* may now be said for many of us, "How extremely stupid not to have thought of that!"

But Queen Victoria did not look with favor upon disruptive

thought. So she never knighted Darwin, as she never knighted FitzRoy.

Lyell, Sulivan, and many others who had been in subordinate capacities were awarded the Queen's favor. But she stubbornly held out against Darwin and FitzRoy.

On the Continent many authorities who felt themselves responsible to a pietistic public also held out against Darwin. The French Academy, after rejecting Darwin for years, finally accepted him only as a botanist. And Darwin, who in spite of his reclusivity was fond of honors, received his belated acceptance by the French in good spirit.

Nevertheless, and in spite of the Queen, to Darwin's cause were drifting in an ever-stronger tide most of the scientists of the world, followed by the rationalists, followed by those who had an instinctive resentment of obligated belief.

In 1876, when Darwin was sixty-seven years old and had lived as a well-tended semi-invalid for most of his adult life, it occurred to him—as it had once occurred to Benjamin Franklin—to write a genial kind of autobiography (recollections and comments) addressed chiefly to his children, revealing, if this needed revealing, the kindly personal side of him as different from the abstract intellectual side that his other books reflected.

In connection with the *Autobiography* his wife, Emma, trumped him. Emma Darwin was always true to herself.

After Darwin died in his seventy-fourth year, ending a hugely productive life that changed the thinking of the whole world, and when a few years after his death it seemed suitable to publish this intimate *Autobiography,* Emma calmly sat down with one of her sons and without any hesitation censored the autobiography, page by page, deleting from it whatever failed to meet with her approval.

Darwin had written: ". . . as I did not then in the least doubt the strict and literal truth of every word in the Bible, I soon

Emma Darwin.

persuaded myself that our Creed must be fully accepted. *It never struck me how illogical it was to say that I believed in what I could not understand and what is in fact unintelligible. I might have said with entire truth that I had no wish to dispute any dogma; but I never was such a fool as to feel and say 'I believe that which is incredible.'* "

Emma simply edited out the part which I have italicized,

leaving in her husband's mouth only the profession of faith without his disavowal.

Darwin had written of his years on the *Beagle:* "But I had gradually come, by this time, to see that the Old Testament from its manifestly false history of the world, with the Tower of Babel, the rainbow as a sign, etc., etc., and from its attributing to God the feelings of a revengeful tyrant, was no more to be trusted than the sacred books of the Hindoos, or the beliefs of any barbarian."

Emma struck that out.

Darwin had written: "Beautiful as is the morality of the New Testament, it can hardly be denied that its perfection depends in part on the interpretation which we now put on metaphors and allegories."

Emma cut that.

And she also cut every perceptive comment Darwin had made about anyone that could possibly be interpreted as a criticism of that person. Then, with the *Autobiography* nicely cleaned up, Emma allowed it to be published. (Fortunately Darwin's granddaughter seventy years later found the original manuscript and restored the deletions.)

WHEN Darwin died in 1882, twenty Members of Parliament petitioned that he should be buried in Westminster Abbey, and Queen Victoria reluctantly decided not to oppose them. He was buried beside England's other greatest scientist, Sir Isaac Newton.

Then, long after Darwin's death and more than a decade after Queen Victoria herself had died, there was interred beside Darwin in Westminster Abbey—in accord with England's uncompromising notion of fair play—the far less well-known naturalist, Alfred Russel Wallace, whose unsupported argument in favor of evolution by natural selection had been submitted to Darwin and had forced Darwin to write *The Origin of Species.*

S A I L in the skies, onetime shipmates!
Jemmy Button.
Robert FitzRoy.
Charles Darwin.

BIBLIOGRAPHY

This story has been in my mind for many years, and the bits of information which I have pieced together to form the mosaic come from a myriad of sources. These include:

Barlow, Nora, ed. *The Autobiography of Charles Darwin, 1809–1882.* London, 1958.

Bertrand, Kenneth J. *Americans in Antarctica, 1775–1948*, New York, 1971.

Braun Menéndez, Armando. *Revista Argentina Austral.* Buenos Aires.

Bridges, E. Lucas. *Uttermost Part of the Earth.* New York, 1949.

Bridges, Rev. Thomas. *Yamana-English Dictionary.* Ushuaia, Tierra del Fuego, Argentina, 1987.

Canclini, Arnoldo. *Allen F. Gardiner, Marino, Misionero, Mártir.* Buenos Aires, 1979.

The Committee of the Patagonian Missionary Society. *A Brief Statement of the Rise and Progress of the Patagonian Mission*, with an Appendix. Bristol, 1860.

Colonial Office papers, Falkland Islands, 1860. Public Records Office, London.

Darwin, Charles. *A Journal of the Voyage of the "Beagle,"* London, 1839.
———*On the Origin of Species by Means of Natural Selection.* London, 1859.
———*The Descent of Man and Selection in Relation to Sex.* London, 1871.

FitzRoy, Robert. *Narrative of the Surveying Voyages of His Majesty's Ships "Adventure" and "Beagle" between 1826 and 1836.* Volumes I and II and Appendix, London, 1839.

Goodall, Rae Natalie Prosser. *Tierra del Fuego*, Buenos Aires, 1979.

Huxley, Julian (with H. B. D. Kettlewell). *Charles Darwin and His World.* London, 1965.

Hyde, H. Montgomery. *The Strange Death of Lord Castelreagh.* London, 1959.

Marsh, John W., and Stirling, Whait H. *The Story of Commander Allen Gardiner, R.N., with Sketches of Missionary Work in South America.* London, 1867.

Mellersh, H. E. L. *FitzRoy of the "Beagle,"* London, 1968.

Moorehead, Alan. *Darwin and the Beagle.* London, 1969.

Mission Scientifique du Cap Horn 1882–1883, Volume VII. Paris, 1891.

Snow, William Parker. *A Two Years' Cruise Off Tierra del Fuego, the Falkland Islands, Patagonia, and in the River Plate: A Narrative of Life in the Southern Seas.* London, 1857.

Ward, Henshaw. *Charles Darwin: The Man and His Warfare.* Indianapolis, 1927.

INDEX

Page numbers in italics denote illustrations.

aborigines of Australia, 8
Adelaide, Queen of England,
    44, 45
Adventure (ship), 65–6, 78, 79–80
Adventure, H.M.S., 32, 36, 65
Alacaluf Indians, 29–31
    language, 136, *137*, 138
Al-Hwarizmi of Baghdad, 16
Allen Gardiner (ship), 110, 127,
    154–60 *passim*, 225, 227
    ransacking of 160, 168–9, 170
    retrieval of, 180–5
American Indians, 9, 18–22, 221–2
anima mundi theory, 206
Araucanian Indians, 91–2
asado con cuero, 69

barometers, 23, 196–7
Beagle, H.M.S., 7, 22–3, *24*, 50
Beagle Channel, *1*, 132, *152*
Bennett, James, 37, 39, 47, 52
Billy Button, 148, 153, 156,
    169–70
Boat Memory, 29–31, 34–5, 36
Bolivia, 92
Bridges, Thomas, 147, 179, 224,
    225, 226–8, 229–30, 232–3

Brisbane (Falklands resident), 68, 77
Bushmen of the Kalahari Desert, 8
Button Sound, *159*

cannibalism, 12, 27
Cape Horn, 6, *58*
    FitzRoy's attempt to sail, 58–9
    naming of, 17–18
Castlereagh, Robert Stewart,
    Viscount, 80–1, 214
Chaco region, 92–3
Church Missionary Society, 39, 88,
    91, 93
Coles, Alfred, 156, 157, 160–1,
    167–71, 173, 190

Darwin, Charles, 48–51, *49*, 59,
    60, 64, 80, 126, 192, 198, *235*
    autobiography, 244–6
    burial, 246
    caricatures of, *205*, *210*
    in Chile, 79, 80, 82
    concentration, capacity for, 193
    death, 244
    evolution, theory of: controversies
        about, 202–4, 207–8;

Darwin, Charles *(cont.)*
  development of, 113–17,
    200–2; refinement of,
    238–9, 241–2
  family life, 118–19
  FitzRoy, relations with, 51,
    69–71, 192–6, 214, 215,
    219–20
  and FitzRoy's death, 219–20
  illnesses, 82, 113–14
  Indians, first contact with, 57
  later years, 237–9, 242–4
  life, view of, 211–12
  Lyell and, 207–8, 209
  marriage, 38
  on missionaries, 123
  naturalist position, appointment
    to, 50–1
  religious views, 70–1
  reunion with Jemmy Button,
    72–6
  scientific approach to natural
    phenomena, 7
  and sexuality, 38
  snuff habit, 242–3
  specimens, collecting of, 67
  Victoria, Queen, and, 243–4
Darwin, Emma, 38, 243–6, *245*
Darwin, Erasmus, 48, 116
Darwin, Dr. Robert, 48, 50, 51,
    114
Descent of Man, The (Darwin),
    241–2
Despard, George Pakenham
  Falklands, arrival at, 142–3
  Falklands settlement expedition,
    preparation for, 127–9
  FitzRoy's views, interest in, 118
  fund-raising, 96
  hired by Gardiner, 93–4
  Jemmy Button: determination to
    find, 109–10; disappointment
    with, 148; vision of, 178–9
  Jemmy's attitude toward, 222–3
  leadership of Patagonian

  Mission, 97, 108–10
  massacre inquiry, 179–80
  massacre survivors, search for,
    158, 159
  mission house at Wulaia, 149, 150
  Okokko and, 185
  resignation, 176–9
  theft incident, 150–1
  writings, 232
Down House (Darwin home), 114,
    115, 193–4, 237, *240*
Duncan, Silas, 68

Egyptian explorers, 15–16
Ellis (doctor), 128, 130, 141
England
  Gardiner's death, reaction to,
    107–8
  massacre of missionaries,
    reaction to, 189–91
  middle-class mood of decency
    and conformity, 110–13
  religious upsurge, 203
English-Indian meetings, 25–7
Erwin, Joseph, 97, 105
Eskimos, 8
*Essay on the Principle of
    Population* (Malthus), 117
evolution, theory of
  development of, 113–17
  natural selection, 200–2
  refinements of, 238–9, 241–2
  religious controversies, 115–17,
    202–7
  scientific controversies, 207–9,
    211–12
  sexual selection, 241–2
  support for, 214–15

Falkland Islands, 65, 66, 67–9, 77,
    129–30, 139–40, *140*
Falklands settlement (of Patagonian
    Mission)

Despard's arrival, 142–3
Despard's plan for, 108–10
FitzRoy's views on, 118
instruction for Yahgans, 146–9
Jemmy, search for, 130–6, 138–9
Jemmy's instruction, 146–8
Jemmy taken to Falklands, 143–5
Keppel Island settlement, 129–
30, 139–42
massacre of missionaries, 156–7
massacre survivors, search for,
158–61
mission house at Ushuaia, 228–9
mission house at Wulaia, 149,
150, 154–6
preparations for, 127–9
Snow's dismissal, 142–3
Stirling-Bridges initiatives,
224–9
theft incident, 150–3
"Trip of Pardon," 224–5
Fell, Robert, 143, 151, 153, 155–6
fevers, Andean, 82, 113–14
FitzRoy, Mrs., 191, 216–20
FitzRoy, Fanny, 42
FitzRoy, Robert, 23–4, *30*, 92, *187*
Adventure, purchase of, 65–6,
78, 79–80
aristocratic stance, 194–5
Brisbane incident, 77
Cape Horn, attempt to sail, 58–9
Darwin, relations with, 51, 69–
71, 192–6, 214, 215, 219–20
evolution, theory of, rejected by,
202–4, 207, 212, 215
Falklands government and, 68–9
global voyage, plan for, 78
Indian languages, work on, 136,
137, 138
Indians in England, care for, 36–
7, 39, 40, 42, 43–5
Indians returned to Tierra del
Fuego, 54, 57–64
Indians taken hostage, 29, 31–2
Indians taken to England, 34–5

mapping work, 55, 65–7, 77
Maury and, 215–216
mental problems, 77–82, 214,
216–19
meteorological work, 191–2,
196–200, 212
on missionaries, 123–4
money troubles, 194–5, 200, 216
New Zealand governorship,
121–6
in Parliament, 120–1
and Patagonian Mission, 118
primitive peoples, fondness for,
211, 213, 214
religious views, 7–8, 51, 71,
202–3
resignation attempt, 81–2
reunion with Jemmy Button,
71–6
second *Beagle* voyage,
preparation for, 47–8
self-defensiveness, 212–13
and sexuality, 38
suicide, 219–20
weather forecasting, 191–2, 196–
200, 212
whaleboat theft incident, 24–5,
27–9
William IV, audience with, 43–5
writings, 119, 200
Franklin, Benjamin, 34
Fuegia Basket, *41,* 73
capture, 29–31
in England, 37, 38–9, 40, 42–5
later years, 229–31
return to Tierra del Fuego, 52–
7, 59, 61, 62–4
voyage to England, 34–5
William IV, audience with, 43–5

Gardiner, Allen Francis, 87, *89*
with Araucanians, 91–2
in Chaco, 92–3
death, 105

Gardiner, Allen Francis *(cont.)*
  missionary work, entry into,
    87–8
  Patagonian Mission, founding of,
    93–4
  ships for missionary activities,
    96–7, 100
  at Spaniard Harbor, 102–5
  Tierra del Fuego, arrival in,
    94–9
  Yahgan Indians, meetings with,
    99–102
  in Zululand, 88–91
Gardiner, Allen Weare, 143–5
gauchos, 69
George IV, King of England, 44,
    81
Germanus, Ericus Martellus, 16
grave-searching incident, 181,
    182–4

Hope Deferred, Not Lost (Despard),
    232
Huxley, Thomas, 204, 206–7,
    243–4

Indians, American, 18–22, 221–2

Jemmy Button, 7, 22, *41, 74,* 146–7
  capture by FitzRoy, 29, 31
  capture by Smyley, 161
  Coles and, 171, 173
  death, 223
  Despard, attitude toward, 222–3
  Despard's desire to find, 109–10
  Despard's vision of, 178–9
  in England, 37, 38, 39, 40, 42–5
  to Falklands, 143–5
  final years, 221–3
  gifts, demand for, 151–2
  grave-searching incident, 181,
    182–4

inquiry testimony, 171–3
  instruction on Keppel Island,
    146–8
  massacre, thoughts on, 222–3
  press's interest in his fate, 83–4
  return to Tierra del Fuego from
    England, 52–7, 59–61, 62–4
  reunion with FitzRoy and
    Darwin, 72–6
  Snow's discovery of, 130–6,
    138–9
  voyage to England, 34–5
  William IV, audience with, 43–5

Keppel Island, 127
  settlement, 129–30, 139–
    42
King, Philip Parker, 32, 36, 65

Lafone, Samuel, 98
Lamarck, Jean Baptiste, 116
land ownership, conflicts over (in
    New Zealand), 122–3, 124–5
Lexington (ship), 68
Londonderry, Lord, 120
Lyell, Sir Charles, 116, 207–9, 211,
    212

MacDowell, Hugh, 157
Magellan, Ferdinand, 17
Maidmant, John, 97, 100, 105
Malthus, Thomas, 117
Maori people, 122, 123, 124, 125
mapping process, 25, 55, 65–7, 77
Marx, Karl, 238
massacre (of missionaries), 156–7
  Jemmy's thoughts on, 222–3
  military expedition in response,
    proposed, 174–6
  newspaper reports on, 189–91
  search for survivors, 158–61
massacre inquiry

board of inquiry report, 173–4, 180

Coles's testimony, 167–71

Despard's refusal to cooperate, 179–80

Jemmy's testimony, 171–3

preparations for, 165–6

Matthews, Richard, 52, 53, 55, 62–3, 123, 223

Maury, Matthew, 158, 191, 196, 198, 215–16, 217

Mawman, John, 46, 47

Mendel, Gregor, 116

missionaries
  Gardiner's experiences, 87–93
  in New Zealand, 123–4
  see also Despard, George Pakenham; massacre; Patagonian Mission; Phillips, Garland

Moore, Gov., 139, 165–6, 174, 175, 176, 179–80

Murray (*Beagle's* master), 28, 32, 39, 52

naturalist position on *Beagle*, 47–8, 50–1

natural selection, principle of, 200–2

Navarin Island, 6, 7, 9, 30

New Zealand, 121–6

nomadic urge, 21–2

Okokko, 153, 170, 184, 185

Ona Indians, 14, 57

On the Origin of Species (Darwin), 117, 200, 201–2, 204, 239

Paraguay, 92

Patagonia, 66, 70–1, 93–4, 108–9

Patagonian Indians, 28, 94

Patagonian Mission
  Despard's resignation, 176–9

founding of, 93–4

Gardiner's mission, 94–107

public reaction to failed mission, 107–8

revival following Gardiner's death, 108–10

see also Falklands settlement

Petersen, August, 150, 156

Phillips, Garland, 128, 129, 130, 141, 148–50, 151–6 *passim*, 222

Picton Island, 103, 131, *132*

Piedrabuena, Luis, 158

Pioneer (boat), 102, 105, 107

Port Stanley, 129, 139–40

primitive peoples, 8
  FitzRoy's fondness for, 211, 213, 214

Ptolemy, 16

Rennie, George, 129

Roman empire, 111, 122

sailor's life, 36–7

Santayana, George, 242

Scott, Sir Walter, 81

seals, *13*, 224

sexual selection, principle of, 241–2

Sheppard, William, 120–1

smallpox vaccine, 34–5

Smith, Augustus, 212

Smyley, William H., 105–7, 158–61, 180–5

Snow, Mrs., 128, 131, 136, 139

Snow, William Parker, *58*, 127–30, 139–43, 171
  search for Jemmy, 130–6, 138–9

Spaniard Harbor, *85*, 102, *106*, 131

Spanish empire, 111, 122

Speedwell (boat), 102, 103, 105, 106

Stanley, Lord, 126

Stirling, Whait H., 224, 225–6, 228–9

Stokes, Pringle, 25
Strait of Magellan, 17, 18

Tierra del Fuego, 5, 6, *26*, 56
  discovery of, 15–17
Trevelyan, George Macaulay, 243

Ushuaia, Argentina, 5, 228–9

Victoria, Queen of England, 111,
  198, 203, 228, 243–4, 246
Virgil, 206

Wallace, Alfred Russel, 117, 246
Weather Book (FitzRoy), 200
weather forecasting, 191–2, 196–
  200, 212
Wedgwood, Josiah (Darwin's
  grandfather), 48
Wedgwood, Josiah (Darwin's
  uncle), 51
Wellington, Duke of, 81
whaleboat theft incident, 24–5,
  27–9
whales, *20*
Wigram, Joseph, 39
Wilberforce, Bshp. Samuel, 204,
  206–7
William IV, King of England, 43,
  44–5
Williams, Richard, 97, 98, 100,
  105
Wilson, William, 39

Yahgan Indians, *163*
  Alacalufs, contacts with, 30–1
  Beagle, first contact with, 22–3
  burial customs, 173
  canoeing, 10–11, *11*, 28
  civilization, contacts with, 15–
    16, 18
  civilizing of, 231–3
  Coles, treatment of, 167–71
  culture (primitive way of life), 7,
    9–15, 136
  diet, 12, *13*
  epidemic of 1864, 223–4
  extermination of, 232–3
  family, concept of, 31
  Gardiner and, 99–102
  hostility to missionaries, 150–3
  language, 13–14, 136, *137*, 138
  massacre of missionaries, 156–7
  mating, 136
  Matthews, treatment of, 63
  origins of, 18–22
  primitiveness of, 7, 9–14
  property, attitude toward, 64
  return of "civilized" Indians to,
    59–64
  seals and, 224
  shipwrecked sailors, assistance
    for, 226–8
  Snow and, 131, 133, 139
  talk, proclivity for, 221–2
  tools and trade goods, attitude
    toward, 28
  violence among, 222
  whaleboat theft incident, 24–5,
    27–9
  wigwams, 9–10, *10*
  women, 29, 230–1
York Minster, *41*, 229
  capture, 29–31
  in England, 37, 38–9, 40,
    42–5
  return to Tierra del Fuego, 52–
    7, 59, 61, 62–4
  theft of Jemmy's goods, 73,
    75–6
  voyage to England, 34–5
  William IV, audience with, 43–5

Zululand, 88–91
Zuni Indians, 21

A NOTE ABOUT THE AUTHOR

Richard Lee Marks has lived in South America, Mexico and
Spain and has traveled extensively through Central
America. He is the author of two novels and a play, and
his short pieces have appeared in *The Yale Review* and
Harper's. He now lives in Topeka, Kansas.

A NOTE ON THE TYPE

This book was set in New Caledonia, a version of a typeface
designed by W. A. Dwiggins (1880–1956). It belongs to the family
of printing types called "modern face" by printers—a
term used to mark the change in style of type letters that occurred
about 1800. Caledonia borders on the general design of Scotch
Roman, but is more freely drawn than that letter.

Composed by The Sarabande Press, New York, New York
Printed and bound by Halliday Lithographers, West Hanover, Massachusetts
Designed by Mia Vander Els

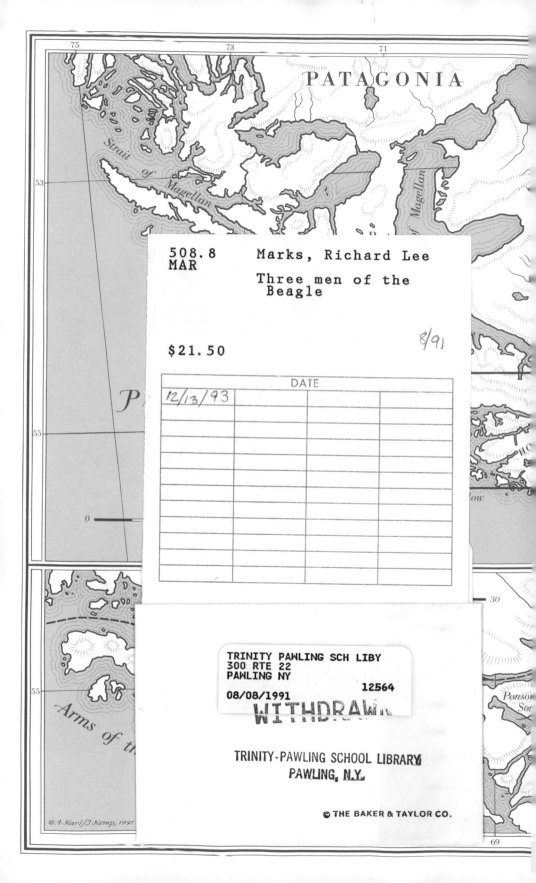

508.8
MAR

Marks, Richard Lee

Three men of the
Beagle

8/91

$21.50